CRITICISM AND POLITICS

CRITICISM AND POLITICS

A Polemical Introduction

Bruce Robbins

Stanford University Press
Stanford, California

Stanford University Press
Stanford, California

Printed in the United States of America on acid-free, archival-quality paper

Library of Congress Cataloging-in-Publication Data

Names: Robbins, Bruce, author.
Title: Criticism and politics : a polemical introduction / Bruce Robbins.
Description: Stanford, California : Stanford University Press, 2022. |
  Includes bibliographical references and index.
Identifiers: LCCN 2021056592 (print) | LCCN 2021056593 (ebook) | ISBN
  9781503630192 (cloth) | ISBN 9781503633209 (paperback) | ISBN
  9781503633216 (ebook)
Subjects: LCSH: Criticism (Philosophy) | Culture—Philosophy. | Politics
  and culture.
Classification: LCC B809.3 .R63 2022 (print) | LCC B809.3 (ebook) | DDC
  142—dc23/eng/20220125
LC record available at https://lccn.loc.gov/2021056592
LC ebook record available at https://lccn.loc.gov/2021056593

Contents

Introduction

What does it mean to call yourself "nonpolitical," as Thomas Mann does in the title of his *Reflections of a Nonpolitical Man*? It might mean a desire to stay neutral when all around you are choosing sides, perhaps too hastily. It might indicate a desire not to be reductive in judging the wild, weird profusion of things that knock at the doors of your perception. It might come out of a wish to preserve politics itself as a meaningful category at a time when the category seems to be expanding too explosively in all directions. According to the *New York Times* of October 28, 2021,

> "You talk to older people and they're like, 'Dude we sell tomato sauce, we don't sell politics,'" said Mr. Kennedy, co-founder of Plant People, a certified B corporation. "Then you have younger people being like, 'These are political tomatoes. This is political tomato sauce.'"[1]

Lately the impulse to describe oneself as nonpolitical has perhaps become more attractive because of the much-discussed polarization of the US electorate. The idea that politics is ugly and sordid—something that entails giving oneself over to uncritical partisanship, forsaking nuance, conforming to a with-us-or-against-us crudeness of thought and feeling, and soiling oneself with unsavory moral compromise—may help explain the republication of Mann's World War I–era volume. For years *Reflections* was not readily available, as I discovered while trying to get ahold of a copy during the global pandemic and closed libraries when I was trying to write this book. Now I find *Reflections of a Nonpolitical Man* not only available again, but reviewed, positively, on the front page of the *New York Times Sunday Book Review*.[2]

As it turns out, *Reflections* was unavailable for so long because it is unreadable. It is not a piece of juvenilia—Mann was thirty-nine when he began writing it and already a well-established writer—but he himself became embarrassed by the positions he took in it and by the over-the-top way he took them. He did not encourage the book's translation into English. As Mark Lilla observes in his introduction to the New York Review Books edition, "Most readers today will find the reactionary political views he expressed in it repellent, as Mann himself eventually did."[3] Whatever nonpolitical means, it's not the word that comes to mind if you consider what Mann is doing here.

Nonpolitical is *unpolitisch* in the original German. It might be better translated as "apolitical" or simply "unpolitical," words that are used much more often in English and are thus more likely to strike a chord, one way or the other, in English-language readers. At any rate, while marching under the nonpolitical banner, Mann did indeed express political views, and to call those views reactionary is something of an understatement. He wrote *Reflections* during World War I, and he did so out of passionate support for Germany, accompanied by a palpable enthusiasm for bloodletting as such. The outbreak of the war had filled him with excitement, as if confirming his sense (shared with other artists and intellectuals of the time) that life could no longer go on in its pathetic, familiar triviality, so really, why not go to war? In a letter to his brother Heinrich, quoted in Lilla's introduction, Mann says, in August of 1914, that we should be grateful for the chance to experience the "mighty things" that the war will bring. Europe, he proclaimed, needed a catastrophe. Channeling Nietzsche in his reactionary content as well as in his high ranting style, he opined that Europe had too much "civilization," meaning too much enlightenment, too much reason, too much democracy. Here you can see the logic of him calling himself *unpolitisch*. In his eyes democracy politicized everything, and that was a disaster. War, the bloodier the better, was a cathartic escape both from "civilization" and from politics.

Mann's enthusiasm for cathartic violence is not currently in vogue. Why then republish his *Reflections*, and in an attractive edition that is clearly not just meant for academics with an interest in the darker corners of intellectual history? To judge from Lilla's introduction, the answer would seem to lie in a second term that, like war, Mann also set in opposition to politics. He opposed politics to culture. Culture, for Mann, was what Germany was fighting for. Culture was dark and demonic rather than peaceful, citizenly, and enlightening. It was profound, enigmatic, perhaps ultimately indecipherable, perhaps ultimately sacred. This general viewpoint ought to be familiar. Unlike Mann's embrace of mass bloodshed, his understanding of culture as sacred mystery has not gone away. Nor has his certitude, which follows logically from that understanding, that in its essence culture can only be profaned by politics. As Lilla says, that is what makes *Reflections of a Nonpolitical Man* a "timely" book.[4]

"Mann wrote at a time, like our own," Lilla says, "when artists were under great pressure to declare their political allegiance and shape their work accordingly."[5] The suggestion is that the present is also a time when many feel pressured to declare political allegiance and that Lilla wants us to learn from *Reflections* to resist that pressure. He does not spell out what exactly we are under pressure to declare allegiance *to*. He quotes a sarcastic passage from Mann that, in his words, "could have been written today": "There is only a 'yes' or a 'no,' sheep and goats, one must 'come forward.' Tolerance and delay would be a crime."[6] Lilla concedes that Mann is inconsistent on this point; after all, Mann ended up saying yes to democracy and no to Nazism, though only after considerable delay and a quietly exasperated tolerance of Hitler that is beautifully captured in Colm Toibin's *The Magician*. If the present contains any bad actors that might be analogous to the Nazis, or situations of manifest injustice comparable to those for which the Nazis are now remembered— actors and situations where a yes or a no might be justified—Lilla does not mention them. As against choice, he opts for "ambiguity" and "resistance to formulas."[7] In the final paragraph of his introduction, he comes down in favor of what Mann calls "aestheticism," which seems to mean an artistic appreciation of life that transcends political side-taking and rules out the making of commitments: "There is more to life than is dreamed of in our values and commitments and causes and programs. Even in times of crisis and great injustice, some inner distance must be maintained."[8]

It would be foolhardy to dispute the value of inner distance. Had there been more inner distance in 1914—distance from the most demanding "causes and programs" of the year, perhaps even enough to resist the clamorous appeals to patriotism and the life-threatening penalties that accompanied those appeals—the massive and meaningless slaughter of World War I might have been avoided, and with it, perhaps, the bigger and even badder war that followed. But producing that sort of distance from the nation's demand for violence would have had to be a political achievement, a result of the shared recognition that there were sides to be taken other than national ones, sides directly opposed to the national ones. It would have been a result of both detachment (from patriotism at home) and attachment elsewhere—for example, the solidarity across national borders that very nearly stopped organized French and German workers from lending their support to the war in which so many of them were to die at each other's hands. It does not go without saying that distance and ambiguity, culture and art should be opposed to politics. It is a sign of the times, however, that this opposition is once again in play.

I have a certain sympathy for cultural critics who register a friction and even an incompatibility between culture and politics. Anyone who has taught the genre of the political novel, as I have, will have noticed how uncomfortable even the genre's classics are with politics—how eager Turgenev is in *Fathers and Sons* to pull his favorite characters clear of it and see them in some other, more personal light, how often Conrad in *Nostromo* condemns it as a dirty business. There is nothing uncharacteristic about Emilia Gould's view in that novel that the "constant 'savings of the country'" are "a puerile and bloodthirsty game of murder and rapine played with terrible earnestness by depraved children."[9] The imperative to be politically engaged is not usually the moral of the story. Even Albert Camus's *The Plague*, often read as an allegory of the need to engage in the French Resistance under Nazi occupation, arguably makes a case *against* joining the Resistance, at least if it would entail violence—as effective resistance to the Nazis most certainly did. More often, the obvious takeaway in political novels has to do with critical distance, ambiguity, the ability to see things from more than one viewpoint—just the virtues celebrated in Lilla's introduction to Mann.

Still, Lilla himself is very much a taker of sides, politically speaking; I pause for so long on his introduction in part because his own pushback against what he sees as the politics of the 60s will prove relevant to what follows. But as I hope this book will show, there are other ways of being political. Mann himself illustrates one of them. Though he quietly renounced the sanguinary German nationalism of his *Reflections of a Nonpolitical Man*, what he did not renounce, as Tobias Boes points out, is that book's "assumption that an author and his country are conjoined by a representational link, and that both the words and the actions of an individual reflect the larger character of the national community."[10] Mann had an "active desire to become representative," Boes concludes, and this desire shaped his entire career.[11] In this sense even Mann's novels can't be enlisted on the side of the nonpolitical. On the contrary, Mann's career offers one answer to a question that has bedeviled cultural politics since 1970, the period I will be dealing with in this book. It suggests that culture doesn't represent only itself, but that it is socially representative, passively displaying truths about its time but also intervening—representing in an active sense—so as to push the social collectivity in a certain direction or directions. If it is indeed representative, it would be the duty of critics to figure out what cultural politics does represent, and how much, and with what effects. Cultivating the habit of observing and reflecting on interesting things that don't immediately fit into a pre-existing political category, as Mann did so skillfully and as any critic will hopefully want to learn to do as well, need not interfere with that political sense of the critical vocation and might even be required by it.

Politics has never been reducible to a simple taking of sides. It has always been an "essentially contested" concept, to cite William Connolly's application of W. B. Gallie's phrase, in which what is contested includes how directly the object under consideration, whatever it is, impacts on the fate of the collectivity in question—but also, for that matter, what ought to count as a side.[12] The playful work of imagining alternatives to a given social collectivity, utopian or dystopian or a mixture of both, can by no means be shrunken to a thumbs up or a thumbs down, yet it too is unmistakably political. For that matter, as will be suggested below, Aristotle's old-fashioned sense of politics as the art of governing may not after all be entirely obsolete. More than one understanding of the political might well discover a legitimate interest even in humble tomatoes—who picks the tomatoes, how much the laborers get paid for that work, what pesticides are touched and inhaled while performing it, and so on.

The need for the would-be political critic to get beyond or behind political cliché is obvious as soon as you consider the multitude of possible targets and causes, each of them willing and able to organize political criticism around its priorities, some of them eager to get along with others, some not so much. Nearest to home, perhaps, is the market. In the academy, as in hospitals and law offices and seemingly everywhere else, there has been increasingly intense pressure over the past decades to accept the logic of the market as absolute. That pressure has been worst at the level of employment, where the proportion of university teaching performed by people without even a minimum of job security or (therefore) the freedom to speak their mind without fear of reprisal is somewhere between two-thirds and three-quarters. But a certain bullying has also been felt at the level of the discipline's self-conception. One effect, natural enough in a generation that no longer feels itself shielded from the market, has been an inclination to seek refuge in the selling points that earlier incarnations of the academy had used to explain their existence to a broader public: uncontroversial values like art, pleasure, beauty, truth—as A. O. Scott does (albeit with considerable irony) in *Better Living Through Criticism: How to Think About Art, Pleasure, Beauty, and Truth*.[13] Another effect, closely related, has been a desire to flee political commitments and claims to representativeness, seen as controversial and likely to alienate the broader public, and in any case as utopian and self-aggrandizing. Thus, for example, Rita Felski accuses "the language of politics" of presenting itself as "the only permissible way of accounting" for literary works—a false accusation, but symptomatic of the times.[14] On the other hand, market pressure can also lead to more serious thinking about political commitments—for example, about how hostility to the market has traditionally been part of what it means to be a critic. Hostility to the market, seemingly hardwired into the discipline, is a source of both energy and confusion. Does it make the discipline anticapitalist? On the contrary, does it make the discipline elitist? Can the discipline be both anticapitalist and elitist at the same time? The ambiguity is a reason why, for most critics of whatever persuasion, the subject of politics does not feel ancillary or accidental.

In the 1970s, two relevant events happened more or less simultaneously. Both turned out to be long-term phenomena. One was the impact of the 60s movements on higher education, an impact that was always controversial even within the academy, let alone outside it, but was eventually quite successful in transforming academic habits. The other was neoliberalism. Neoliberal policies of austerity have their own historical trajectory, but they won support for the defunding of public services, including higher education, in large part thanks to the culture wars of the 1980s and 1990s, which took the post-60s politicizing of the humanities as an opportunity to stoke the rage of the "silent majority," with special indignation directed at movements for racial and gender justice. Indignation is perhaps too strong a word for Mark Lilla's version of this argument, but he has certainly presented attention to racial and gender justice as a political mistake, in large part because it added to the rage of the white majority and alienated the so-called Reagan Democrats among whom he grew up. It's a well-populated position.

The 60s movements and neoliberalism also intersect in the sense that this defunding of public institutions of higher learning helped undermine the job market for humanities PhDs. And what affects the job market also affects the consciousness of those facing that job market. This context too helps explain why anyone in or near the discipline will recognize "criticism and politics" as an established and even unavoidable subject for reflection and debate.

As its title suggests, this book is intended both as an introduction to the subject of criticism and politics and (like Mann's *Reflections*, though shorter and hopefully more readable) as a polemic. The immediate stimulus to indulge in a polemic came from a series of theoretical proclamations over the last decade or so associated with so-called surface reading and post-critique—proclamations that from my vantage point looked like attempts to depoliticize the practice of criticism and even to carry forward the right-wing culture war's attack on the humanities, which seemed to peak in the 1990s but has remained a significant part of national politics. I felt "called out," so to speak, provoked by these proclamations to mock what I saw as self-betraying silliness, maybe even, at worst, an impulse to repeat the errors of the *unpolitisch* Thomas Mann and some of his friends in 1914.[15] I tried to put my own contrary assumptions on the table. I published several short pieces. They threw further fuel on the fire, and I can't say I was entirely displeased to see the sparks fly.

Here is a sample, from a *PMLA* roundtable on Rita Felski's *The Limits of Critique*. Felski writes:

"Anyone who attends academic talks has learned to expect the inevitable question, 'But what about power?' Perhaps it is time to start asking different questions: 'But what about love?'" [p. 17 in *The Limits of Critique*]

And I respond:

Power has sometimes been used, it is true, in vague and intellectually sloppy ways. But when the over-critical critics of whom Felski disapproves talk about power, they are most often trying to talk, successfully or not, about injustice. If you think of power as shorthand for injustice, you will perhaps hesitate before calling for it to be decommissioned. The word *injustice* does not appear in the index of Felski's book. Would she maintain that it is an inappropriate or a played-out topic? A flower can be beautiful. The photograph of the corpse of a child on a Syrian beach, beautiful or not, will also have to be discussed in terms of injustice. Is it clear to *PMLA*'s readers that the task of literature, and therefore of critics of literature, is to talk about flowers rather than drowned Syrian children or to see such photographs as if they were flowers? I am curious to know whether Felski would go ahead and make the case. I am also curious to know why society should pay for us to make this substitution.[16]

This remains pretty much my position. But in the process of meditating on this back and forth—leading me to pronounce that the "limits of critique" project amounted to a "corporate restructuring" of criticism and leading Felski to respond with comparable asperity—I came to feel a need to engage, historically and philosophically, on a deeper level than the pugilistic roundtables the hastily convened periodical venues would permit. Hence the project jettisoned some of the local squabbling and metamorphosed into a book-length hybrid, a mid-size polemical introduction. My aim shifted from the very likely ephemeral controversies of the moment, as I reframed the persistence of such controversies, bringing in some voices from earlier periods and thus laying out a more lasting and responsible position about how criticism has and has not been a political enterprise. I also attempt to explain, for those entering the profession now, what they ought to be thinking about and the larger meanings of their personal commitment to it.

I recognize a certain tension between the ambition to write an introduction—a work that claims to be cool, fair-minded, and authoritative—and the ambition to write a polemic—a work that is obliged to try to be livelier and to that end can afford to be less restrained in expressing its true opinion of its opponents. I have tried and (as I bring this project to a close) am still trying to find a suitable balance between the two. It doesn't seem to me impossible.

To begin with, this project entails some work of historical contextualization. Chapter 1, "Criticism in the Wake of the 1960s," discusses the heritage of Matthew Arnold as I encountered it when I entered graduate school at Harvard (admittedly not a perfectly representative institution) in the early 1970s and the dramatic collision between the Arnoldian model of humanistic criticism and the demands of the 1960s emancipation movements, which were little by little working their way into the humanities in the 70s and 80s and introducing a fundamental concern with race, gender, sexuality, imperialism, and other highly political topics. A collision of sorts did happen, with much of the resistance to the 60s influence framed in Arnoldian terms. And yet (so I argue) there were also deep continuities between Arnold's notion of criticism as a sort of permanent opposition and the new style of opposition encouraged by the 60s movements, continuities that help explain both why the influence of the 60s "took" in the academy and why that influence assumed the form it did (particular, limited): for example, criticism that is political in the sense of being anti-reformist and anti-institutional. I offer Lionel Trilling as a relevant example.

At another level, the project of assessing the relationship between criticism and politics also requires a clarification of language. Chapter 2, "Criticizing," begins with a discussion of the word "criticism" as it appears in Raymond Williams's book *Keywords*, with attention to the difference between criticism there and in Williams's earlier *Culture and Society*, the book that established Arnold as a central figure in a left-wing oppositional tradition. Williams (born in 1921) and Judith Butler (born in 1956), though of different generations, are discussed as central figures in the new left-wing oppositional tradition that came out of the 1960s, embodying a relationship to the 60s movements and negotiating between those movements and the institutional form that criticism had previously assumed. I put a discussion of Butler's thinking on "critique" (in dialogue with Talal Asad) together with Williams's on "criticism," relating both to the charge that criticism is political in the sense of being merely negative, a form of faultfinding. Is faultfinding a decisive element in the legacy that the 60s movements left to criticism? Is it the necessary consequence of so-called identity politics? I argue that it is not, emphasizing Butler's differences from Asad (whom I take to represent a disavowed but real identity politics). On the other hand, I also reinterpret the "historicist/contextualist paradigm" (Joseph North's phrase) as an effect of what remains most desirable in identity politics—an effect that is irreducible to faultfinding.

I argue as well that the supplying of historical context represents a form of defensible expertise (expertise as such being a sine qua non of academic work) that more or less reconciles the anti-elitist, anti-expertise impulse of the 60s with the generation's political goals. That those goals were never reducible to identity politics in any sense can be illustrated by Edward W. Said (born in 1935), the chapter's final figure "of" the 60s generation, who helped define the decade's influence on the characteristic intellectual procedures of the following decades. Colonialism in general, and Zionism in particular, being popular and populist in their appeal to their respective constituencies, how could academic critique of them ever have bowed supinely to the sensitivities of any given constituency, as the critics of identity politics accuse it of doing? On the contrary, Said's distinctive and influential mode of critique reveals a commitment to universalism—a commitment that played a much larger part in the movements of the 60s (so I argue) than is usually recognized.

Even more than Williams, Butler, or Said, the figure who is most central to the self-conception of criticism in the decades after 1970 is Michel Foucault. Chapter 3, "Lost Centrality," takes Foucault as the successor to Matthew Arnold: the next general guide to work in the humanities and to the understanding of what criticism has come to be and why it is worth doing. The chapter begins with a close reading of Foucault's treatment of "commentary" in his lecture "The Order of Discourse." That section (one of Edward Said's favorites) deserves to be seen as perhaps the richest and most troubling discussion of the paradoxical nature of criticism, and (coming as it does in 1970) it makes a useful landmark for those tracing the trajectory of criticism and politics over this period. The chapter reads several recent critical enterprises (for example, "surface reading" and criticism-as-performance, as in Andrea Long Chu's *Females*) as implicit responses to the dilemma Foucault laid out. As theorist of disciplinarity, Foucault also permits a structural comparison between the place of criticism in literary studies and the methods and objects of other disciplines. Does disciplinarity explain the coherence or incoherence of political claims for one's work? Are the claims made by literary critics different in kind from those made by the practitioners of other disciplines? Are they more or less persuasive?

The chapter then takes up John Guillory's argument (one of the most serious advanced during the culture wars) that it is the marginalization of the humanities that has generated their political claims, which should be understood not in terms of the politics they articulate but rather as a collective cry of disciplinary pain. Against this argument, I bring forward Guillory's own account of the discipline's lost centrality. According to Guillory, critic/journalists of the eighteenth century made claims to general social significance that were largely valid, since (by Guillory's own account) these proto-critics played the socially significant role of codifying the norms by which the emergent middle class could identify itself *as* a class with common interests and a common destiny—the destiny of ruling. There is a striking parallel, I suggest, with the criticism of the 60s, although that parallel is obviously imperfect. In addition to class, the divergent interests and perspectives to be reconciled include race, ethnicity, gender, and so on. The goal of instituting a new mode of rule—building a new inclusive common sense that is respectful of all and yet remains open to communication and cooperation with older habits of thinking—has remained inarticulate, to say the least. Still, the analogy is intriguing and valuable, if only because it offers resistance to the tiresome tale of criticism's or the humanities' decline into irrelevance. Tellers of that tale must be reminded that it presupposes a real centrality that was there to be lost. On what was that presumptive public significance ever based? If criticism's significance *had* a base, even if what was erected on it was something less than centrality, it becomes at least theoretically possible to imagine that it can have one again. That theoretical possibility leads us straight back to the notion of discovering common interests and ambitions among what seem to be the dramatically divergent perspectives of identity politics.

Chapter 4, "Aesthetics and the Governing of Others," returns to Foucault. Foucault describes critique (in the essay "What Is Critique?") as "the art of not being governed *like that*."[17] I read this description as a gesture of antinormativity. To point one's finger with a "*like that*" is to refuse to state a principle or norm in the name of which one is objecting. The refusal of normativity is a refusal not merely to be governed, but also to govern, since governing, for Foucault, is what norms are inevitably guilty of. This refusal helps explain Foucault's attraction to aesthetics, which is widely seen as a refuge from normativity. This is another point of convergence between Foucault and the 60s liberation movements, which are known for their own refusal of aesthetics, seen as falsely universalizing and falsely authoritative, but which also entertained (as it is easy enough to show) a much more positive attitude toward aesthetics. The central argument here, however, is trickier: that the "disinterestedness" of the Kantian aesthetic, which serves as a procedure for self-abstraction or self-problematization, is also an essential part of the *politics* of the 60s liberation movements and their inheritors. Given the divergent identities and interests that had to be considered and reconciled if the movements (plural) were to come together and function, even intermittently, as a single collective political force—as "the movement"—some degree of self-abstraction was a necessity, and the legacy of that critical habit is to be seen in the current status of the term "intersectionality." Neither then nor now is freedom an absolute value. "Force till right is ready," Matthew Arnold's ominous phrase from "The Function of Criticism at the Present Time,"[18] does not simply refer to Arnold's willingness to use state violence against the rioters in Hyde Park; it can also be stretched so as to read, or so I suggest, as a commitment to see the aesthetic do the work of governing—the work of governing better.

Chapter 5, "Grievances," focuses on the political movements that helped women's studies and ethnic studies programs win acceptance from the academy in and after the 60s. Were these programs forced upon the academy by the sort of outside pressure that some within the academy (including those who hold that criticism is "too political") feel should be discouraged now, and perhaps should have been discouraged then? Beginning with the history of Native American studies, this chapter argues that there were principles on which the academy welcomed these programs, principles of importance both to the way in which disciplines are constituted and legitimated and to the way in which the project of democracy makes its own demands outside the university. This is one of the more important senses in which politics is not external to the university. The university's somewhat hidden *desire* for ethnic studies programs (some more than others) is illustrated with reference to Kenneth Warren's reflections on the field of African American literature and Benjamin Schreier's reflections on the field of Jewish American literature. For both, the principles involved turn out to be higher than mere demography or diversity—and these standards are not always met.

Yet the traditional logic that called for the preservation and transmission of the cultural heritage also remains operative when the cultural heritage is pluralized, as it is after the 60s movements, and for that matter when it is extended beyond the nation. What's at stake is democracy. At the same time, the example of Edward W. Said demonstrates that democracy as it exists, on a national scale, is not sufficient to legitimize new intellectual work or for that matter to dictate the responsibilities of the intellectual. Reading Said through the lens of Noam Chomsky's essay "The Responsibility of Intellectuals" (which Said greatly admired) and against Said's own (exilic) theory of the intellectual, I present him as "organic" (in Gramsci's sense) to Vietnam-era antimilitarism, a strain of 60s thinking that requires a geographical stretching of democracy as well as a rethinking of elitism and expertise.

Chapter 6, "The Historical and the Transhistorical," argues that from a political viewpoint, Walter Benjamin's wildly influential imagination of the "angel of history" is not a useful paradigm. This is in part because it abandons the concept of progress that was essential to the entry of ethnic and women's studies programs into the academy and that ought, so I suggest, to continue guiding their efforts, and the discipline's. Instead, ethnic studies and queer studies have largely made an uneasy peace with the discipline's dominant mode of temporality and dominant affect, which is melancholy. Rather than a general or indiscriminate reverence for the dead *as* the dead, an affect whose antecedents are theological, this chapter argues for a sense of history that is political because it focuses on meaningful links between past and present. Is this so obvious as not to need repeating? No, I argue, given that constructionism, the practical disciplinary common sense that "X is a construct," encourages the critic's freedom to reconstruct the world only by assuming that the world comes in the form of a chaos of meaningless particulars on which meaningful narratives can then be freely imposed. Our freedom to impose narratives depends on the premise that the world, unimagined, is meaningless.

The strange premise that history is widely seen to be meaningless in itself is also traced through the chapter's subsection entitled "History Versus Fun." Here "fun" stands for the assumption that human nature is everywhere the same, the assumption (again, theological) of the right wing in the culture wars maintaining that it was only in those terms that the value of the Greek and Latin classics could be defended. Great literature was fun because there was no "context" to interfere with the reader's pleasure; the reader in the present was free to identify with characters from the distant past without any knowledge of moral and cultural differences between then and now getting in the way. History does not or should not make a difference. The notion that history should and does make a difference emerges here as part of the political program of the 60s movements. And the recently expressed desire to get that paradigm out of the way so as to allow for crowd-pleasing entertainments and unalloyed reader identification emerges as a continuation of the populist politics of the right.

Yet history is not composed only of differences. If it were, it would truly be meaningless. Page duBois's spirited attempt to take the Greek classics back from their right-wing champions reveals that the case cannot be made without attention to sameness as well as difference. Sameness, I will argue, can and must be understood as something other than a convenient and unexamined humanistic given—indeed, it too, properly conceived, is a valuable part of the legacy of the 60s movements. If history is properly conceived, transhistorical sameness *is* historical—as historical as difference is. This argument is pursued by a reflection on Fredric Jameson's 1981 proclamation, in *The Political Unconscious*, that the cultural past can be only be retrieved if it can be seen as belonging to a single great collective story. This unfashionable sentiment is subjected to a certain doubt even in Jameson's own subsequent work, and with good reason; the small and apparently innocuous word "great" in Jameson's phrase commits the critic to making room for ample dark amoral violence, abusive power so extensive that it comes very close to meaninglessness, even if it doesn't ultimately stop there.

Chapter 7, "Cosmopolitical Criticism in Deep Time," takes as its premise that criticism's new global scale, an effect both of capitalist globalization and of the 60s movements of international solidarity, has been accompanied by a corresponding expansion of temporal scale. Going back before 1500, before modernity, so-called deep time relativizes European colonialism and the core-periphery model. It thereby makes room for the subdiscipline of world literature, which emerges after 2000 as a candidate to replace postcolonial studies. But it also makes room for a new interest in the culture of Indigenous peoples, many of whom consider themselves as having been colonized *by non-Europeans*. It is too soon to assess the moral and political implications of this shift, which both rejects and sustains impulses of the 60s movements. Examining world literature in relation to developments in world history, this chapter considers two non-Eurocentric options: on the one hand, the moral shallowness that might result (once again) if criticism uses this opportunity to flee from context, and on the other hand, a more positive revaluation of anticolonial culture both in Europe and elsewhere, seen now in a truly worldly perspective as one site of what has to be thought of as a narrative of moral progress. The chapter ends by reflecting on the contrast between criticism's generally anti-progressive stance in theory and the claims critics often make for progress *in their own work*. Stuart Hall, perhaps the single finest example we have of an organic intellectual of the 60s movements, helps me draw the moral: that in order to believe in progress in the world as well as in their work, critics need to belong to the world in something like the way they belong to their work, and ensure that their work makes changes in the world.

That's what I think critics are for.

As should be obvious, this book is not meant as a survey of criticism, even criticism over the last fifty years. It is not a guide to better living, like Scott's, even an ironic one. It is not a how-to book for would-be critics trying to master the craft. It is meant as a brief introduction to how and why conceptions of what criticism is and does have changed, with commentary added about how we should feel about those changes from a political point of view. In trying to combine a slender but hopefully clarifying outline with a vigorous polemic that does not spill over into a rant, I find myself defending certain aspects of the profession as it was formed in the last half century—defending it because it has been attacked, and attacked in particular for what it has taken from the legacy of the 1960s, but also because, somewhat to my surprise, I find it worth defending. But the book is polemical in the sense that certain practitioners will not recognize themselves in it or be pleased by what they do recognize. Even at its most creative and constructive, as when it imagines alternative ways of being and feeling, politics is nothing if not divisive.

1 Criticism in the Wake of the 1960s

From 1970 to 2020

When I began graduate school in English in 1972, we incoming students were invited to purchase and familiarize ourselves with Walter Jackson Bate's 719-page anthology, *Criticism: The Major Texts* (1952), which had just come out in an updated edition in 1970. As of this writing, the anthology is ranked at 2,989,597 on Amazon. That's in the same humbling range as my own books. I suppose the number could be worse. But it's nothing to write home about. The one Amazon review, while full-throated in its admiration, laments mildly that the book's moment is over: "In this day and age of splintered and broken schools of literary theory, where nobody seems to agree what is the right way to go about reading and discussing literature, W. J. Bate's *Criticism: The Major Texts* is a wistful reminder of the days when critics were far more certain."

Were critics so very certain, in 1970, about the right way of reading and discussing literature? It seems unlikely. As I remember, different options loomed, and the ones that were attractive (for me, these would not include the Jungian hunt for universal myths and symbols) were attractive in distinct and confusingly contradictory ways. I felt I was being asked to choose, for example, between interpreting a text in its historical context—like interpreting *Paradise Lost* as an epic poem about the English Civil War, which is to say about the success and failure of the world's first revolution—and so-called close reading, where we were supposed to uncover a poem's ambiguities on our own, without access to its context—the assumption being that context was a crutch we should not learn to lean on. Both of those had their appeal. Professor Bate—who was a charismatic figure on campus, ran the first-year colloquium, and had won a Pulitzer Prize for his biography of Keats—identified himself with what he called "humanism." Humanism seemed to be something else again, although it too downplayed historical context—even in the biography of Keats—and played up, correspondingly, the ability of a work of literature to speak its piece loud and clear, unhindered by the passage of centuries. Bate's humanism came to us suffused with a certain man-will-always-be-a-sinful-creature conservatism, but that atmosphere never solidified into any actual discussion of politics, conservative or progressive. And most of the time, it's true, we were not plagued by fundamental doubts. Our professors asked us to read George Eliot or T. S. Eliot in order to figure out what the authors were really saying, and that's what we tried our best to do.

Today, the uncertainty does seem more intense. Many critics and critics-in-training give the impression of being unpleasantly up in the air as to what they have signed up for and why. Both the uncertainty of the what and the uncertainty of the why seem somehow entangled in politics. Politics has the positive appeal of connecting what academics do with matters of pressing interest to people outside academia, but it is rarely mentioned without provoking confusion. The question of what criticism is meant to be or do, politically speaking, therefore seems worth re-opening.

As a way of getting this inquiry jumpstarted, I propose a glance back at Bate's anthology. What has happened in the roughly fifty years since its publication? If there used to be more certainty about criticism and if that certainty has indeed been shaken, one would like to know what has shaken it. Does the fault lie with the advent of literary theory, its schools broken and splintered? Or was theory (itself pronounced dead on more than one occasion) perhaps only part of something larger, and even something that is still showing signs of life? There have been other doubt-inducing trends and movements in the half century since 1970, some of them involving politics. I argue that a more plausible agent of change might be sought in the social movements of the 1960s. In 1970, the various liberation movements—which either were or were not united, depending on whom you asked, in what was then called, hopefully, "the movement"—were widely perceived to be slowing down and perhaps even stopping. But in another sense, the 60s were arguably just beginning—beginning, for better or for worse, their influence on thinking in the university and on criticism in particular.

The "for worse" side of this explanation ought to be familiar. The premise that the 60s had a large, disruptive, and undesirable impact on American life has been a staple of mainstream conversation at least since the culture wars of the late 1980s and 1990s, and it has never gone out of fashion. The decade has been blamed for a variety of sins small and large, from a loss of certainty about the value of the humanities to narcissism, relativism, postmodernism, neoliberalism, consumerism, wokeness, victim studies (now an actual degree program), cancel culture, and critical race theory. In *The Age of Entitlement,* Christopher Caldwell—who declares that "for two generations, 'the sixties' has given order to every aspect of the national life of the United States— its partisan politics, its public etiquette, its official morality"—blames the decade for setting up a "rival constitution" that makes race "the central concept in the country's self-understanding" and is thus incompatible with the true Constitution.[1] Most often, as for Caldwell, the accusing fingers point at those who pay too much attention to race. The most unsparing accusations complain about the hegemony of identity politics, as in Walter Benn Michaels's *The Trouble with Diversity: How We Learned to Love Identity and Ignore Inequality*: "for thirty years, while the gap between the rich and the poor has grown larger, we've been urged to respect people's identities—as if the problem of poverty would be solved if we just appreciated the poor."[2]

The more general charge, though by no means the most severe, is that the political energy of the 60s was misdirected, as when Richard Rorty mentions "the English department left" or when Russell Jacoby announces that "radicals captured the Modern Language Association."[3] If you are a dues-paying member of the Modern Language Association, as I am, this seems an overstatement—just try, as I did, to get a resolution through the MLA condemning Israeli mistreatment of Palestinian academics. But the sarcasm still smarts. Nevertheless, on these topics, more thinking is called for than has been offered. Behind what was not yet called snark lie political questions that, if taken seriously, would require stepping back to consider not just the place of the university in American life and the place of literature within the university, but more generally what has and has not been attainable, politically speaking, over the past decades, given both good intentions (which were often quite real) and the particular resistances that had to be overcome on particular issues. A key example is economic inequality. People need to be reminded that getting the rich to cough up even a paltry share of their ill-gotten riches was and is a lot harder than getting almost any other political concession on any other issue. In *Achieving Our Country*, Rorty decides finally to grant, without apparent sarcasm, that the "cultural Left" succeeded in diminishing the total quantity of "sadism" in America. That would seem worth counting as an achievement, and an achievement that has had direct material effects.[4]

In any event, why not peel the sarcasm away and have a look at the thing itself? If something like the capture of a department or a discipline or a professional association did indeed happen, even a partial one, it would be helpful to know what the results were, how much of a change it wrought. Could such a change be described as genuinely political? Is a politics something that a collective entity like a discipline, a department, or a professional association can properly be said to possess? And if so, can that politics be described as progressive? Did the reincarnation of the 60s in the academy, such as it was, betray what was truly progressive in the movement, or did it merely inherit the movement's political confusions and weaknesses? Was the influence of the 60s erased by countervailing ideological forces within the discipline, continuities that ran deeper than a few shouts in the street, and dictated that there would be a conservative core to its ongoing assumptions and operations? Or were the continuities, assuming they existed, not after all so very conservative? These questions deserve more reflection than they have received. Even if they can't all be answered, it's worth something merely to prop them open and let in some light and air.

As a first hypothesis, let us imagine that what has happened in these fifty years can be measured by the stark contrast between what criticism meant in Bate's anthology and the very different animal that criticism became afterwards, in large part under the influence of the 60s movements.

As it happens, the 60s make a cameo appearance, late in the anthology, when Bate introduces R. P. Blackmur, one of the prominent mid-century critics added for the updated 1970 edition. Bate writes:

> The original movement of the New Criticism, insofar as it differed from Arnold, was primarily a movement toward a stricter and more involved formalism. But when it found itself in the 1960s faced with a militant anti-elitism—sociological in its interest rather than formalistic—it began to return to the Arnoldian fold, at least in general spirit, and despite justifiable pride in what it had done, in something of an autumnal mood.[5]

This is Bate's anticipation of the Amazon reviewer's loss-of-certainty story. He places enduring certainty about how to read literature not in "formalism," like the context-averse close reading of the New Critics, but in Matthew Arnold, whose concerns are humanistic, which is to say less formal than moral. What has ended the New Critics' experiment, Bate suggests—unsettling their commitment to formalism and returning them to the solid certainties of the Arnoldian fold—is not literary theory, which is not yet on Bate's radar, but rather the "sociological" interest of the 1960s, a sociological interest that Bate sees as also militantly anti-elitist.

I hazard an unadventurous translation: in the 60s, certain marginalized social groups have been audibly demanding institutional recognition for themselves while also complaining, consistently, that a criticism that did not recognize them would have to be described as elitist. Bate sees them as opposed to humanism, which here seems to mean respect for the timeless universality of human nature, and thus also the universal validity of the literature that explores and reflects on human nature. Trying to see the same logic from the point of view of these social groups, one might say that, in their eyes, humanism claimed to speak for everyone at all times and places. But this was a false claim, since they had never been consulted about either their moral or their aesthetic values, both of which might well be different. It's time for a consultation.[6]

It's time for a consultation—that's not the worst way of describing the polite memo humanism had received, or for that matter a way of describing the new norms of courtesy that seem to have crystallized little by little over the past decades. According to Stefan Collini, one of Arnold's more sympathetic commentators, it is Arnold's sensibility as much as his ideas that captivated his followers: his "cast of mind" and his "temper," his "poise," his "finesse and tact."[7]

If so, it seems worth speculating that there is some analogous sensibility among the members of the more recent generation—among those, let us say, who have been similarly captivated since 1970 by Michel Foucault. Foucault, I would argue, has come to play much the same vocation-defining role that Arnold had played for an earlier generation. He is not commonly associated with finesse and tact, and yet it seems likely that, among those inspired by him, there is in fact a new temper, a new poise, a new set of unwritten rules concerning the proper tone of voice to adopt, when and where to display concern or on the contrary to withhold one's concern. If such a sensibility has not been articulated, it has surely been parodied and even perhaps awarded a prize for "bad writing." Readers will perhaps grin knowingly, indicating that they recognize the object of the parody. But why not also try to articulate that sensibility, staying agnostic for the moment as to whether sarcasm is or is not in order? Why not look for a finesse or tact that, like Arnold's but now taking a different form, today determines both lexical and syntactic choices and, more generally, that determines who and what needs to be consulted if one's professional statements are to be received as both polite and intellectually responsible? The tacit model of good scholarly manners is surely out there, whether one feels comfortable within it or on the contrary feels prevented from blurting out the impolitic things that most urgently need to be said.

Bate echoes a much-repeated complaint about what its critics came to call identity politics. So is that the issue? Is it Bate's humanist universalism against an identity-politics particularism that draws its inspiration from the movements of the 60s? To some extent, yes, of course. But that is not the end of the conversation. For starters, it is better not to take for granted that identity politics is an adequate umbrella term. Does it really cover the full range of impulses and commitments that animated the 1960s? In "Periodizing the 60s," Fredric Jameson marks the true beginnings of "what will come to be called the 60s" not with movements for racial and gender justice in the first world but "in the third world with the great movement of decolonization in British and French Africa."[8] The "most characteristic expressions of a properly first world 60s"—he mentions the predictable flower child references: sex, drugs, and rock and roll—all come later. The student antiwar movement, on the other hand, not only borrowed from third-world models but "found its mission in resistance to wars aimed precisely at stemming the new revolutionary forces in the third world."[9] Like the movements of national liberation (at least much of the time—Négritude was of course a powerful force) and what was then called the "ecology" movement, the antiwar movement made its case in unabashedly universalistic terms.

"Universalizing" was basic to French third-worldism, according to Kristin Ross, and third-worldism in turn was a neglected but important element in May 1968. All it meant, Ross says, was "giving a name to a political wrong," a name that mobilized both the subjects and former subjects of colonialism (in France in the 1960s, the Algerians were a highly charged example) and "students and others in the west."[10] In his compelling resuscitation of mid-century humanism and his account of the "big bang" of the 60s that eventually ended it, Mark Greif observes that much of what is politically most powerful in the decade, like the rhetoric of Martin Luther King Jr. continues to make use of "universalist rhetoric" in arguing for the recognition of minorities, like African Americans, and of women.[11] "The New Left, up through the early 1960s, still centrally used the language of man as universalistic, morally unimpeachable, and the ultimate reference of political and moral improvement." Greif is especially interesting on what Joan Wallach Scott calls the "paradoxes" of female speakers who continue to appeal to universalism even though as they are well aware it has excluded them, and on how American feminists of the 1960s like Betty Friedan let "universalism announce its own thoughtlessness or grammatical incoherence, falling apart by itself." Friedan, he says, "both preserves and dissects" universalizing rhetoric.[12] Identity politics, understood as a rejection of false human universals in favor of the truth of social particulars, is one genuine impulse of the 60s, as in Black Power and "difference" feminism, but as a putative representation of the whole it is drastically misleading. In those contexts, universalism was (and arguably still is) worth fighting for.[13] It is a political as well as a historical error to allow universalism to be claimed by the other side. Here is one reason, then, for being careful about the hypothesis of a simple clash between criticism as it came out of the 60s and criticism as it is represented in Bate's anthology.

Bate worried that attention to the social groups and social hierarchies behind or around or within or shut out of literature threatens to distract attention from literature's value—not its supposed value in itself, as for the aesthetic purists, but its ultimate value (as he would say) for life, or for us.[14] Literature's ultimate value: that's another line of demarcation with the 1960s. Most of the major figures Bate includes in his anthology rephrase, in different vocabularies, the common proposition that literature matters a great deal. He has little patience for anything that gets in the way of that proposition. As if unwilling to waste any time in getting to a conclusive explanation for *why* literature matters, Bate remarkably puts Aristotle first in the anthology, as if he were answering Plato, although Plato was almost half a century older. Aristotle shows that the "poetic," which was not yet called "literature," possesses unity of form and that its unity of form makes it into a special and permanent kind of knowledge, higher and more enduring than the chaotic contingency of mere historical events in the sequence in which they occur.

For Bate, and not just for him, this answer still commands considerable assent. (Consider for example what "narrative" means to the Marxist critic Fredric Jameson, to be discussed in a later chapter.) Given that commitment, it's to Bate's credit that the anthology jumps from Aristotle to Longinus. The concept of the sublime in Longinus ignores both Aristotle's unity of form and (in so doing) literature's contribution to knowledge. Instead, it addresses itself to intensity of feeling. It bestows on literature a different kind of value. Sublimity tears us apart, doing so not with unified wholes but with jagged disunited fragments that anticipate, as Bate comments, Matthew Arnold's "touchstones." One of Longinus's illustrations is brief but still dazzling: the two short sentences "Let there be light. And there was light." (For Longinus, the Bible counts as literature.) Later Kant would argue that sublimity too is a kind of knowledge—knowledge of the limits beyond which the conceptual categories we bring to the world cannot go. In the decades since Bate's anthology came out, that sublimity-based case for the value of literature has become increasingly prominent: what literature knows about, we now say with a hint of paradox, is ways in which knowledge is limited, and especially the limits to our knowledge of others. That sort of knowledge or anti-knowledge, acknowledged as valuable outside as well as inside the discipline, has given a boost to the discipline's prestige in other fields.

The Dignity of Opposition: Matthew Arnold

If this book were intended as a historical survey of criticism rather than a polemical introduction to it, I could offer myself the pleasure of lingering over each of Bate's selections and then adding some of my own from the half century that followed. Instead I will summarize drastically. The Bate anthology skips the Middle Ages, presumably because Bate thinks religious belief in that period was too all-pervasive to permit an autonomous or secular case to be made for literature. The succeeding highpoints are explicit defenses of secular literature, as in Sir Philip Sidney, Percy Bysshe Shelley, and (more surprisingly) the wonderful, progressive, and under-appreciated Romantic critic William Hazlitt. The story then comes to a climax in Matthew Arnold. In so doing, it also makes a major turn. For though Arnold sees literature as taking over the socially necessary role in the world once played by religion, and thus winning for itself something of religion's social significance, he doesn't celebrate literature alone. He also celebrates criticism. This includes, of course, the criticism of literature. But the decisive reference is to criticism *as such*, as an activity in its own right, independent of what it is criticism of. What Bate values most in Arnold, he says, is "his constant support of the dignity of critical thinking."[15]

The phrase "critical thinking" has come to sound portentously empty, as if inviting the wrong people to celebrate its emptiness as a kind of authoritative neutrality. University administrators can't seem to do without it.[16] But Bate, glossing Arnold, reads it to mean something administrators might hesitate to embrace. Criticism for him is a kind of permanent opposition. It assumes that something is fundamentally wrong with the culture of the present and that its task is to make that wrongness known. This assumption is a strong argument for the dignity of criticism, maybe even the most consistently influential argument the discipline has enjoyed. Following Arnold, criticism becomes a natural vocation of any and all who, in the world of books and ideas, see that something really must be done, even if Arnold and his followers tend to be vague about what exactly that is or why it is so needful. The vagueness is certainly a drawback, but it has been both disciplinarily productive and, as I can testify, personally seductive. Arnold, Bate says, is "an *apologist* for literature, who tried to assert essential ends at a time when Western thought—in criticism as in almost everything else—was becoming increasingly absorbed in means for their own sake."[17] Means for their own sake, with no thought of essential ends—this is not exactly a condemnation of the capitalist system. But it could pass for one, if one were eager enough for institutional approval of one's own anticapitalist politics. It could pass as confirmation that those of us who were out demonstrating in our spare time had made the right choice of what to study the rest of the time.

Once again, therefore, a contrast that looked like it was going to be clear and decisive turns out blurry. For if what Arnold stands for is opposition, then there is obvious common ground between Bate and the liberationist projects of the 60s. Those projects were nothing if not oppositional.

In 1970, how could one avoid aligning oneself with the opposition? In 1970 we saw the publication of Kate Millett's *Sexual Politics*, a manifesto of feminist literary criticism whose author was hailed by *Time* as "the Mao Tse-tung of Women's Liberation."[18] There was a cultural revolution brewing here at home, and patriarchy being as pervasive and as noxious as we were discovering it was, self-scrutiny was becoming an obligation, even for women but especially for us men. What you had to oppose might well be yourself. Or your country. In May 1970 student demonstrators were shot and killed at Kent State by the National Guard. All that spring B-52s were engaged in the massive carpet-bombing of Cambodia, an escalation secretly authorized in 1969 by President Nixon. The operation is estimated to have killed approximately 100,000

Cambodians while rendering some 2 million homeless. By thus encouraging the overthrow of the Cambodian government, the bombing also led to the rise of the Khmer Rouge and thus to the genocide of 1975–1979, in which 1.5 to 2 million died. Indirect causation, perhaps, but who could confidently claim that American responsibility was negligible? America did not claim responsibility for the genocide.

In 1970, a commitment to Arnoldian opposition did not stretch so far as to require self-questioning attention to gender or genocide. I do not remember much discussion of Aristotle's classification of women or slaves, or for that matter of the atrocities committed by Athens in acquiring and maintaining its own empire, like the massacre of all the adult males on the island of Melos, an island asking only to be left alone during the Peloponnesian War. All this was known by scholars, of course. But in the most profound sense, it didn't matter. The mattering came afterwards, as the lessons of the 60s very gradually sunk in—a process that is arguably still happening, with all its attendant questions attached and some new ones. The process and the questions still engage those critics who continue to feel that opposition is part of their job description.[19]

The danger of slipping back into a contrast between the sensibility of the 60s and the sensibility of Arnoldian humanism is hard to avoid, especially where it is literature as criticism's specific object rather than criticism as such that is in question. How could the 60s bestow on literature the single-minded veneration that Bate did? In the 60s, the overriding project of liberation meant that literature, though glorious, had to share its glory with other forms of expression, some of them grounded in ordinary social life and, in that sense at least, yes, both "sociological" and "anti-elitist." One handy example is the genre of the demonstration. Even those who neither participated in demonstrations nor, given the opportunity, would have wanted to participate in them find it hard to recall the political theater of the 1960s without some acknowledgement of its creative energy and hopefulness. Think of Martin Luther King's "I Have a Dream" speech at the Lincoln Memorial in August 1963, or Norman Mailer's nonfiction novel *The Armies of the Night*, about the 1967 march on the Pentagon, or the barricades of Paris in May 1968 and the poetic surmise that under the cobblestones you might find the beach.

A century earlier, Matthew Arnold had had his own opportunity to acknowledge the creative energy and hopefulness of a democratic demonstration, but he declined it. In 1866 there was a large march outside London's Hyde

Park, during agitation for the Second Reform Bill (which eventually granted suffrage to most of the male working class). The marchers broke down the railings around the park, perhaps accidentally. Unsympathetic observers thought the crowd was out of control. Property had been damaged. Arnold spoke sardonically of "a little rioting, and *what they call* popular demonstrations" (my italics). In the first edition of *Culture and Anarchy*, he repeated (citing his father) the recommendation that in cases like this, it would be best to follow the Roman example by flogging the rank-and-file and flinging the leaders from the Tarpeian Rock. That passage was deleted from subsequent editions, but Arnold did not delete his complaint that the working-class marchers were putting into practice "an Englishman's right to do what he likes; his right to march where he likes, meet where he likes, enter where he likes, hoot as he likes, threaten as he likes, smash as he likes."[20] This is more or less Bate's reaction to the "militant anti-elitism" of the 1960s.

For the variety of criticism that came out of the 1960s, literature continues to matter, but demonstrations also matter. After all, demonstrations were one way in which people whose voices often did not make it into print (in the case of Hyde Park, this meant those who had been excluded even from the vote, though some of them did in fact manage to get published) were attempting to make their voices matter. If mattering is a pie, literature gets a smaller slice. In that sense, literature matters less. Thus the door swings open for Stuart Hall and what will come to be called cultural studies, which adds other cultural objects and practices to the scholarly and pedagogical agenda. Even in literature departments that claim no special affiliation with cultural studies, there is a broader understanding of what kinds of scholarship and teaching are acceptable. In most departments, literature remains the major subject, but room is also made, and increasingly so, for film, music, new social media, and other sorts of cultural activity. Bate resists this opening up. Notice, however, that Bate's personal resistance does not follow logically from what he tells us about Matthew Arnold. Arnold's position, to repeat, is that what really matters is *criticism*, and criticism is an independent activity. It sometimes takes literature as its object, but it always and necessarily aims at life. (Poetry, in Arnold's much-repeated formula, is a criticism of life.)

As many commentators have remarked, Arnold became the single most influential guide to the meaning of English-speaking literary criticism although his most-taught essay, "The Function of Criticism at the Present Time," speaks very little about literature and makes no mention of any work of English literature at all. Arnold may not have found any value in the Hyde Park demonstration, but that demonstration was nothing if not a criticism of life as the nineteenth century was living it. Finding features of that demonstration to reflect on and admire (or even to deplore) would be completely consistent with how Arnold teaches his readers to practice criticism. Again, a clear and simple contrast between Bate's anthology and the 60s ends up hard to sustain.

Such a contrast might also be sought in the different importance each gives to history. That contrast seems likely to be decisive. On the one hand, the movements of the 60s made critics feel that they were *making* history, or at any rate that history was open for the remaking. It was also literary history that was being remade: the creative energies that went into the demonstrations were also channeled into a new literature, much of it the self-expression of previously un- or under-recognized groups. Contemporary literature therefore mattered, and mattered a lot. However, in that first-year colloquium in 1972, contemporary literature was not a focus. Why was the literature of the present not more interesting? Because it was not imperiled. We were there to rescue the literature of the past, which (it was strongly suggested to us) *was* at risk. Yet Bate does not say, as one might have expected him to, that being a classical humanist means believing that history is irrelevant because human nature is more or less the same in all times and places. He does not say that it is because human nature is more or less the same in all times and places that the literature of the distant past can speak to us as freshly today as it did in its own time. (Bate was then working on his biography of Samuel Johnson, which came out in 1977 and also won a Pulitzer, and he seems to have shared with Johnson the opinion that human nature *is* more or less the same in all times and places.) He does not say that literature matters because, in some fundamental sense, history does not matter. Nor does he say that for the 1960s, history *does* matter, and that this is a mistake—that for the 60s the truth of history is the incommensurability of different periods, the insuperable differences they imposed on how life is experienced, and that is what blinds the 60s to transhistorical sameness.

Here the contrast has to be nuanced. Is that necessarily why or how history matters? In the aftermath of the 60s, history did seem to stand in for a necessary relativizing of all apparent universals. When Susan Sontag castigated the highly successful touring photography exhibit *The Family of Man*, in a 1973 review and then again in 1977 with *On Photography*, she did so in history's name:

By purporting to show that individuals are born, work, laugh, and die every-where in the same way, "The Family of Man" denies the determining weight of history—of genuine and historically embedded differences, injustices, and conflicts.[21]

As I will argue below, however, it is a mistake to think that the commitment to history is simply a commitment to incommensurable difference, hence to what is very loosely called relativism. Literature's power to speak across the ages is not absolute (even Arnold admitted that), but it is real. In that sense and to that extent, its transcendence of history is perfectly historical. But this is a paradox that the criticism that followed the 60s has been slow to unpack, a proposition it has been slow to affirm or articulate.

Another nuance: Why doesn't Bate insist on this generational disagree-ment over whether history matters? Perhaps because history does in fact mat-ter to him, if only in a backhanded way. When he mentions the return to Matthew Arnold on the part of New Critical formalists like Blackmur, he adds the phrase "in something of an autumnal mood." The word "autumnal" had already come up in his introduction to Northrop Frye, where it links Frye to the decline theories of Spengler and Toynbee—that is, to a historical vision that is larger and more linear than the cycle of the seasons. "Frye is essentially in the Arnoldian tradition as an 'apologist' for literature," Bate writes,[22] and he explains:

[W]e think of Arnold especially because he was at the threshold of the central problem that the humanist in our own century faces: How to preserve the precarious legacy of the humanities in the face of the twentieth-century rush of technology, population crowding, and paralysis or breakdown before the task of mass education. To put it more specifically: how do we save the great classics of Western literature—and save them not only for the elite but even, once again, for popular use?[23]

How to "save the great classics," how to "preserve": Why is *that* "the central problem" for the humanist? Because the truth of history is spoilage. Putting aside the particular value (and values) of the classics, it is clearly assumed that history is moving, and moving in the wrong direction—moving away from whatever those values are that the classics transmit and embody. This prem-ise ought to set off any number of alarm bells. There are ways of despising the present that are themselves despicable, and perhaps even more despicable than the present is.[24] In his own account of how history is going wrong, Bate seems embarrassingly hazy, random, and unconvincing, though perhaps no more so than other humanists. A list of factors like the "rush of technology, population crowding, and paralysis or breakdown before the task of mass education" seems not very well thought through. No clear contrast emerges here with, say, what Arnold valued in ancient Greek drama.[25] But there is no doubt that Bate sees history as in motion, sees that motion as relentlessly destructive, and sees its destructiveness as an explanation for why society needs the preservationist work of the humanist. The destructiveness of history explains why criticism is important.

In the abstract—forgetting for the moment what it is exactly that each objected to in the present and the difference between Bate's pessimism and the relative optimism of the 60s—the same could be said on behalf of the criticism that came to prevail in the succeeding decades. Criticism is important because the society of the present is in a very bad way. Again, the contrast with the 60s is relative, not absolute. If history is in motion for the 60s, history is also in motion for Bate, not despite his self-declared classicism but as a founding premise of it. And if the historical situation makes it incumbent upon the critic, in the wake of the 60s, to take an oppositional stand, the same is again true for the sense of the critical vocation that Bate derives from Arnold. These continuities may not be unimpeachable, but they had and have a certain weight.

Defending Arnold against his many critics on the left, Bate writes, "disinterestedness is always liable to be censured as intellectual flabbiness by critics who are dominated by compelling and rigid preconceptions acquired through accident or despair."[26] Despair was a striking theme of Bate's teaching. It's as if it were all too easy for Bate to imagine the accidents or the despair that might have compelled him, too, to take a political position. Despair means, etymologically, hopelessness.

As someone who turned eighteen in 1968, a hopeful age in a hopeful year, I should not have been such a sucker for despair.[27] Could I have really thought (as was being insinuated) that hope is naïve because nothing ever changes for the better? I was no leader or activist, but I did some thinking and following; I thought of myself as at least somewhat political. If politics is about changing for the better the terms on which a society is constituted, then a *permanent* opposition is not, strictly speaking, a *political* opposition. The fundamental premise of politics is action oriented toward a different future. A permanent opposition denies that premise: it denies political achievements that deserve to be praised and preserved, recognizing only that which deserves to be criticized. The permanence of permanent opposition is a version of the permanence of humanism. My cohort of graduate students was not necessarily asked to declare our belief that nonliterary achievement is always illusory, that political action is therefore a waste of time, and that history makes no difference—that in effect history is meaningless. But the bleakness of that founding belief was not discouraged. It served as a guarantee of the enduring value of the literature of the past. In any event, we did not risk reprimand if we temporarily overlooked the optimism of the 60s movements, whether revolutionary or reformist, and instead adapted ourselves to a disciplinary posture of wised-up rejection, like Arnold's rejectionist stance toward the reforms of the nineteenth-century liberals, his hesitation to acknowledge any meaningful political gains or accomplishments. The present being what it was, it was always respectable to display discreet signs of despondency. Faced with anything that looked like progress, we were apt to decide with Arnold that progress was not in fact what had happened, and that we, an elite minority, were in on the secret. We were being flattered. The flattery has continued to work. One major reason for Foucault's success in becoming the discipline's next Matthew Arnold is his very Arnoldian certainty that supposed efforts at reform are at best unworthy of much political respect, and at worst sinister expressions of a new regime of domination. Foucault's work is rich in exactly the kind of proposition at which Arnold taught us to nod with uncritical approval.

Let's sum up where we have gotten thus far. Criticism's premise in 1970 was that something was urgently wrong with the present. Before it assimilated the impact of the 1960s, then, criticism already had an oppositional politics. That politics was obviously not very specific. It was inexplicit about what exactly was wrong, and it did not specify what was to be done about it. Specifying what is to be done is arguably the very heart of politics in the strict sense.[28] In many instances criticism's politics is also self-defeating. When it does specify what it opposes, its examples often include the forms of political action themselves, like group think, party loyalty, and mass demonstrations, just what would have to be mobilized in order to make a change. In *Culture and Anarchy*, Arnold set the characteristic tone by expressing an "indifference to direct political action."[29] For Arnold, it was urgent that something be done, but culture was not meant to equip or inspire anyone to do it, at least not directly:

"for my part I do not wish to see men of culture asking to be entrusted with power."[30] Still, this self-qualification was something Arnold was more or less obliged to add. His concept of criticism had put politics into play, and that concept helps explain why politics of some sort has stayed in play ever since.

A Gun to Our Heads

One day, as I remember, Bate asked the members of the first-year colloquium what we would say if a businessman held a gun to our heads and demanded to know why we were studying literature. Or perhaps it was why society should pay good money for us to become literary critics. All I am absolutely sure about is the businessman and the gun to the head. That would have stuck in my mind even if I had not had a father, a businessman, who sold curtains and drapes, who had not gone to college, and who had a very limited idea of why, having gone, I seemed never to have left. It also sticks in my mind today because of its ambiguity. Were we expected to think of an answer that the businessman *as* businessman—that is, as someone who could not afford to ignore the profit motive—would agree with or at least appreciate? Did our rationale for doing what we were doing have to persuade the holders of capital to fund our discipline, a discipline that some of us might hopefully imagine as anticapitalist? This would lead us up against what I have called the paradox of empowered dissent—perhaps more accurately, here, the paradox of *subsidized* dissent. Why should society pay for anyone to dissent from society? Or should we have been clear that, given Bate's choice of interlocutor, an indignant dismissal of the profit motive was not the answer he wanted? Or is the point something else entirely?

For Arnold the task of criticism, in Stefan Collini's words, is to "try books as to the influence which they are calculated to have upon the general culture."[31] As Collini says, this is not a task for a specialist,

> or even a team of specialists. It requires the exercise of cultivated judgment, formed by engagement with work of the highest standard. "Literary criticism" is the name Arnold was here giving to this task of general judgment.[32]

Today, the uncertainties of criticism include uncertainty as to whether we could even imagine agreeing on what "work of the highest standard" is, or what should count as (in Arnold's famous phrase) "the best that is known and thought." The highest from what perspective? The best for whom? The best by what criteria? It is these widespread and entirely plausible uncertainties, and not one or another theoretical dogma proclaimed from on high, that help account for why Arnold no longer holds the preeminent position of leadership he once held. And yet it does not follow from Arnold's sense of the task of criticism—to "try books as to the influence which they are calculated to have upon the general culture"—that what one would need, in order to do this, is knowledge of and access to "the best." The more obvious thing one would need is a well-developed sense of the general culture itself, however obtained. Otherwise, how could one pretend to know what would be good for it and what would not? Knowledge of what would be good for the general culture could evidently come from all sorts of sources. Those sources would include writing on various subjects, academic and not, literary and not. There would be an obligation to listen to people who were not writers as they analyze and debate the perhaps quite burdensome conditions under which they were obliged to live. There might be an obligation to converse with threatening businessmen. The canon might be finite, but the stream of statements and opinion-makers, victims and beneficiaries of the current state of society, topics and issues to which we were asked to be attentive in order to assess responsibly the influence of books and ideas on the general culture—that was and is unending.

When he led us through Matthew Arnold, Bate was also teaching us, perhaps with some reluctance, that even the strongest principles are not immune to the insidious contagions of history. He singled out for us the section in Arnold's "The Function of Criticism at the Present Time"—a title that already insisted that the function of criticism is relative to its historical moment—where the liberal Arnold praised the conservative statesman and thinker Edmund Burke. After wrathfully attacking the French Revolution, Burke had written:

> If a great change is to be made in human affairs, the minds of men will be fitted to it; the general opinions and feelings will draw that way . . . and then they who persist in opposing this mighty current in human affairs, will appear rather to resist the decrees of Providence itself, than the mere designs of men. They will be not resolute and firm, but perverse and obstinate.[33]

If the opponents, like himself, simply stand on principle, that is, they will lose their audience; they will sound like they are ranting. And Arnold comments: "That return of Burke on himself has always seemed to me one of the finest things in English literature, or indeed in any literature."[34] It does this passage an injustice to conclude, as Lionel Trilling does, that Burke's anticipation of Arnoldian disinterestedness did not stop Burke from ranting against the French Revolution. Nor did Arnold's admiration for Burke's "return on himself" stop Arnold from ranting against the Hyde Park marchers. For that matter, Trilling's admiration for Arnold did not stop Trilling, the most eloquent Arnoldian of his generation, from ranting against the demonstrations at Columbia University in 1968, when a farcical "WANTED!" poster was circulated by wryly angry students with Trilling's photo in the center, demanding the arrest of Lionel "Trains" Trilling.

The point about the value of self-scrutiny survives these disappointments. None of these three humanists paused to scrutinize themselves in the light of where history seemed to be going, but that gesture is nevertheless what we were being encouraged, reading all three, to approve and imitate. Whether the mighty current of human affairs beyond the gates turned out to be revolutionary or not, the moral seemed to be that as critics we would not be rewarded for refusing to attend to it and instead keeping our eyes trained on the text itself and nothing but the text. We were tasked with paying attention to our time.

According to Jameson's "Periodizing the 60s," my first semester of graduate school in 1972 roughly coincided with the end of the decade's political momentum.[35] Jameson cites a splintering of the Black and women's movements, the formulation of the (abruptly quite moderate) Common Program of the left in France in 1972 and the rise of Eurocommunism, the Chilean coup against Allende in 1973 as well as the Yom Kippur War in Israel/Palestine and the US withdrawal from the Vietnam War in the same year, the end of the draft and the beginning of the oil crisis.[36] In the realm of criticism, Jameson cites Lionel Trilling's Charles Eliot Norton Lectures, delivered at Harvard in 1970 and published the next year as *Sincerity and Authenticity*. Jameson describes *Sincerity and Authenticity* as "an Arnoldian call to reverse the tide of 60s countercultural 'barbarism.'"[37]

I attended those lectures as an undergraduate. I remember Trilling coming up the aisle in Lowell Lecture Hall with a green bookbag slung casually over his shoulder, looking much cooler than his later reputation for pomposity would have suggested (I was twenty and didn't know the reputation yet). At the time I did not understand the lectures as hostile commentary on the 1960s, but looking back at *Sincerity and Authenticity* now, I see they were, especially toward the end. Trilling took Sartre to task for encouraging the naïve and misguided aspiration to authenticity. Norman O. Brown, R. D. Laing, David Cooper, and Michel Foucault (yes, already), also thinkers of major importance to the 60s, were criticized for idealizing and politicizing madness: "who that has spoken, or tried to speak, with a psychotic friend will consent to betray the masked pain of his bewilderment and solitude by making it the paradigm of liberation from the imprisoning falsehoods of an alienated social reality?"[38] Like Bate's businessman-with-a-gun scene, this perhaps hypothetical scene of encounter with a psychotic friend gave Trilling's point an existential leverage that that made it hard to forget. Sometimes, he was saying, disease is just disease. Disease is not political. On the contrary, it sets the limits beyond which politics should be smart enough not to make any claims. Like death, like tragedy, disease is part of the dark truth of the human condition, essential and immutable. The implication is that our real business as humanists is with that dark and permanent truth.

At the same time, Trilling's version of humanism was much more directly engaged than Bate's both with politics and with history. In a 1950 review of *The Liberal Imagination*, Blackmur writes that Trilling "cultivates a mind never entirely his own, a mind always deliberately to some extent what he understands to be the mind of society."[39] This concern with "the mind of society" follows the Arnoldian playbook in a way that Bate did not.

The Norton lecture I remember best is the second, especially the parts on *Rameau's Nephew* as read by Hegel, and the idea that once upon a time, the dominant idea of happiness was aristocratic—"a visionary norm of order, peace, honour, and beauty."[40] This rhymes with Arnold's disinterestedness, which offered the middle class a chance to renounce its distinctive ideology of economic self-interest and identify instead with an ideal that in the past only landowners had been able to afford. I too was being invited to identify with that ideal—in literature, and in a vocation devoted to literature. The invitation again had a class meaning: upward mobility for me, as for the nineteenth-century middle class. And it was not revoked merely because for a thinking person, as Trilling went on to say, that visionary norm of happiness was no longer available. Like Hegel and Marx, we now knew too much of the bleak truth of self-estrangement. This too was a reprimand to the 60s. Paradise now? If that's what you were expecting, you were clueless.

Trilling, unlike the characteristic voices of the 60s, favored delaying gratification, even delaying it indefinitely. As Amanda Anderson notes, he was something of a fan of unpleasure. Readers should no longer expect happiness from the greatest literature, which was modern or modernist. Modernism's abandonment of the classical goal of audience pleasure, Trilling argues, makes the counter-offer of "a higher, more significant life."[41] But the stress falls on the Freud of *Civilization and Its Discontents*, which Freud "first thought of calling," Trilling tells us, "'*Das Unglück in der Kultur*,' 'Unhappiness in Civilization.'"[42] The "view that life in civilization is largely intractable to reasonable will is profoundly alien to the prevailing ideology . . . [and] cannot fail to offend the established moral sensibility."[43] Trilling sees himself as alone in realizing, along with a few of the elect, that civilized life is intractable to reason or political will. Liberation is nowhere in sight.[44]

Trilling was not trying to rescue an ever-receding past of literary greatness from the mean-spirited sociological self-interestedness of identity politics. His target was much larger. What he hated about the 60s was not the excitement with which that generation inhabited modernity, but its failure to face up to modernity's true bleakness. Trilling's engagement with the great works of modernism, which he took to convey this bleak message, allowed him an engagement with history itself that had no counterpart in Bate. In the Norton lectures, this engagement showed. In tracing the emergence of a historically unprecedented ideal of sincerity (in *Hamlet*, Rousseau, Goethe, and Austen) and then its rapid hollowing out, Trilling does not cast the counter-ideal of authenticity as the villain of the tale. On the contrary, authenticity helps disabuse us of the notion that what we say in society can ever be the same as what we feel within. It makes tragedy visible. In Conrad's *The Heart of Darkness*, we are taught to doubt that our deepest desires can ever be realized in social life. Despite Trilling's "strong warning against the glamorization of madness and schizophrenia as authenticity," Amanda Anderson notes, he has "legible sympathies with authenticity's conceptual force and scope," in particular its function as "at heart an oppositional concept."[45]

In this sense Trilling, like Bate, did not set himself up in simple hostility to the 60s. Looking forward to what criticism after the 60s was to become, however, there is a more important point. Trilling exhibited in the Norton lectures a version of historical scholarship, in the lineage of Matthew Arnold, that could continue to inspire those (like me) who were seeking a model for our chosen vocation. He took the values of sincerity and authenticity, which continued to serve the culture at large, traced their intellectual history, explored their ambiguities, and evaluated them, as Arnold had advised, in terms of their influence on the "general culture" of the present time. It was breathtaking as a display of hard-won expertise. And as a *kind* of expertise, it was also an answer to Bate's businessman with a gun.

Expertise and Sensibility

What kind of expertise? Trilling combined literary history with intellectual history, both of them animated by an oppositional commitment to the present. Social history, or history-from-below, was just emerging in the 60s and had not yet made the decisive impact it would make later on. Literary history in the less ambitious, sources-analogues-and-influences sense is there (for example, in the section on Hegel's reading of Diderot) but only in the background. That style of literary history is one of the pre-60s critical schools parodied in Frederick Crews's surprise bestseller of 1963, *The Pooh Perplex*, which also has some fun imagining what myth-and-symbol hunting, psychoanalysis, Marxism, and the judgmental, canon-policing seriousness of F. R. Leavis, among others, would do with Pooh, Piglet, Kanga, Eeyore, and the other characters of A. A. Milne's classic. Unless I am mistaken, however, one school of criticism that is *not* parodied in *The Pooh Perplex* is historical contextualization as such, where "historical" would signify anything and everything, the life as well as the works, social class and location as well as literary tradition, that might be perceived to help elucidate the text. Irving Howe's still unsurpassed *Politics and the Novel* (1957) is an example that, for all its idiosyncratic brilliance, makes a bridge across the 60s that extends all the way to the present. As does James Baldwin's argument with Richard Wright in "Many Thousands Gone" (1955).

In discussing the quarrel of the new "critics" with the previous generation of "scholars," in the early to mid-twentieth century, Gerald Graff in *Professing Literature* insists on the New Criticism's pedagogical benefit:

> [P]utting the emphasis on the literary text itself also had a more humble advantage: it seemed a tactic ideally suited to a new, mass student body that could not be depended on to bring to the university any common cultural background—and not just the student body but the new professors as well, who might often be only marginally ahead of the students. The explicative method made it possible for literature to be taught efficiently to students who took for granted little history by professors who took for granted little more

history. . . . Reading the text itself in a vacuum was an all too inviting expedi-
ent in an institution where no contexts could be taken for granted because
nobody could be assumed in advance to know any one thing, where nobody
knew what anybody else knew, and where nobody talked to others on a consistent enough basis to find out.[46]

If it's true, as Graff argues, that the New Criticism redefined expertise for a
massive and non-elite student body that could no longer be expected to know
either the history of the relevant languages (philology) or the history of literature itself, then Trilling was unabashedly pushing back in the opposite
direction, making a display of historical knowledge that was also an implicit
argument for historical knowledge itself as the true and most valuable sort
of expertise, even if only a few might be capable of attaining it. The tension
between such expertise and the commitment to democracy is another thing
Trilling shared, despite his own inclinations, with the sensibility of the 60s.

To Bate, the imperative to see our work as critics against a backdrop of
life outside the university would probably not have meant seeing it in relation to democracy. Though Bate and his mentor Douglas Bush repeatedly
invoked "the common reader," the rationale for the Great Books curriculum
was "fundamentally incompatible" with democracy.[47] Still, Bate had prepared
us to replace the pushily interrogative businessman with another interlocutor, this time a collective one. Our appointed interlocutor would be the social
movements of the 60s, which spoke in democracy's name. They too could be
imagined (or could not *not* be imagined) asking us intrusive and unsettling
questions about what we thought we were doing. Even without the gun to
the head, it was an inevitable substitution. And answering the 60s questions
might well be just as hard. Democracy was a tough interrogator, especially
on claims to expertise. As the Bate anthology correctly noted, the democratic
impulses of the 60s included "militant anti-elitism." Kristin Ross describes
May 1968 as "a mass movement that sought above all, in my view, to contest the domain of the expert."[48] In "'68, or Something," Lauren Berlant presents her desire to keep faith with the 60s a quarter century later as resistance
to "current pressures on intellectuals and identity politicians in the U.S. to
adopt a 'professional' voice of expertise in some putative public sphere."[49] She
is refusing to play the role of expert.

If the 60s were indeed allergic to expertise, it becomes almost inevitable
that the eventual convergence of the decade and the academy, in the years

that followed, would be narrated either as the victory of the academy over the 60s movements or as a self-betrayal of the principles of those movements. As Russell Jacoby writes, "In the end it was not the New Left intellectuals who invaded the universities but the reverse: the academic idiom, concepts, and concerns occupied, and finally preoccupied, young left intellectuals."[50] Or, in Richard Rorty's version (which this time does not resist the temptations of sarcasm): "As Todd Gitlin put it, we academics marched on the English department while the Republicans took over the White House."[51] The White House was much better defended, of course. And even the English Department was no pushover. Some would argue that it successfully resisted all assaults.

These may seem like quibbles, but the point is a serious one. On the one hand, the 60s generation's cultural politics were better suited to make demands on an institution devoted to the study of culture than on Washington or Wall Street. On the other hand, many of the voters who put the Republicans in the White House detested the 60s cultural politics—detested in particular the ideals of gender and racial justice and solidarity with the victims of American violence abroad—and detested that politics more than they loved their own economic self-interest. There was thus a backlash. That is quite a different explanation of why national politics turned to the right. The culture wars that flourished during the Reagan, Bush, Clinton, and Bush administrations would never have been so passionately divisive or so long-lasting without the widely advertised notion that the universities, now in enemy hands, were refusing American patriotism, disrespecting the classics of Western civilization, and stuffing syllabi with works chosen solely on the basis of the race and gender of their authors. A shameless misrepresentation, as one would expect from the heat of the cultural battlefield, but it had traces of truth in it.

It also needs to be said that within the movement, expertise was always a matter of controversy, and sometimes a matter of self-contradiction. Trying to make sense of the fact that so much of the New Left of the 60s came from what they called the "Professional-Managerial Class," Barbara and John Ehrenreich noticed an "ambiguous mixture of elitism and anti-capitalist militance."[52] The contradiction on expertise was flagrant: "Credentialing barriers would tumble. The rule of the experts would be abolished—by the young experts. . . . It was at best a difficult approach to sustain."[53] Perhaps it would be better to say that the authority of expertise had first to be gained in order then to be relinquished, if only relinquished in part. In many cases it was not relinquished at all, but only redistributed or redefined. New areas of knowledge had become necessary as new areas of concern opened up, and thus some of the old ones now seemed less pressing or even sank gradually into the background.

But not everyone would see this redefinition as a betrayal of the 60s. Even the anti-elitism was not uncontested. Perhaps, as the skeptics allege, it could not have gone uncontested if those who came afterwards were planning on working within the institutional structure of the university. In any event, a certain elitism was almost certainly there to be detected among us Harvard first years. In society as we know it, it is a rare privilege to be offered the con-viction that a meaningful vocation awaits you. A meaningful vocation doesn't await everyone. And most people know it. In this sense and others, we were privileged. It is no coincidence that disinterestedness, which Arnold presented as the centerpiece of culture, is a value historically associated with the aris-tocracy. We new champions of disinterestedness were encouraged to see our-selves as rising above middle-class self-interest and thus earning the right to become a sort of new aristocracy. It was a hard kind of flattery to resist even if one fancied oneself a radical democrat.

Uncertainties around expertise and elitism, historical difference and his-tory-transcending sameness, are among the structural tensions to be found on both sides of the half-century divide between 1970 and 2020. They lead into the heart of the question of what criticism is and should be. The chapters that follow have a good deal to say about Michel Foucault as well as Mat-thew Arnold because, as a key site for these issues, Foucault is the figure who comes closest to summing up the guiding messages the discipline took in and worked over from the 1960s. That's what it means to say that he is the closest thing the last half century produced to a Matthew Arnold. And again like Arnold, Foucault is perhaps better conceived not as the discoverer of an area of expertise—who is better known for skepticism about expertise?—but as the center and exemplar of a certain sensibility.

In *Bleak Liberalism*, Amanda Anderson makes an inventive pairing between the sensibility of Foucault and the sensibility of Trilling:

> Trilling privileges hesitation over commitment, appreciation of complexity over action. Foucault also produces a mode of intellection and ethics that stresses a delicate suspension. . . . As in Trilling, an apprehension about the

very use of political power is met by a turn toward a morally heightened attention to the self's relation to the self.[54]

Anderson uses this "coincidence"—both prefer the ethical to the political—
in order to pull Foucault into the liberal camp: "For Trilling and other bleak
liberals . . . there is a chastened recognition of the limits of human aspiration,
not only natural limits such as illness and death, but the fact of aggression
and violence, what in Reinhold Niebuhr takes the form of sin."[55] But the privi-
leging of "hesitation over commitment" and the "appreciation of complexity
over action" seem less characteristic of the particular political philosophy of
liberalism than of academic thinking in general. The essence of the academic
habitus, according to Pierre Bourdieu, is "the posture of the scholar feeling
free to withdraw from the game in order to conceptualize it."[56]

The appreciation of complexity and the hesitation to act on any extra-academic political commitment are two complementary aspects of the overarching commitment to scholarly autonomy; Anderson calls it "detachment."[57]
Scholarship's allegiance to autonomy ought to be clear. It is perhaps less clear
that, at least in the humanities, scholarship cannot claim *only* autonomy.
Imagine trying to offer "detachment" as an answer to Bate's businessman.
Detachment falls well short of even Arnold's criticism-as-permanent-oppo-
sition. Opposition is necessarily *attached* to what it opposes. One has to be
attached to something first in order for detachment to become a virtue.[58]
Commitment of some kind is equally necessary—if not to the great works
of the ever-receding past, then to *something*. Commitments are also essential to scholarship, and this is in a structural, politically neutral sense. That's
why it is unsurprising that surprising continuities keep popping up, like those
between the oppositionality of the 60s and the oppositionality of both Bate
and Trilling, neither of whom had anything good to say about the 60s.

Of course, not all scholarly sensibilities are the same. And as I said above,
it's to be expected that the Foucauldian sensibility will differ in important
respects from Arnold's "tact" and "poise" even while displaying a certain tact
or poise of its own. But since the critical sensibility that comes out of Foucault
and the 60s is likely to be associated most readily with incivility, as in accusations of cancel culture, or with a refusal of rational dialogue, it seems worth
pausing to put some flesh on this idea.

In *The Way We Argue Now: A Study in the Culture of Theory*, her prequel to
Bleak Liberalism, Anderson paints an unflattering portrait of that sensibility.

She objects to what she calls, more precisely, the "ethos" of contemporary criticism, an ethos that she attaches to the impact of "theory" but that follows the same rough periodization I have identified with the impact of the 1960s. Her central figure too is Foucault. "In the case of Foucault and his admirers," she writes, "the appeal to ethos functions to trump, eclipse, or subordinate the claims or value of rational or impersonal argument."[59] Anderson does not object to the existence of an ethos as such; she does not demand rational argument that would be totally separated from collectively developed habits of tact or manners or finesse, *habitus* or sensibility. Her objection is to the particulars of this ethos. In her view, (1) it is excessively respectful of the opinions of others, a respect based on nothing more than identity, and (2) it has carried respect for the opinions of others so far as to discourage and even disable the exchange of rational arguments. To disable rational argument is to rule out the scrutiny and evaluation of scholarship that rational argument is depended upon to provide. This is disciplinarily self-defeating. If a discipline disables rational argument, allowing the fruits of scholarship to pass unscrutinized because of the value attributed in advance to the identity of the knowledge producer, it diminishes the value of the knowledge produced.

Is this a fair assessment? The hypothesis is not totally ungrounded. Where rational argument is severely restricted, Anderson suggests, as she thinks it is by identity politics, the work of argument will be carried on instead by other, less transparent means. These include characterology, or casting aspersions on the supposed character types of those who champion particular schools or styles of critical thought. Anderson makes an amusing collection of them: "hermeneuts of suspicion are paranoid; feminists are, as we well know, angry and humorless; rationalists are uptight purists; and multiculturalism has introduced a particularly onerous version of piety in the form of the politically correct person."[60] But she clearly has a special place in her heart for the accusations against pragmatism, which she lists more than once: "Pragmatists are accused of being, among other things, smug, complacent, cynical, blithe, and dismissive."[61] Each of these adjectives seems worth pausing over. If you call someone smug, complacent, cynical, blithe, and dismissive, you are presumably claiming not to be any of those things yourself; you are probably assuming that you are the very opposite of those things. What would it mean to be the opposite of those things? Not being smug or complacent would mean being dissatisfied with yourself, worried about yourself, unwilling to appear self-righteous. Not being cynical would mean something like being earnest, perhaps a little naïve, but certainly respectful. Not being blithe would mean, again, being troubled. Not being dismissive would mean being attentive, caring, and again, respectful. What Anderson provides, in sum, is a mirror image of the sensibility to which the theoretically informed but insufficiently rationalist criticism of recent decades would seem to aspire, whether or not its members can be said to have achieved it.

One cannot help but notice, however, that while excessive respect for the opinions of others (not being cynical or dismissive) fits perfectly with Anderson's objection to the critical ethos that refuses rational argument in the name of the identity of the other, the same cannot be said of worry, troubledness, and self-dissatisfaction (not being smug, complacent, or blithe). On the contrary, each of these suggests a sort of perpetually unsatisfied self-scrutiny. To judge from this perhaps unrepresentative sample, the harshness of scrutiny has not after all been banished from criticism's current ethos or sensibility, as Anderson suggests when she complains about the reluctance to engage in rational argument. Anderson may be right about that reluctance. But rational argument is a means rather than an end in itself. The desired result of rational argument is exposure to scrutiny and critique, eliminating the possibility of smugness, so that the truth that prevails has been properly tested, exposed to the eyes of a maximum of potential stakeholders. Exposure to scrutiny seems to be exactly what the critical sensibility of the present values most highly. Perhaps even too highly—it is of course possible that the desire not to offend anyone could shut down potentially valuable avenues of discussion.[62]

Readers will of course want to check this argument against their own impressions of the prevailing critical sensibility. They may also ask: Whose scrutiny? Has anyone been forgotten? Other adjectives than Anderson's might be thrown into the mix. The sketch above overlaps with the prevailing caricature of political correctness, which is taken not only to discourage the honest exchange of views but to build hesitation into its characteristic rhythm of relationship, discouraging any speech at all until the would-be speaker has scanned and eliminated all possible grounds for offense, a process that can be inhibitively time-consuming. But this *is* a caricature, and the best way to show it is to remind the reader of the vigorous internal debate that the 60s and post-60s sensibility has provoked and sustained.

Susan Sontag's 1964 essay "Notes on 'Camp,'" which made her reputation, announced that a sensibility "is the one of the hardest things to talk about" and that in her case talking about camp is harder still because camp is the site of "a sharp conflict in my own sensibility."[63] Exposing and dramatizing her ambivalence, she stages an argument with herself—an argument over just that "detachment"[64] that Anderson sees as definitively liberal. Sontag identifies detachment, rather, with a particular constituency, in fact one of the very constituencies of the disadvantaged that were soon to become definitive of the 60s movements:

> homosexuals, by and large, constitute the vanguard—and the most articulate audience—of Camp. . . . The two pioneering forces of modern sensibility are Jewish moral seriousness and homosexual aestheticism and irony.[65]

Since Sontag can claim both identities, though she is not eager to do so, it's clear that she cannot be entirely pleased to declare that "the Camp sensibility is disengaged, depoliticized—or at least apolitical."[66] Nothing could be further from the 60s demand for politicized authenticity than camp's appreciation of stylization and artifice. Yet nothing could be more characteristic of the 60s than the moral seriousness of acknowledging the neglected voice of a minority that has suffered long and terrible injury, even if what that minority seems to be affirming is stylization and artifice. Instead of demanding justice for the injured or demanding that they demand justice for themselves, Sontag appreciates their good bad taste. And she displays the resulting uneasiness. Over the decades that followed, her argument with herself would be magnified by the LGBTQ debate in which, as Michael Trask puts it, "many post-Stonewall commentators . . . have felt the need to derive a politics from camp based on what they take to be its dominant feature: a manifestation of sensibility (progressive) or an attention-grabbing performance (reactionary)."[67] This has made camp "a wedge issue within gay liberation"[68]—not identity politics, but the question of whether or not identity *is* politics.

As the canon expanded after the 1960s, some of the criticism that did the work of that expansion was of the same nature as Bate's biographies of Keats and Johnson: expository, informative, appreciative, willfully nonideological—trying simply to establish the worthiness of additional great works and additional great authors. Who would not want Wright, Ellison, Baldwin, and Morrison, say, to get the same largely admiring life-and-works treatment that their white predecessors had gotten? But that is not the whole story. There was also "Many Thousands Gone," Baldwin's life-and-death argument with Wright over the proper representation of Black existence. In the many essays inspired by Baldwin's, argument is not suppressed in order to avoid trespass or grievance. There is polite recognition that injured feelings are possible, but the politeness does not stand in the way of engagement.

How characteristic is this engaged, dialogic mode? The examples I think of are, again and again, not essays that go silent in order to avoid giving offense but essays that build the likelihood of offense into their argument. Rather than reporting, with strident outrage, a violation of one's own identity, criticism's dominant sensibility, as I see it, prefers to look at one's own identity from the outside. Its characteristic gesture is like Sontag's: to add another collectivity's set of eyes and then explore the more complex view that emerges from the extra level of scrutiny—as when Hortense Spillers adds gender to race in "Momma's Baby, Papa's Maybe," or when Laura Kipnis adds class to gender in her account of *Hustler*, or when Gayatri Chakravorty Spivak adds imperialism to class and gender in "Three Women's Texts and a Critique of Imperialism." Lauren Berlant writes:

> American academic feminism operates out of fear, I believe, of repeating the definitional exclusions, violences, and imaginative lapses of feminism since '68, of repeating American/white feminism's imperialist, racist, heterosexist, class-biased, culture-bound, and overoptimistic parochialism.[69]

It is not the desire to cram every conceivable theorist into every conceivable paragraph that gives Spivak's or Berlant's or Judith Butler's writing its characteristic difficulty (when indeed it is difficult, which is not always), but rather an acute sense of responsibility not to forget a relevant and pressing category of injustice. When Berlant speaks of the cultural capital that "a decorous intellectual, writer, or speaker might gain by speaking for 'diversity' or 'difference' from within the legitimating forms of a dominant culture,"[70] the point is both that diversity should not be seen as an unexamined good and that even if it *is* a good, the holder of cultural capital or institutional legitimacy has also got to examine their championing of it, and the position from which they do their championing, as a part of the whole picture—not as damning guilt and disqualification, but as one more element in a complex whole. This is one way in which complexity and hesitation, which Anderson sees as defining the sensibility of Lionel Trilling, continue to define the more political sensibility that succeeded him.

Criticism today may be unjustifiably proud of its ethos of self-scrutiny, as Ian Hunter has argued.[71] Its sensibility does not absolutely repel parody even when it is being "sober and restrained," as Viet Thanh Nguyen has said Asian American criticism had to be in order to overcome the hostility that initially greeted it.[72] But there is a case to be made for its one obvious rule of politeness: true respect for identity lies in never assuming that anyone can or should be wholly identified with that identity, whatever it may be. The emphasis should perhaps fall on the fact that this sensibility or code of politeness is now widely shared and widely taught—in effect, it is a form of expertise. In its embrace of self-scrutiny and its refusal to accept simple identitarian self-interest, it is unexpectedly continuous with Arnoldian disinterestedness. In that sense, among others, it is also of some small use to democracy.[73]

2   Criticizing

At the age of seven or eight, my daughter was asked what her father did for a living. Having heard the expression "literary criticism" around the house and having a certain personal experience of which she perhaps wanted to make sense, she replied, "Daddy is a criticizer."[1]

As usual, my daughter was right, mainly—not just about her father but about the sort of work done by literary critics. On the one hand, most of what literary critics do from day to day is still, as it has been in the past, appreciative. It involves finding creative and persuasive reasons for praising texts that critics find praiseworthy. On the other hand, there is criticizing in the everyday, parent–child sense—call it faultfinding. Faultfinding is also a major component of what we do. One point of this book is to explain to literary critics and interested others how and why our discipline criticizes and why such work is worth doing, even when it doesn't seem very nice.

As noted above, the idea that critics are not as nice as they ought to be, or as nice as they used to be, was a staple of the culture wars of the 1980s and 1990s, and it has returned intermittently since then. One still hears that literary criticism used to be more appreciative and has become more negative, more critical, in fact excessively so. It has become more critical because it has come to focus on things like race, gender, and sexuality and class, power, and imperialism. It has become too critical because it has become too political.

I don't imagine anyone is eager to sit through a blow-by-blow replay of the culture wars, and I do not propose to inflict such a thing on you. Still, one large point ought to be uncontroversial. Although the Young Turks of that time are now following the former Old Guard into oblivion, those decades remain a live part not just of the history of the academy but of the history of the country.[2] In the third decade of the new millennium, we in the United States are living in the midst of compelling evidence—in matters like the splitting off of white, and especially male, voters from the Democratic Party and the defunding of public education—that the Republican cultural offensive was remarkably successful. And as the same "too critical" charge has returned, it is hard not to see hints of a political continuity—hard not to suspect, in other words, that it too has to be linked up with the political right at least in the sense that it fulfills a right-wing agenda.

This time around the accusation has not come so much from hostile journalists, speaking in the name of common sense and against newfangled critical vocabularies and styles of evaluation, as from fellow academics, many of them eager to drape themselves in the shimmering mantle of novelty. Some, like the right-wing culture warriors, find other critics arrogantly lacking in reverence for the artifacts they are privileged to curate and imagine nothing more daringly up to date than a posture of humility (about our work) and fervent appreciation (of literature). Others merely suggest that, for better or worse, the once-newfangled has run its course and has now become old-fashioned and uncool. The dépassé thesis is often dated to Bruno Latour's 2004 essay, "Why Has Critique Run out of Steam?" Though Latour's title was a cheap shot (after all, are we so sure critique *has* run out of steam?), at the time this essay was not just a fashion statement: It had a political purpose, and a progressive one. Latour was concerned that certain left-wing habits of mind, including his own, were no longer publicly effective, faced with popular right-wing projects like climate change denial and the then very recent 2003 invasion of Iraq. The hypothesis was and is contestable, but it also was and is worth trying out. After the presidential election of 2016, many self-identified progressives made versions of the same argument. Critique, however cogent, didn't seem to work on Donald Trump's voters. We need to try something else. The proposition has remained interesting even as events in the political sphere have moved on.

Raymond Williams on Criticism

The entry for "criticism" in Raymond Williams's *Keywords: A Vocabulary of Culture and Society*, first published in 1976, gives "the predominant general sense" of the word as "faultfinding." A more specialized sense, Williams says, relates to criticism of "art and literature." Aesthetic criticism is more complex. But this specialized artistic sense is both "confusing" and too negative. As an alternative, Williams declines the more positive and "softer" term "appreciation."[3] "Appreciation" too is a term for judgment, he argues, and the real problem is "the assumption of judgment as the inevitable and even natural response" to literature.

Why is judging the wrong a critical operation? Williams does not answer at length; his entry is brief and primarily genealogical rather than theoretical. Nor does he engage directly with the enormously influential figure of F. R. Leavis, whose insistence that criticism *is* judgment was certainly on Williams's mind. Instead, he offers two relevant lines of thinking. One is that criticism is better thought of as a "practice" alongside "all other practices." This can be plausibly understood to mean that criticism is not essentially juridical or censorious, which is to say not a matter of judging after the fact. That would leave open the possibility that criticism is a non-evaluative form of explanatory decoding, making available texts that are often obscure to those without higher education. In this sense criticism would be mildly democratic in form but otherwise politically neutral. It seems more likely, however, that Williams was saying criticism is a form of politics in the following senses of that complex word. Considered as a practice among other practices, criticism appears as (1) one part of an effort that is shared with non-critics, and (2) relevant to the urgencies of its moment. Put these together, and you get criticism as a practice to be undertaken and understood along with, rather than apart from, other ways of facing, or choosing not to face, those same urgencies. In each of these respects, criticism can be distinguished from judgment. Leavis, who was notoriously allergic to politics, would have agreed with the second sense—that criticism is relevant to the urgencies of its moment— but probably not with the first—that criticism is part of an effort shared with non-critics and with other practices.

Williams's other line of thinking proposes that, while moving away from simple "censure," the specialized literary sense of criticism has attributed to the critic an officially sanctioned, authoritative, quasi-judicial posture that is undeserved. After all, who says that a critic is entitled to sit in judgment? "The notion that response was judgment depended, of course," Williams writes, "on the social confidence of a class and later a profession."[4] Linked terms like "taste," "cultivation," "culture," "standards," and "discrimination" appear to justify certain responses, but not others, on the basis of possessing a particular sensibility or having attained a particular scholarly expertise or set of professional credentials. Those who do not belong to the designated profession or class, Williams implies, should not be surprised to see their responses, perhaps anomalous and even shocking responses, go unrecognized while a range of other responses, coming from inside that class or profession, are taken as generically acceptable. And that lack of recognition, as Williams feels no need to add, is a problem for a society that wants to think of itself as democratic. The difficulty is on display within the single word "discrimination," split as it is, Williams notes, between "good or informed judgment," on the one hand, and on the other "a strong negative sense of unreasonable exclusion or unfair treatment of some outside group."[5]

At a time when the discovery of left-wing indulgence in criticism-as-faultfinding is being marketed as a garden-fresh scandal, it is good to be reminded that Williams was already taking some distance from faultfinding in 1976, and doing so as a critic explicitly writing from the left. The need for a reminder echoes the strange trajectory of the phrase "political correctness": right-wing users who gloatingly peddled the putdown during the culture wars largely failed to observe that they were borrowing the phrase from the left, which, rather than defining itself by an absolutist "it's not funny" self-righteousness, had been circulating "politically correct" for decades as a wry self-warning against precisely that moral absolutism.[6] In the case of faultfinding, too, there is a historical record that begs to be set straight.[7]

That said, however, Williams's argument against the faultfinding model of criticism does not seem entirely satisfying. In fact it's a bit of a shock, given the position he so influentially laid out in *Culture and Society,* published in 1958, the book whose enterprise *Keywords* ostensibly continues. The main idea of *Culture and Society* is that the concept of culture arose and flourished in the years following the Industrial Revolution because it could serve as a standard by which to judge the society newly created by industrial capitalism.[8] Figures who might not otherwise be considered progressive, from Edmund Burke through Matthew Arnold to T. S. Eliot, could be reclassified and appreciated accordingly because of what they had contributed, despite their explicit political affiliations or their bias against politics as such, to the concept of

culture, which Williams argues has become an indispensable tool of anticapitalist critique.[9] Via culture Williams made them over into voices within a left-
wing tradition.

Itself a classic of the tradition it assembled, *Culture and Society* could incidentally stand as evidence, if further evidence were needed, of how the left's
best critics have tended to do criticism that is appreciative and even redemp-
tive of writers who are not its political allies. But bolstering that case was not
Williams's own intention. In 1958 the "too negative" charge did not yet need
to be rebutted.

In *Culture and Society*, then, "criticism" does not mean criticism of literature and art, as in the *Keywords* entry, but criticism *of society*. Society is
assumed to be a place where injustice thrives and demands immediate attention. This is not an outlandish assumption. It would not be hard to defend if
it should come to pass that those who quietly hold the contrary assumption,
like the "limits of critique" and "surface reading" schools, were willing to
stand up for their own apparent belief that (to put words in their mouths)
things are not perfect, no, but they are more or less okay, so why get all political about them? But if society is taken as a place of thriving and multifarious
injustice, then culture is opposed to it, as Williams's title suggests. This is
also contestable from another direction. Opposition to society is not implied
by the anthropological meaning of the word "culture," as a whole way of life.
As a whole way of life, culture like society is also an *object* of critique. And in
that case, where would the subjects or performers of critique come from? The
question is worth a conversation. For now, however, let us agree that if culture
is opposed to society, then so too is criticism.

For the culture-and-society tradition, criticism is a methodology adapted
to the culture concept and determined by service to that concept. That is
true whether or not cultural criticism also interprets works of literature. As
we have noted, in Arnold's "The Function of Criticism at the Present Time,"
perhaps the single most important text for Williams's new disciplinary back-
story, there is almost no reference to literature. The essay's most memorable
phrase, "Wragg is in custody," is a quotation from a newspaper. Newspapers
and other public media would henceforth be part of the proto-discipline's
archive, providing raw material that permitted critics to do versions of what
Arnold was doing: locating society's callousness toward the misery of a working-class single mother in an ordinary, apparently innocuous instance of nonliterary discourse. Whatever else he was doing, Arnold was also helping to

found a new style of finding fault. In *Culture and Society* words like "culture," "standard," and "judgment" give Williams pause, it's true, but in that book his reservations about them are secondary. His primary purpose is to compose those terms into a new paradigm of criticism: criticism as a reaching for perspectives on and imagined alternatives to a categorically unacceptable status quo. For *Culture and Society*, building on Arnold, political faultfinding is in criticism's DNA.

Williams thus takes two antithetical positions on faultfinding: pro- in *Culture and Society*, anti- in *Keywords*. This disparity might be resolved in one of several ways. Williams might have had a change of heart between 1958 and 1976, perhaps as a result of disappointment with the actual prospects for the discipline's rearticulation around a critique of capitalist society. Williams's argument against criticism-as-faultfinding in *Keywords* could be less an argument against faultfinding as such than an argument against the particular faultfinding practiced by the critical establishment of Williams's day, whether the hierarchical ranking of texts by the Leavisites (and their exclusion of so many texts from the so-called great tradition) or a faultfinding that penalized the opinions and values of his working-class family, friends, and comrades. The distinction could also be widened between the *literary* critic (whom Williams discourages from sitting in judgment) and the *cultural* critic, for whom judging is essential to the job description—judging not literature and art but the larger social and cultural worlds in which they are produced and received. Literary criticism pays attention to two nonidentical objects, literature and culture, which overlap, are at work simultaneously, and yet generate different kinds of knowledge. This deep doubleness helps explain why doing criticism is not as easy as it may look.

The most useful explanation for this apparent contradiction, however, is that Williams simply had mixed feelings about faultfinding. It's hard to know for sure—Williams did not spend much time displaying his feelings—but it seems plausible that he did. And in these mixed feelings I think he is more representative than he may seem—representative not just of the New Left or of his post-war generation (he was forty-seven years old in 1968), but of the profession as it exists today, a profession that appears to have gone in other theoretical and methodological directions. I hope it will not be taken as special pleading on behalf of the profession (or the profession as it presently exists) to say that like other affects, Williams's feelings have their own high intelligence, an intelligence that is visible even in their seemingly permanent irresolution. For him and for the discipline, ambivalence toward standards of judgment has been energizing. It is not something the discipline could surrender easily.

As I suggested above, the anti-faultfinding position is a logical expression of Williams's presumed feelings—coming to Cambridge University from the Welsh working class and perceiving that the standards of judgment applied to literature and its interpretation at Cambridge were not in perfect harmony with the collective experience of that class. One major figure at Cambridge during his student years, and perhaps a representative one, was E. M. W. Tillyard, Tory author of *The Elizabethan World Picture*, a book that reminded the modern era of a medieval understanding of hierarchical order, cosmic order, and, naturally, also social order, that heroically persisted into a disordered modernity.

But class injury is of course not the only kind of injury that might lead to this rejection of criticism-as-faultfinding. The feminist philosopher Judith Butler, author of *Gender Trouble: Feminism and the Subversion of Identity*, was invited to deliver the Raymond Williams Lecture at Cambridge University in May of 2000. She chose the title "What Is Critique?" (borrowed from Michel Foucault) and returned, in her opening remarks, to Williams's worry "that the notion of criticism has been unduly restricted to the notion of 'faultfinding.'"[10] When Williams suggests that response is better thought of as a practice rather than a judgment, Butler says, he unexpectedly comes together with Foucault, "since 'critique' for Foucault is precisely a practice that not only suspends judgment for him, but offers a new practice of values based on that very suspension." A quarter century after *Keywords*, Foucault had already come to serve the discipline of criticism much as Matthew Arnold had served. He was the single most foundational thinker not just for criticism but across the humanities, and even for certain social sciences; it is arguable that he has not yet surrendered that place. Butler was ventriloquizing him so as to work out the new theoretically informed common sense of a great number of scholars across the disciplines, most of whom had taken their cue from feminism and queer theory. That common sense, she says, is that judgment must be suspended.

But judgment does not so easily cede its place. In an effort to avoid it, Butler distinguishes between *criticism*, which does find fault, and *critique*, which for her (as for Kant and Adorno) pursues a higher-order aim and thus need not lower itself to faultfinding. The proper object of critique is the rules and conditions by which faultfinding is governed. Criticism makes judgments, judgments that (in Butler's words) subsume "a particular under an already constituted category." Critique, on the other hand, "asks after the occlusive constitution of the field of categories themselves." But can a focus on critique resolve or escape the problem of criticism? Or does it just kick the can down the road? The words "asks after," which Butler calls upon to replace the activity of judging, look more like a *disavowal* of the judgments that her version of critique is in fact making, negative judgments marked here by the adjective "occlusive." Practically speaking, what's the difference between calling a field of categories "occlusive" and saying, if at all possible (and if it is not possible, why go to the trouble of mentioning it?), that field of categories should be replaced by a more transparent or enlightened or otherwise desirable one? The point of critique as it's presented here can only be to determine *what's wrong* with those categories and the questions those categories permit so that the categories and questions can be exchanged for better ones. Butler is setting up the practitioner of critique, like the practitioner of criticism, as a maker of judgments. Which is to say that, like Williams, she too seems to have positive as well as negative feelings about faultfinding.

According to the anthropologist Talal Asad, writing in the 2009 book *Is Critique Secular?* that he co-authored with Butler, Wendy Brown, and Saba Mahmood—a book to which I will return, as it serves as a reminder that the stakes in this seemingly peripheral topic include the most fundamental questions of how to do any and all intellectual work, and how to do it on a global playing field of extreme inequality—Butler's feelings about faultfinding are *too* positive. Taking off from the Danish cartoon affair of 2005, and in particular from European incomprehension of the Muslim sense of injury and outrage at the satiric cartoons published of the Prophet Mohammed, Asad argues that the practice of judging has to be dealt with much more harshly. There is in fact no distinction, Asad says, between criticism and critique. Critique *is* criticism, and criticism in just the sense that Butler tries to repudiate. (This was my point as well.) Critique too is a normative practice. But Asad is harder on that practice than Butler is; he describes its norms as unspeakably violent and indefensible. For Asad, critique in its essence is an all-out Western assault on the non-Western world. As a rubric for the sins of which critique is guilty, faultfinding is thus much too gentle. As if trying not to appear to be rendering judgment on it, Asad sends up a smokescreen of interrogatives and repetitions of "may be": "critique as the drive to truth *may be* motivated by delight in the sheer exercise of power over another (torture is only an extreme case of this), and conquest *may indeed be* critique's primary function. How should one compare these motivations of critique with those of faultfinding?"[11] (my italics). But on occasion he allows a simple declarative to blow through the fog of evasiveness, revealing a simple and almost unequivocal condemnation: "Critique is no less violent than the law."[12] Violence, conquest, torture, the exercise of power over another: these are the ultimate truths of critique as seen, according to Asad, from the viewpoint of its Muslim victims.

Victims—that's the key to the case. The Muslims of Europe for Asad, women and what has come to be called the LBGTQ community for Butler, the working class for Williams: in each instance the case against criticism-as-faultfinding seems organic to a social collectivity that has been the victim of discrimination. This may seem embarrassingly obvious, too obvious to bear repeating. My reason for repeating it nevertheless is to suggest that the ill repute into which faultfinding has fallen has a logic that is not merely theoretical, but socio-historical. Right or wrong, it results from the still recent self-assertion and still fragile politicization of groupings of the disadvantaged, those whose shared baggage has included the collective experience of having faults found in them. The case against faultfinding expresses the shared subjectivity of the discriminated against. This is why anyone addressing the question of criticism and politics today can't avoid coming to terms with the emancipatory movements of the 1960s and their aftermath.

Yes, but. Yes, the case against faultfinding expresses the shared subjectivity of the discriminated against. But this is misleading in the sense that it runs together the movements of the 1960s, which were largely based on subjectivity, with the politics of class, as in Williams, which is arguably based on interests that are more objective than subjective. Also, the demographic weight brought to bear against faultfinding is in itself no guarantee that the case against faultfinding deserves anyone's full and unconditional support. It is no guarantee—here I am trying to make a turn in my argument—that the case against faultfinding indeed *receives* unconditional support even from those who make it. If there is widespread impatience with judgment on the part of the discriminated against, there is also widespread impatience with that impatience. And justly so.

In her response to Asad in *Is Critique Secular?* Butler speculates that perhaps after all Asad is *wrong* to "suspend the question of evaluation, or 'judgment.'"[13] Suspension of judgment, you will recall, is just what she herself had proposed, via Foucault, in the Raymond Williams Lecture. Here the suspending of judgment is no longer what she advocates. To claim that the Danish cartoons inflicted "a kind of structural injury" on "religious and racial minorities," as Asad does, is itself "to make a strong normative claim."[14] Making strong normative claims is criticism. It is what Asad is doing, Butler insists, beyond his useful meta-critical work in exposing the hidden categories that structure Western discourse, and he is right to do it. In discussing Asad's book on suicide bombing (which showed, correctly, that Western liberals cannot trust their gut feelings about terrorism without falling into utter inconsistency), she reminds us, "I have sought to make the case for Asad's normative commitments, despite his very interesting and confounding protestations to the contrary."[15] In *Is Critique Secular?* she returns to Raymond Williams's comments on the restriction of criticism to faultfinding, and she suggests, if only implicitly, that Asad is wrong to reject Williams's aspirational link between criticism and "liberation."[16] This fits her own endorsement, in the Raymond Williams Lecture, of "strong normative commitments that appear in forms that would be difficult, if not impossible, to read within the current grammars of normativity."[17] For all her impatience with its current grammars, Butler has clearly not given up on normative commitment as such.

Victims and Contexts

On reflection, Butler's argument that Asad is faultfinding in spite of himself will surprise no one who is not an unqualified supporter of identity politics.[18] Identity politics is of course the kind of politics Asad is engaging in: for him, as for Samuel Huntington's "clash of civilizations" thesis, civilizational identities like "the West" follow religious allegiance and remain essentially unchanged through history. Civilizational identity, rather than any other principle or attachment, determines what Asad fights for and fights against. Asad rails against those who find democracy and free speech "intrinsic to 'European civilization,'"[19] and he's right to do so. But each of his own arguments is an emphatic insistence on what is "intrinsic" to European civilization.

Identity politics and faultfinding are not incompatible. On the contrary. It was of course always possible that the victims of what Williams called discrimination (meaning victims both of educated taste and of social exclusion) might become judges in their turn, and perhaps unforgiving ones. Given the Soviet-influenced judgments of art delivered in the name of the working class during Williams's lifetime, judgments that tended to be quite sure of their own righteousness and uncompromising in their denunciations, it is striking that the *Keywords* entry does not reflect on this eventuality. It was not merely hypothetical. It had already happened. More to the point, it is something that has also happened since. It has happened not as a result of the class upheaval Williams hoped for, but as a result of the relative success of the new social movements of the 1960s and after, movements of liberation that mobilized women and sexual, racial, and ethnic minorities, among others. Williams gives no sign of imagining a future, two or three decades later, when those accused of wielding judgmental authority and thus finding fault with others would be, broadly speaking, his own students. Yet that is a rough outline of the generational story with whose consequences we are now living.

As is well known, the generational story has been caught up in fierce polemic, much of it extending beyond the academy. "In [a] radical extension of the politics of the late Sixties," Todd Gitlin writes, "difference and victimization are prized, ranked against the victimization of other groups. We crown our good with victimhood."[20] Gitlin may be overstating the case, but he is not inventing from whole cloth. In *Achieving Our Country*, Richard Rorty writes:

> The heirs of the New Left of the Sixties have created, within the academy, a cultural left. Many members of this Left specialize in what they call the "politics of difference" or "of identity" or "of recognition." The cultural Left thinks more about stigma than about money, more about deep and hidden psychosexual motivations than about shallow and evident greed.[21]

Ten pages later Rorty prophesies that the errors of that cultural or "English Department" left—in particular its excessive concern for minorities and non-citizens, its refusal of patriotism, and its negligence of economic inequality at home—would one day encourage the rise of an authoritarian populist strongman who would be a national disaster. Twenty years later, in his 2017 *The Once and Future Liberal: After Identity Politics*, Mark Lilla continues the same line of accusatory thinking. He blames the 2016 election of Donald Trump on "identity politics," a "romantic sensibility that "took political form in the early 1960s" and became crystallized in the phrase "*Speaking as an X.*"[22] Reviewers have not universally admired Lilla's analysis of the 2016 election, but in calling out the 60s generation Lilla is not entirely wrong: there is, as he suggests, a connection between national politics and trends in academic criticism that can be traced back to that generation.[23] There is no doubt that representatives of the disadvantaged, inheriting authority from the relative success of the liberation movements, rose in the academic ranks and are now themselves acting as judges, feeling empowered both by their identities and by their institutions—empowered to denounce and dismiss. Their judgments not only have a formative effect on the next generation of students and teachers, but are sometimes public enough to be commented on in the press. For better or worse, they have come to wield a non-negligible social influence.

For better, or for worse? How should we feel about that influence, such as it is? The best observers have found it difficult to pronounce. Consider for example Simon During's re-telling of this same story in "When Literary Criticism Mattered." "By the time that poststructuralism and identity politics were reorganizing the discipline in the 1980s, criticism in its modernist form was no longer at the center of what actually went on in English departments."[24] Why not? Because

> Leavisism had no room for any cultural politics that insisted on expanding the canon or the curriculum to include works by (what we might now call) minority writers just on the grounds that they were minority writers. . . . Leavisism's cultural politics were incompatible with the cultural politics embraced by the seventies and eighties emancipation movements, in which people of color, women, and queers struggled for cultural justice and recognition. This turned out to be unacceptable within an academy drawing its students from different cultures and enabling them to affirm their difference.[25]

During does not sound very sympathetic to the new dispensation. He seems to assume that in the post-Leavis period, criticism does *not* matter anymore, which is a serious loss; he hints that works by minority writers made no claim to inclusion in the canon on the basis of their aesthetic or moral value, but only because they "*were*" by "minority writers," a hint that he would probably prefer to have back; he suggests that it's the academy's new demographics ("drawing its students from different cultures") and its role as an enabler of difference that led it to judge criticism in the older sense "unacceptable" (an adjective that suggests undue severity on the part of the arbiter) and thus got it banished.[26] But he does not condemn the admission of "students from different cultures" into the academy or their "struggle for cultural justice and recognition," and he does not call for a return to Leavisism's "antirelativist and antipluralist spirit," though he may want to. What he says he wants is criticism that offers "critique of the present"[27]—a vision that Leavis and Williams shared.[28]

Generalizing about the meaning of this half century of history for the discipline of criticism is hard to do in a purely analytical rather than a partisan and polemical spirit. I can't say I have succeeded at this so far myself, or even made a good faith effort. But one can be passionately polemical in more than one direction. Students, teachers, and observers of the academy will have their own favorite examples of scolding and even cancellation that are ill considered enough to cast doubt, in their eyes and the eyes of the public, on what criticism does or has become. One of my own favorites is an essay by a feminist critic at an illustrious university announcing that she will no longer read the novelist David Foster Wallace, not because of the putatively repulsive treatment of women in Wallace's novels, novels that are barely mentioned in the essay, but because of (to the essay's writer) Wallace's morally repulsive dating habits. If an author's dating habits now count as a standard of judgment, if chastisement like this can pass as anything other than an embarrassment to the chastiser, then identity politics deserves at least some of the extensive bad-mouthing it has received. And this is especially so because its confident judgments are now invested with considerable authority, embraced (for example) by university administrations eager to show off their enlightened tolerance, thus avoiding both race and gender litigation and more politically costly demands (for example, demands for divestment from fossil fuel companies and corporations complicit in the Israeli occupation of Palestine). It is tempting to reach for the old chestnut about power corrupting.

If the phrase "identity politics" sounds a bit outdated to the academic ear, it's because much of what it fought for is now uncontroversial, firmly ensconced in criticism's institutional status quo. The debate has died down. Does it really need to be revived? Well, yes. For one thing, "identity politics" is a misleading designation, and that mistake needs to be corrected. And for another, the new controversies that have arisen to replace it make more sense if one starts from the generational story that extends out from the 1960s and if one is attentive to complications that have not been registered in the public wrangling over that story.

As noted in the previous chapter, for the past decade critics have argued for example over the value of "historical context" in interpreting literature. In her 2015 *Limits of Critique*, Rita Felski declared with attention-grabbing simplicity (and another nod to Bruno Latour) that "context stinks!" In his

Literary Criticism: A Concise Political History, Joseph North names the problem as "the historicist/contextualist paradigm" and locates criticism's wrong turn, again, in the academic success of the 60s generation:

> [T]hough the turn to the historicist/contextualist paradigm has generally been understood as a local victory for the left over the elitisms of mid-century criticism, this has been largely an error. In fact, it is better to say that the opposite is true: in its most salient aspects, the turn to the current paradigm in the late 1970s and early 1980s was symptomatic of a wider retreat of the left in the neoliberal period and thus a small part of the more general victory of the right.[29]

Like many others, North is sloppy in his invocation of neoliberalism as an all-purpose, virtually omnipotent explanatory context. If the "historicist/contextualist paradigm"—more on this below—triumphed in the academy *at the same time* that neoliberalism was triumphing outside the academy, it can only be because the true essence of what seemed to be left-wing scholarship was in fact right-wing, or more precisely neoliberal.[30] Ignoring the institutional specificity of the university, North relies upon the crudest possible model of "historical context." Simultaneity is treated as if it were causation.

Why did the "historicist/contextualist paradigm" come into being in the 1970s? North does not try to tell his story without referring to the marches and demonstrations of the 1960s, to the resistance to racism and the Vietnam War, to the vitality and persistence of the civil rights movement and the other movements inspired by it. He notes them, and he says he admires them. But he skips over all that with the scantest of gestures in order to argue that the 1960s movement was immediately and conclusively betrayed by what he calls "scholarship"—a desire to give up on changing the world, a desire that he locates in "criticism" (and, weirdly, in I. A. Richards), in favor of merely interpreting the world. It is telling that, for North, the rejection of Richards and practical criticism is not identified with any women or people of color. If North had identified that rejection with critics who were women or people of color, it would have been clear that it was not breaking from but, on the contrary, continuous with one major impulse of the 1960s—the impulse to question a supposedly universalistic aesthetics that in fact spoke (as Richards did) almost entirely for white men, and white men of a certain class. Instead, North personifies the shift from criticism to scholarship in—four white men.

White men are safer targets. It's as if North did not want to say, to his readers or perhaps to himself, what his target really is.

One of the four men North sees as not true leftists, Raymond Williams, has already been discussed, though much more might have been said about his strenuous personal efforts to change as well as interpret the world, efforts that hold up pretty well against those of I. A. Richards and company. Another white male leftist, Fredric Jameson, will be discussed at length in a later chapter. But let me say something here about a third, Terry Eagleton. North's point about Eagleton is that in his attack on aesthetics and practical criticism, Eagleton was beating a dead horse. Neoliberalism had already decided to withdraw funding from both. Its supporters no longer defended "highbrow taste" as part of the symbolic infrastructure of class hierarchy; instead, they posed as "democratic levellers of aesthetic distinctions," defending "individual consumer preferences."[31] So North (who wants us to unlearn our dependence on historical context) accuses Eagleton of an error of historical judgment. North may be right that capitalism has found new ways of propping up class hierarchy. But even if he is, the fact that neoliberalism no longer wants to celebrate or fund highbrow taste is not an argument that highbrow taste is worth celebrating or funding. Why does North assume it is? That case would have to be made. And any account of what a highly educated taste should value would have to include input from people, like Eagleton, who (as North neglects to mention) had not been extensively consulted in the era of I. A. Richards.

In a different but not entirely contradictory telling of the story, more might be made of those, like Eagleton, who arrived at Oxford as working-class students of Irish ancestry. However solid their prior schooling, Eagleton and his fellows were arguably less prepared than others of other backgrounds to affirm, say, that (to quote Eagleton) "the tone of a Yeats poem veers from defensive hectoring to grimly resilient resignation."[32] The confident sensibility to which this critical vocabulary would testify—whether one considers it proof of serious training in Richards's practical criticism or merely characteristic of a certain class, ethnicity, and ideal of refinement—is arguably less available to anyone who is not in all these respects already a cultural insider. Cultural outsiders, who might want to apply some other vocabulary to Yeats and to the intricacies of Irish politics in the colonial period and might even ask the poem another set of questions altogether, might well feel they were being hectored by their teachers into grimly resilient resignation, resignation to a false universality. Surely you too feel this, do you not? If you are the kind of talented student I fully expect you are, a student of whom I have such high expectations, then surely the poem's words themselves deliver to you the defensive hectoring and the grimly resilient resignation?

Maybe not.[33] Subtract the word "defensive," and the line becomes a tiny pedagogical allegory of the depoliticizing process to which new students were subjected, or criticism's passage away from politics (hectoring) to a grim but better-educated resignation to the status quo. What I. A. Richards took as the benefit of learning how to read poems, good and bad, was "ordering our minds"—North quotes this clause. He understood this as an equilibrium of the mental faculties that leaves the reader, in John Paul Russo's admiring account, "without any tendency to action."[34] Neoliberals could not have any objections to such reading.

The rise of "context" (and with it, the rise of "theory") coincided with the decline of "close reading" in the manner of I. A. Richards and F. R. Leavis, which North celebrates and Eagleton, in the passage above, affectionately mocks. This rise was never simply a matter of how to understand the past. It was never simply about what North calls, disparagingly, historical scholarship. Yes, historical scholarship got an inflection and a boost from the left-wing ideas of the epoch. Both scholars and activists should be glad that it did. But context was also the people sitting next to you in class. Context came to matter to the literature of the past because it was suddenly felt to matter in the face-to-face present. The liberation movements—for women's liberation and sexual liberation—the civil rights movement, the movements of national independence from colonialism, and so on—these were objecting to a criticism that was in the unconscious but quite arrogant habit of pretending it had the authority to speak about tones of defensive hectoring and grim resilience for everyone. Women, working-class students, and minorities began, hesitatingly, to suggest, around the seminar table as well as in the streets, that they had not been consulted, that those who were in the habit of speaking for everyone were not necessarily speaking for *them*. It seems worth speculating that the notoriously awkward abstractions of theory-speak, for example, served as a way of opening up critical language to people who are native speakers of languages other than English and who might not have an equal and instinctive sense of what constitutes grim resilience or defensive hectoring, but on the other hand can learn and "deploy" theoretical abstractions as an accessibly transnational critical language, like mathematics or digital code. It too was universalistic. "Theory" offered up, against "close reading," both an impulse of anti-universalism and an impulse of counter-universalism, geo-graphically broader and more sociologically attentive.

By a logic that I'm not sure was ever articulated at the time, at least within literary studies (social history was different), it came to seem self-evident that we have to *think of the past* with the same respect for those who may have been neglected or ignored then as we have for those who are neglected or ignored around us *in the present*. Interrogations and protests and raised eyebrows were now also guides to historical investigation. Didn't the same sort of attention have to be paid, in literary works of the past, to voices that had been silenced or marginalized or perhaps were always there to be heard, however faintly, by those, like Horton in Dr. Seuss's *Horton Hears a Who*, who were prepared to listen with big ears and unusual care? And wouldn't it make a difference to those in the present who *did* learn to listen, thereby also learning something about themselves?

One all-important thing that needs to be said about the so-called histori-cist/contextualist paradigm is that the supplying of historical context defines a form of professional expertise. It tells the lay reader something that in all probability the lay reader would not otherwise know, and that enriches and perhaps changes that reader's understanding of what they are reading. Some-one reading or watching a performance of Shakespeare's *The Merchant of Venice*, for example, and contemplating the most famous portrait of a Jew in Western literature, might benefit from the knowledge that the Jews had been banished from England since 1290, so it is unlikely that Shakespeare's contemporaries had ever met one, though Roderigo López, Jewish physician to Queen Elizabeth I, has been proposed as a possible model for Shylock. This bit of information may not totally transform the sense you make of the play or of anti-Semitism (anti-Semitism is a fault to be found there, even if you don't think it spoils the play), but it adds value to your understanding—publicly understandable value. And without *some* form of public value-added, socially recognized expert knowledge (not necessarily historical), criticism could not continue to exist as an academic discipline. Why else should society support it, even to the minimal extent that it does, as more than a private hobby or pastime? Expertise of some sort is an absolute requirement.

This requirement should be obvious. It nevertheless needs pointing out, and even expanding upon, for two reasons. First, not every proposed vision of what criticism is, or should be, in fact recognizes it or includes a way of satisfying it, and forgetting to fill in that blank will disqualify the submission.

And second and more important, *any* idea of expertise, political or not, will conflict to some degree and in some way with the case against standards and faultfinding that Williams makes in *Keywords*. Democracy, at least in its strongest formulations, has a long, troubled history with expertise, and vice versa.

Criticism and the Limits of Democracy

The conflict between democracy and expertise deepens the confusion that surrounds criticism and politics. But without taking it into account, one has little chance of understanding what goes on beneath the surface of our discipline, or of any discipline. Ambivalence about expertise was (and is) real. One troubling side of the 60s movements, as Gitlin says, is "a certain tendency toward know-nothing leveling. One hears the assumption that all knowledge is bankrupt, all claims to authority or objectivity fraudulent, all expertise a mask for raw power."[35] It seems logical, then, to tell the story of this generation's move into the university as its capitulation to the university's protocols. The simplicity of this narrative arc is especially attractive to those who are proudly writing for the general public and don't have to worry about the quibbling over details of their fellow academics. In *The Last Intellectuals*, Russell Jacoby writes, "In the end it was not the New Left intellectuals who invaded the universities but the reverse: the academic idiom, concepts, and concerns occupied, and finally preoccupied, young left intellectuals."[36]

This version of the story does a disservice to the New Left. It is true that the generation that was empowered by the movements of the 1960s could not have occupied a position within a profession or discipline *without* embracing some version of expertise, some systematic method or methods (in the case of criticism) of adding value onto the non-expert experience of reading. And that expertise would necessarily bring with it some standards of professional knowledge and judgment—standards that exclude or diminish the responses of the noncredentialed, which find fault with them. Does that mean, however, that the generation of the 60s betrayed itself when, coming into professional or disciplinary power, it failed to reject faultfinding and indeed got into the habit of finding fault itself? To tell the story in this way is to make a fundamental error about that generation and, more important, about what the present has inherited from it. When that generation is understood to have betrayed its principles, the assumption seems to be that it was committed in principle, committed absolutely, to the shared values and beliefs of particular disadvantaged collectivities, collectivities that were scorned or neglected by the dominant culture.

The model here can again be Talal Asad in *Is Critique Secular?* Rita Felski, who has led the charge against criticism-as-faultfinding, finds Asad "persuasive" when he accuses critique (in her words) of "its ignorance of faith, its disdain for piety, its inability to enter imaginatively into a lived experience of the sacred."[37] Following Asad, she chastises Western intellectuals (in reality, she only attacks those on the left) for a "smugness of tone that can be harshly dismissive of the deeply felt beliefs and attachments of others."[38] One might, of course, think of the "deeply felt beliefs and attachments" of, say, white supremacists and wonder whether they really ought to be protected from critique. Shouldn't it matter *which* beliefs and attachments you are protecting? And how are you going to decide which beliefs and attachments to support and which to deny without having recourse, on occasion, to something like critique?

It is my own belief that we need critique in order to decide which beliefs and commitments to support and which to hesitate about. But I am not the only one attached to that belief. It expresses, I think, the majority sentiments of my profession and my generation. Felski defends all forms of particular belonging against any judgment that would claim to be universal, or more universal than they are. I hesitate to use the term "moral relativism" about her position, since that phrase has been used so sloppily in polemics over what used to be called postmodernism, but here it seems, unfortunately, pertinent. Felski's moral relativism looks like the logical but unacknowledged endpoint of a certain line of 60s thinking. To the extent that the 60s generation concluded, based on the faults found by the mainstream in its own disadvantaged collectivities, that faultfinding itself had to be rejected, it would have produced a rejection of critique very like Felski's. In that sense, Felski's *Limits of Critique* is a true if belated expression of 1960s ideology, but her position is representative of only one ideological impulse of the 60s generation. Sympathetic (or uncritical) acquiescence to the beliefs and attachments of others as long as those others are somehow society's victims, or at any rate not its rulers—that is at best a very partial reading of the 60s movements.

How could it have been their overriding principle? As theorists of the new social movements like Chantal Mouffe and Bonnie Honig have insisted again and again, would-be followers and activists were exposed from the outset to the awkwardness of others who had quite different identities and different complaints against the status quo. In practical as well as theoretical ways, they were obliged to consider the limits as well as the possibilities of their solidarity with others. For some, of course, any compromise on their own sense of their identity would count as self-betrayal. But the extreme insistence on identity tended to bear that group away from politics. For identity *politics*, or more precisely for an *effective* identity politics, a working intimacy with those with whom one does not share every aspect of one's identity is a prerequisite—as is knowledge of the multitude of different identities that intersect in each of us, consciously or unconsciously, not all of them worthy of uncritical solidarity. What has come to be called *intersectionality*, properly considered, was already being negotiated, sometimes quite painfully, within the 60s movement.[39] Intersectionality (more on that concept below) makes it less plausible for anyone to insist that any one identity is fully adequate and conclusive. To put this otherwise, the rule is *not* that no one can be critical of anyone else.

Asad, on whom Felski relies, reserves his most acidic treatment for critique as it is theorized and practiced by Edward Said. Let us have a quick look, then, at Said (1935–2003), considered for the moment as a representative of the long generation in question. Said was not representative at all in some respects (he was thirty-three in 1968, and not at that time an activist), but for that very reason he is perhaps a better guide to its core and long-term significance.

Writing about Jonathan Swift as an intellectual, Said finds ways of separating Swift from his disregard for democracy and his explicit Toryism—in this respect, Said's approach, like that of Williams, of course refuses the dull predictability of a certain faultfinding. One way of valuing Swift positively is by seeing him as "an intellectual engaged in particular limited struggles of a very limited sort" rather than "a man who formulated, defended and owned a consistent set of ideological values."[40] But Said also tries another tack that is all about having a consistent ideological value. He praises Swift for his antimilitarism. Yes, it was Tory policy to "delegitimize the Whig politics of war,"[41] but Said suggests that Swift's position was not really partisan. On the contrary, it opposed "anything connected with human aggression or organized human violence,"[42] whatever the party behind it. Thus Swift "never had a good thing to say" about "war," "conquest," or "colonial oppression."

Notice that though these targets would not get any partisan political label assigned to Swift in the eighteenth century, they are crucial to the politics of the 1970s and 1980s, when Said was writing. They are crucial to the Vietnam generation to which, loosely speaking, Said belonged. But they are not issues of identity. More important, they explain why, like Swift, the Vietnam War generation could not give any identity or collectivity their wholehearted support. As we know, the enterprises of war, conquest, and colonial oppression have always been quite popular, at least in the countries that undertook them. Often they have been almost hysterically popular, and even most popular among those who stood to profit least from them and indeed were more likely to lose their lives by taking part in them. This has certainly been true in America, whether the subject was seizing land from Native Americans or passively accepting Zionism's "for a people without a land, a land without a people."

Antimilitarism was not and is not a populist position. Depending on the scale at which you theorize democracy, it may not even be a democratic one. Given its self-defining attention to war, conquest, and colonial oppression, therefore, the generation of the 60s, 70s, and 80s could not in good conscience surrender itself unconditionally and uncritically to what Felski calls, following Asad, "the deeply felt beliefs and attachments of others," however victimized those others might feel. History had demonstrated and was continuing to demonstrate that those beliefs and attachments might turn out on inspection to be very unpalatable ones. They might produce their own victims. Zionism is by no means the only example, though it was a forceful one for Said, and it remains a forceful one today.[43]

Democracy was of course a strongly positive value for the 60s generation. But it could never be an absolute value. The idea that difference might be inviolable was regularly violated. Judgment and standards of judgment could not be done without, even if (or because) those judgments and standards conflicted with the beliefs and attachments of a given collectivity. Impatience with faultfinding was and is real and valuable, but it could not be a satisfactory excuse for surrendering the obligation to find fault. The 60s generation would not be betraying itself, therefore, by accepting in one form or another the standards and protocols of judgment defined by expertise. Expertise, which always involves some relativizing of the commitment to democracy, was not alien to it. When Joseph North disputes the idea that "the turn to the historicist/contextualist paradigm" was "a local victory for the left over the elitisms of mid-century criticism," he does not quite deny that that mid-century criticism was elitist, though he elsewhere seems unperturbed by the arrogance of its assumption that its critical mode spoke for everyone. But he might have said that for all its greater pretensions to democracy, there is also an elitism in the left-wing criticism that followed it. If there is contention over the legacy of that generation, then, it should not center on expertise as such. What needs to be talked about, rather, is the particular nature and contents of expertise. The real question is there.

After the depredations of COVID-19, it ought to be clear that expertise must on occasion be defended, and perhaps on many occasions, and perhaps even to the death. We have seen where disrespect for expertise can lead when the popular prejudice against it is loudly supported in the highest places and enacted as policy, or the lack thereof. But the basic argument is not new. In *Secular Vocations: Intellectuals, Professionalism, Culture*, my own minor contribution to the culture wars, I suggested that the left should not run screaming from the recognition that professional status confers on them, as it does on everyone who attains it, a degree of legitimate authority and power.[44] In considering the connection between criticism and politics, we will have to pursue that line of thinking further. That means considering both what the word "politics" means and what the word "power" means. You cannot decide what side you are on simply by listening to those who describe themselves as disempowered. They may be a lot more empowered than they say or even think they are. Nor can you decide whom you oppose simply by deciding whether they hold power or not. The category of holders of power may include yourself, and you (and others) may be glad of it and wish the power were greater.[45]

What to think, then, about Williams's objections to faultfinding in *Keywords*? As I said above, Williams objected to his own objections. Standards, culture, and judgment are not always the villains of his argument. When Williams refers to the victims of discrimination—those whose naïve, untrained responses are presumably rejected by "good" or officially sanctioned taste— standards as such seem to be on the side of the oppressors. And it would seem to follow that Williams is calling for standards to be rejected. But if the victims of discrimination wanted to rebel against officially sanctioned taste, they would not necessarily rebel against standards as such. They would also rebel in the name of *another* standard. That other standard might be (1) an entirely different one, defined this time by the former victims' own distinct values and experiences, or perhaps (2) merely an extended and modified standard, a sensibility that would retain some of what had passed for good taste under the regime that excluded them but that would now also factor in the values and perspectives that had previously been excluded. Neither of these options would involve rejecting standards, judgment, and culture as such. Indeed, option one corresponds more or less to Williams's most positive account of "culture" at the end of *Culture and Society*. Culture could work as a standard for the judging of capitalist society, Williams concludes there, because it was an organic expression of the worldview of capitalism's victims. It supplied just those principles of wholeness and solidarity that bourgeois individualism had driven out of social life. It represented, precisely, "the social confidence of a class"—not this time the confidence of the aristocracy or the bourgeoisie, however, but of the working class.

As I see it, the bulk of *Culture and Society* in fact aligns much more closely with option two. And that alignment helps explain why the culture-and-society paradigm has flourished as much as it has. It has won broad approval not by expressing the distinct worldview of the working class, but by forging a synthesis or coalition of otherwise conflicting worldviews, not all of them critical of the same things or critical in the same way. For example, that paradigm implicitly encourages *pre*-capitalist literature to be counted as *anti*capitalist literature. That's not exactly wrong; the literature of earlier periods can certainly be seen as a vehicle for the experience of alternative ways of being. Still, capitalism was not what that earlier literature was contemplating, and the formula makes for some strange bedfellows in the period of capitalism as well. As Williams wrote in the "culture" entry of *Keywords*, "Politically, . . . [culture] veered between radicalism and reaction and very often, in the confusion of major social change, fused elements of both."[46]

If Williams had not allowed so much diversity of perspective under his umbrella, however, it seems unlikely that *Culture and Society* could have succeeded as a disciplinary rationale, a narrative sustaining long-term public support for an empowered or least a precariously viable academic field. If he had, say, repudiated any literature or criticism not authored by the working class, rather than laying out for criticism a kind of Popular Front in which both bourgeois and feudal literature had a valued place, his line would not have been so acceptable. Nor would it have served the cause of the left. After all, why should society permit the existence of (let alone pay for) a discipline whose raison d'être was *nothing but* the critique of that very society? Whatever else the word "politics" means when fastened to the unlikely object of literary criticism, it designates the zone of possible answers to that question: Why is the discipline allowed to survive, to the extent that it is?

What Do You Mean, Politics?

There is no entry for "politics" in Williams's *Keywords*. Perhaps in 1976 the term seemed too obvious or too unproblematic to warrant genealogical discussion. This lack is corrected, however, in the updated and supplemented edition, *Keywords for Today: A 21st Century Vocabulary*, published by Colin MacCabe and a team of colleagues in 2018. The new edition opts to trace the adjective "political" rather than the noun "politics," and it grounds this choice in the recent trajectory of both words: a move away from politics in the sense of a single, central, all-determining arena, Hannah Arendt's "public sphere of active citizenship," and toward the political as something that "can take place in many different arenas, with many different types of agents participating simultaneously."[47] This focus on the political is a tribute to the contemporary moment. One thing the generation of the 1960s and its inheritors are generally agreed to have accomplished, for better or worse, is getting the world to see the personal as the political, as the 70s feminists first declared. This formula multiplies the zones and sites where politics of a significant sort is agreed to happen. That said, however, the *Keywords for Today* entry also recognizes in the history of "political" a certain decline. The adjective "politic" once "connoted that which was prudent, sensible, and sagacious."[48] In the eighteenth century "political" suggested the "elevated and righteous, often contrasting the perceived benefits of constitutional governments against the characteristics of despotism or tyranny."[49] In the same period, however, another set of meanings was arising that connoted cunning, temporizing, calculation, and partisanship. In short, there has also been a "semantic fall from prudence to mere expediency." "To call someone 'political' is rarely a compliment."[50] This genealogy overlaps with Arendt's sense of politics as something noble that was lost as modernity began "to look inward rather than outward, intent on the private pursuit of happiness and wealth."[51]

Politics would probably already have counted as an "essentially contested" concept, to cite William Connolly's application of W. B. Gallie's phrase, before the generation of the 1960s, but it was this double movement that made the contestation inescapable. Suddenly politics seemed to be everywhere. And thus politics was also nowhere—the site of a tragic disappearance. One reason it was nowhere in an actionable sense was that it seemed to have disappeared as the result of a longer and more complex historical development, the turn toward "the private pursuit of happiness and wealth." It is the longer and more complex development, whose obvious referent is capitalism and the subjugation of politics by economics, that is neglected by culture wars polemics blaming the loss of politics in the true sense on the 60s generation's exaggerated concern for such cultural matters as gender, race, and sexuality. I have already quoted Richard Rorty's charge that "the heirs of the New Left of the Sixties" were wrong to "specialize in what they call the 'politics of difference' or 'of identity' or 'of recognition,'" thereby distracting from more directly or truly political matters like money and greed, labor unions and the institutions of the welfare state, and "laws that need to be passed"—in short, "things that need to be done."[52] Rorty chooses to ignore the longer-term trends that make the sorts of labor action and law-passing he favors much more difficult but that are not in any sense the fault of a cultural left or indeed of anything either done or left undone in the academy. As Francis Mulhern writes in *Culture/Metaculture*, the decisive point was made by Georg Lukacs in 1919:

> Bourgeois civilization has exalted politics in socio-economic conditions that sooner or later thwart all but the best-adapted of programmes. This historic paradox, which has intensified over the decades since Lukacs wrote, with the widening of popular claims to entitlement and participation in public affairs, has done more than any local disappointment or scandal, however great in itself, to discredit the very idea of politics.[53]

Mulhern goes on, explaining his rejection of identity politics' sloppy slogan:

> [P]olitics is never everything. . . . It is normally deliberative in character, governed by the question, What is to be *done*? Political utterance, then, is always injunctive, regardless of the medium, occasion, or genre. It wills, urges, dictates. Its aim is to secure assent (a process in which issues of identity are indeed central) and, failing that, compliance, of which coercion furnishes the last guarantee.[54]

Let us note, for future reference, the appearance here of the menacing term "coercion," a "last guarantee" and perhaps for that reason a kind of determining instance of politics. At any rate, coercion seems to offer a maximum contrast with culture, which in Mulhern's words "may offer an infinity of moral discriminations, in mutually irreducible patterns. No meaning or value simply translates any other."[55] The implication is that politics in his injunctive, "what is to be done" sense, happens only when moral discriminations, meanings, and values *do* translate, thereby allowing themselves to be gathered up into a shared program or action, the end result of which may be or look like coercion.

The most common site of such translation, though by no means the only possible site, is the state. As *Keywords for Today* suggests, faithful in this to the practical legacy of Williams, responsible thinking about the political requires responsible thinking about the different locations where politics is happening right now and the different forms and limits that those locations impose on it. It is politics at the level of the state that Rorty clearly has in mind when he speaks of passing legislation, and he may even be conceding that the cultural left has not been totally indifferent to this level of politics when he gives it credit for "extraordinary success" in making humiliation on the basis of identity less routine than it had been, or decreasing "the amount of sadism in our society."[56]

After the experience of COVID-19—when a centralized policy protecting the health of citizens from the pandemic would have had to be formulated at the top and enacted through existing agencies, including a certain degree of coercion (mask wearing, social distancing, mandatory vaccination) and when the blatant failure of the state (which includes a failure of its citizens to pressure it into better behavior) was measured in hundreds of thousands of unnecessary deaths—the idea of discussing the political significance of any phenomenon, even one as unlikely as criticism, *without* attention to politics at the level of the state seems almost grotesque.

3 Lost Centrality

Foucault on Commentary

Criticism, as we have seen, has two objects of knowledge, not one. Even when preceded by "literary," criticism as it is usually understood by critics is defined by a relation to culture as well as by a relation to literature. There are various ways in which literature can be considered political, but culture has more points of connection to the urgencies of the present, and thus to politics. Deciding on criticism's proper or desirable relation to politics therefore does not depend solely or perhaps even primarily on discovering its proper or desirable relation to literature. Still, there has always seemed to be something mysterious about the relationship between those who comment on literature and the field of literary objects on which they comment, something different from the relations that historians have to history or sociologists have to society. No one has shined a brighter light into this disciplinary murkiness than Michel Foucault.

Foucault's "The Order of Discourse," his inaugural lecture at the Collège de France in 1970, lists a number of procedures for "controlling and delimiting discourse" that do not control or delimit in the most obvious sense—that is, by prohibiting the saying of certain things. One such procedure is what Foucault calls "commentary." Every society, Foucault says, has its "major narratives" that are repeated and recited, a set of utterances chosen (he does not say how they are chosen or by whom) to be "preserved because it is suspected that behind them is a secret or a treasure."[1] As opposed to the vast majority of utterances, which in the normal course of things simply vanish without a trace, there exist a small number that, once said, *continue* to be said, giving rise "to a certain number of new speech-acts which take them up, transform them or speak of them, in short, those discourses which, over and above their formulation, are said indefinitely, remain said, and are to be said again."[2] Among these utterances, selected to be preserved and commented upon, are legal and religious texts, "but also those texts (curious ones, when we consider their status) which are called 'literary' and, to a certain extent, scientific texts."[3]

From this angle, literature can be thought of as a set of texts that are chosen to be "said" again and again. Literature is not some enigmatic metaphysical or anti-metaphysical essence; it is what gives rise to forms of commentary like literary criticism, literary history, and so on. In this respect literary texts resemble legal, religious, and scientific texts, which also give rise to commentary. But literature is unlike them, and indeed "curious," because of its "status." By "status" Foucault presumably refers to literature's framing by the aesthetic—as shorthand, let us say it is framed by an unpronounced "as if." To read a literary text "as if" means—in the discipline's dominant, Kantian tradition—to read it in a state of relative indifference as to whether what the text represents actually exists outside literature or not. Isobel Armstrong reminds us that we need this "as if" in order to distinguish adequately (as Catherine MacKinnon does not) between the representation of a gang rape and the physical acts of violence themselves.[4] Abiding under the sign of "as if" would seem to separate literature off from the more direct, literal, or applied authority exercised by science, religion, and the law—though their forms of authority, too, are open to further questioning.[5] For contrast, we might call that other authority "as *is*." Being understood to exercise "as is" authority explains why law, religion, and science give rise to so many new speech acts. There is a lot riding on what they are agreed to have said or to be saying. The same cannot be said of literature.

The main point of the Foucault passage, however, is to insist that this difference in social status is not as important as it might seem. Foucault's interest is in the basic structure of commentary, and that structure overrides such differences. Literary critics tend to see literature as distinctive, and distinctive in the kind of commentary it elicits, precisely because it does not excommunicate or imprison, feed people or poison the environment; its status or authority goes no further than aesthetic semblance. Foucault seems to be suggesting the opposite: that however the aesthetic is defined (as non-instrumental imagination, defamiliarization, the deliberate intensification of already existing indeterminacy, the distribution of the sensible, "as if," or whatever), it is only one subset of a wider social mystery, a mystery shared with religion, law, and science. What is profoundly mysterious here is commentary as such, not the distinctiveness of the literary text or of the particular commentary called literary criticism.[6]

For Foucault, commentary is defined by a hierarchical relation between primary texts, the ones that demand to be commented on, and secondary texts, the ones that comment on them, are chained to them, are obliged to serve them. Secondary texts cannot say whatever they like; they have no choice but to comment on primary texts. This seems natural and self-evident. But it leads Foucault to lay out a paradox, and for critics an intimate and unsettling one:

> On the one hand, [commentary] allows the endless construction of new discourses: the dominance of the primary text, its permanence, its status as a discourse which can always be re-actualised, the multiple or hidden meaning with which it is credited, the essential reticence and richness which is attributed to it, all this is the basis for an open possibility of speaking. But on the other hand the commentary's only role, whatever the techniques used, is to say at last what was silently articulated "beyond," in the text. By a paradox which it always displaces but never escapes, the commentary must say for the first time what had, nonetheless, already been said, and must tirelessly repeat what had, however, never been said.[7]

If repeating and saying for the first time are the two things that commentary is compelled to do with its primary texts, then the literary critic's first thought is probably: I *knew* there was a reason why writing feels so hard. When I sit down with my laptop, I am unconsciously trying to obey imperatives that contradict each other. How do my colleagues manage to pull it off? Bless Foucault for finding words for the frustration I feel when I try to perform the professional duty everyone else sees as natural and expects me to perform—and keep performing.

On second thought, however, the contradiction that Foucault installs at the heart of commentary may seem less motivated by sympathy for the struggling critic than by exasperation with the object that sets the rules and imposes her struggles. After all, it is literature, invested with the special honor that society has agreed to bestow upon it, that makes criticism seem like an impossible mission. Since it is literature that requires criticism to do nothing but repeat, expose, display what has both already been stated and somehow also has never been stated, the obvious moral, if Foucault's thinking here can be reduced to a moral, would be that the category of literature, defined as it has been defined, should be abandoned. If it could be abandoned (a fantasy that Foucault himself holds at arm's length), then criticism, released at last from the quiet desperation of its servitude, would have metamorphosed into something else entirely. It would now be free to make more interesting and creative statements of its own. It would have won the right to speak freely. Foucault seems to be offering criticism an allegory of political emancipation.

Gesturing toward the longest perspective on his subject, Foucault refers to Greece in the sixth and fifth centuries BCE. In that period, he says, truth was redefined. Truth had been a matter of discourse—who speaks and how. Now it became a relation between an utterance and its referent. In the time of Plato, the Sophists lost out, and discourse took on something like its modern structure: "the highest truth no longer resided in what discourse was or did, but in what it said."[8]

Following Foucault's lead, critics have discovered in Plato's *Ion* a sort of creation myth for criticism.[9] Socrates happens upon the rhapsode, a professional performer of Homer's poetry, as Ion is returning from a festival where, as he is not too modest to observe, he has won first prize for his performance. Socrates congratulates him on the victory and on not merely memorizing all those lines but also understanding Homer's thought, since that's surely what he must have done in order to succeed. Socrates then proceeds to demonstrate that in fact Ion understands nothing at all—that his ability to entertain his audience as a performer of Homer does not entail any of what Socrates and even Ion himself would recognize as knowledge. In speaking up for knowledge that is separable from performance, Socrates can be thought of as inventing philosophy. For the smaller purposes of our discipline, he can also be said to be inventing literary criticism: criticism considered as a form of knowledge about art (here, Homer) that is distinct from what the performer or perhaps even the artist would have access to.

Ion is not quick on the uptake—he is not among the most formidable of Socrates's opponents—but the dialogue brings into view a possible line of defense for him that he himself does not make use of. He lets drop, with Donald Trump-like vanity, that he has the "finest things" to say about Homer.

Socrates says he'd love to hear them. Ion says, you must, you really must come and watch me perform. Like the community around him, Ion assumes that knowledge comes embodied in performance and does not otherwise exist; no division has opened up as yet between them. Socrates then tries to separate knowledge off from performance. He says he'd love to see Ion perform—one of these days. But in the meantime, perhaps he can just answer a few questions.[10] Answers to questions asked while supposedly awaiting a performance that he will never attend—that is how Socrates redefines knowledge. Knowledge, suddenly disembodied, no longer inheres in performance.

The same two-step—from watch-me-perform to answer-my-question—happens again later in the dialogue. Socrates has said that when Ion has such a wonderfully potent effect on his audience, he must be mad or possessed—that is, in a state of divine inspiration in which "reason is no longer in him" because "the deity has bereft [him] of [his] senses" and knowledge is not really relevant.[11] Ion says Socrates wouldn't think he was mad or possessed if he "heard me speaking upon Homer." Socrates replies, "I really do wish to hear you, but not before you answer me."[12]

What Ion does not say for himself, but the generation instructed by Foucault and other Continental theorists would one day say for him, is that Socrates's method of question-and-answer—call it philosophy, or call it criticism—is not, as Socrates implies, a form of knowledge that is external to performance and is more reliable for that reason. No, it is its own kind of performance, and all the more compelling because asking questions and demanding answers pretends not to be a performance at all, but only a transparent and innocuous means of arriving at truth, truth defined precisely by its independence of all the embodied or affective factors—the music, costume, and tone of voice and the emotion all these combine to produce—that allow performance to override rationality.

The repudiation of criticism/critique in *Is Critique Secular?* replays Plato's dialogue, laying out just the position that Ion can't catch hold of for himself. Asad equates Socrates's simple asking of questions and demanding of answers with insufferable political oppressiveness. Saba Mahmood defends Islam from criticism/critique by redescribing it, like Ion's performance, as a "practice" that is "affective" and "embodied." Each would have reason to enjoy one of the dialogue's funnier moments: Ion, bowled over by Socrates's arguments, admits toward the end that Socrates must after all be right. Why? Because "somehow you touch my very soul."[13] Even as Ion surrenders his position, he continues to equate possessing decisive knowledge with the ability to produce, as Socrates has, a powerful and inscrutable affect. He clings to just the identity he is in the act of surrendering.

If criticism can be thought of as a kind of performance, hence not fundamentally different in kind from the literary performances it discusses, it would presumably have escaped from the dilemma of commentary. It no longer has to say for the first time what the primary text had already said while repeating what the primary text had somehow never said. Fidelity to the (primary) text would no longer be crucial. A performative criticism could only be judged by some other criteria—for example (Ion's example), the ability to touch the soul of the other. At the same time, however, redefining criticism as a mode of performance would involve a considerable risk. The secondary text takes its value from the honor that society attributes to its primary text. Literature is what bestows such value as it has on literary criticism. The logic is so blatant that, keeping to a Foucauldian perspective, one might well see "literature" as an object of knowledge invented by critics and invested with authority by them precisely because of the reflected radiance it would then confer upon their own words. (The inevitable analogy is with priests and religious scripture.) From this angle, the point is not the difficulty the concept of literature imposes, but the significance it bestows. For those who are attracted by the idea of a performative criticism, the question that arises—a question that takes us abruptly outside Foucault's perspective—is therefore the following: *Can or should the significance that literature bestowed on criticism be replaced with some other form of significance? If so, what would that be?*

We can perhaps glimpse the beginning of an answer to this question in some of those recent critics who have gone down the performative path, rejecting to some degree the secondariness of commentary and offering various sorts of theoretical and/or first-person experiential writing as a new combination of the critical, or secondary, with the creative, or primary. Maggie Nelson's *The Argonauts* and Andrea Long Chu's *Females* are two brilliant and notable examples. *Females* makes an ostentatious show of how little authority the writer gets, *or needs to get*, from her primary text—in this case, an unpublished and perhaps unpublishable play by Valerie Solanas, the would-be assassin of Andy Warhol. Chu's tongue-in-cheek commentary on the play would be hard to describe as wishing to redeem her primary text. The real authority her commentary commands comes from the highly performative first-person account of her sexual transition and the theorizing about gender and sexual identity she ties to it.

Where such revisions of the unspoken formulas for critical writing are concerned, the patience of colleagues cannot be expected to be infinite; there are no doubt limits, whether we have arrived at them or not, on how far this first-person tendency can go before it comes to be seen as indulgent and unprofessional. Yet *Females*, which is arguably quite professional (in a positive sense of the word), suggests some surprising and praiseworthy flexibility in the logic of professionalism. The deficit of authority that results from dethroning the primary text is compensated for by the new authority of the personal experience offered. And to the extent that that experience is taken as authoritative, it's because it is not merely personal. Readers are invited to see the experience of sexual transition as a matter of urgent significance to society in general. Injury, or what Chu calls dysphoria, becomes a form of intellectual capital.

This logic has of course become familiar. If it is mentioned, it is most often mentioned with contempt, or cynicism, or even righteous indignation, whether as a jibe at an individual critic or as an expression of general annoyance (again) with the legacy of the 1960s, a legacy summed up as something like "grievance studies" or "victimology." Should scholars in the humanities be treating victimhood as a professionally profitable form of intellectual capital and thus encouraging their readers (including aspiring members of the profession) to identify with and publicly perform the status of victim? The argument has only been made by those for whom the answer is an unambiguous and thunderous no.

Readers who have been patient enough to get this far will have realized that, despite the undoubted examples of poor criticism that have little more than putative victimhood to trade on, my own answer is, perhaps polemically, less negative. In principle, the logic that transforms suffering into intellectual capital seems to me legitimate. If criticism is fundamentally about justice (a point and a word on which not everyone will agree), there ought to be no sense of scandal when someone cashes in on injustice or personal victimhood. The claim to victimhood can obviously be abused, but it requires skill to cash in on it successfully—the skill that Chu demonstrates and that deserves sympathetic or at least neutral commentary.

A phrase like "victimhood culture" is no doubt a microaggression in itself, and yet the deep truth of the matter is that, skillfully and responsibly performed, criticism can *work* if it mixes in the right proportions a (some-what diminished) attention to a primary text with a (somewhat augmented) attention to a personal experience of injustice.[14] In so doing, criticism comes to share some of the "as *is*" authority of law, religion, and science. One might say that in replacing a theological investment in the primary text with, say, the dysphoria that demands gender transition or a representation of African American life under the system of mass racialized incarceration that Michelle Alexander calls "the new Jim Crow," the discipline is in effect going back to society, which was the silent partner backing up the discipline's original investment in the primary text, and asking: Aren't gender dysphoria and mass racialized incarceration equally worthy of your investment? The investment metaphor may be awkward, but the point nevertheless seems clear. Society's backing has not been unanimous, but it has been adequate. A new set of pro-tocols for satisfactory scholarship, laying claim to a new source of authority, has been approved, if only a bit ambivalently, and put into practice, if only at a time when the humanities themselves are suffering a loss in public value. The criteria for acceptable critical discourse have stretched, making room for more personal testimony, and perhaps even for books trading on a cute remark made by a seven- or eight-year-old family member.[15]

These paragraphs on performative criticism were not so much a detour from my argument as a way of recalling its larger outline. But let's return to where we were. A performative criticism would seem to be an emancipated criticism. But if so, what exactly would it have been emancipated *from*? From "literature" as such? Or perhaps only from a certain style of subservience to literature? Thinking back to our discussion of faultfinding, it seems worth noting that the true onerousness of criticism's secondariness to literature, at least as Foucault lays it out, comes from the burden of producing "apprecia-tive" readings—readings of propositions that the text itself wanted to make, would have been proud to make, and did make even if it also somehow with-held them. It would not be equally burdensome to produce "political" or "critical" readings. As citizens of the present, we are already presumed to pos-sess, without any special training, standards of political judgment that we are prepared to apply to anything that crosses our path. It can be safely assumed that, as history moves along and social values move along with it, critics in the present will never suffer from any dearth of opportunities for the pass-ing of negative judgments on the past. There will always be moral principles, honored in the present, that the literature of the past did not honor to our satisfaction. There will always be matters of urgent concern to the present that the literature of the past can be seen to have neglected. If that's all it takes, then criticism's mission would not be so tough after all. Making new statements would be relatively easy. If new statements are *not* easy to make, as in practice they are not, it's of course because criticizing the past for not being the present is not (and never has been) an adequate formula for the production of acceptable criticism.

The onus of producing new statements would be much heavier, on the other hand, if these new statements had to invent new ways to appreciate or admire works that have been appreciated and admired many times before and if the grounds for appreciation have themselves relocated and are now distant from the grounds on which those works used to be appreciated. From this perspective, the discipline's perceived shift from "appreciative" to "critical" readings—which has been only a very partial shift, as anyone familiar with the profession will know—looks like another escape from Foucault's paradox, but an escape in a different direction. Foucault imagined (though he didn't exactly propose) exploding the hierarchy of primary and secondary texts once and for all. The so-called historicist/contextualist paradigm is a successful method for generating new statements *without* exploding that hierarchy. It keeps the primary texts primary, on the one hand, while on the other hand it dodges the obligation to say, admiringly, nothing but what that text has already said. It says things the text did not say or perhaps was unable to say. Yet by the discipline's unspoken rules, it can still claim credit, for it does not do away with the primacy of the primary text.

There is a good reason why, as long as criticism maintains something like its present set of protocols, the shift away from the "appreciative" could *not* have been more than partial. Even negative or critical statements about a primary text depend for their own value on the prior value attributed to the primary text. Who would care about negative or critical statements about primary texts that no one cares about? Foucault's subtle and rigorous analysis leads all the way back to a crude but inescapable question: Why should anyone care? It's a question to which, as I suggested above, performative criticism has a better answer than, say "I satisfy my narcissism." Any new version of criticism would need such an answer.[16]

The same question disturbs so-called surface reading, one self-nominated candidate to replace "political" or "contextual" reading. Seen through Foucault's lens, surface reading again makes sense as an attempt to escape the paradox of commentary. While flirting with the idea of a return to a (supposedly neglected) appreciative or even reverential attitude to the primary text, it rejects the premise that the primary text *hides or withholds* its statements. It sees the hiding or withholding as a cheap and unconvincing way of ensuring that the primary text contains something that has never been said. Interpretation, it implies, should not be like an Easter egg hunt where the rules of the game do not include the possibility that there are no eggs to be found. What if the primary text is all surfaces, no depths? What if you withdraw the premise of hidden treasures and what you see is what you get, whether what you get turns out to be worth treasuring or not? These are reasonable questions. The large and perhaps insuperable problem that accompanies surface reading as a way out of Foucault's dilemma, however, is that the secondary text will itself seem less valuable, and perhaps not valuable at all. If it has not found anything that was hidden, what *has* it done? What has it done that any untrained reader couldn't do? Has it brought to light anything *worth* bringing to light? What expertise does it entail or require? As we have said, without some exhibition of expertise, the discipline empties of whatever publicly verifiable worth it had preserved, thus inviting a declaration of redundancy that might have been awaiting it in any case. Always eager to slash public budgets and make education a matter of private investment in consumer preference, public decision-makers might decide they can dispense with such an esoteric and unprofitable branch of knowledge production.

As recent experience emphatically shows, it cannot be taken for granted that the institution of criticism will continue to exist—that people will continue to be hired and paid to perform the duties associated with the profession. And this is all the truer if we are no longer making any effort to seduce our public with the promise of some sort of hidden treasure. But assuming criticism does persist, there is the potential benefit that a criticism oriented toward surfaces rather than depths would adopt a more modest understanding of itself.[17] Modesty is morally attractive. It is less attractive, however, if it seems to be forced. And that is arguably the case here. Criticism would *have* to be more modest, for it would offer the public less knowledge, less value. (The same logic—greater modesty only because there is less public value to boast of—nips at the heels of criticism-as-performance, demanding a demonstration that some sort of value has indeed been generated; this is a demonstration that Andrea Long Chu successfully makes.)

Sharon Marcus and Steven Best, in their introduction to the 2009 issue of *Representations*, claim to be writing "out of a sense of political realism about the revolutionary capacities of both texts and critics."[18] They recognize with admirable honesty that "[t]o some ears this might sound like a desire to be free from having a political agenda that determines in advance how we interpret texts, and in some respects it is exactly that."[19] The phrase "a political agenda that determines in advance how we interpret texts" is less admirable. Indeed, it is misleading and specious. From a citizenly rather than a strictly academic point of view, it is not a mistake to have thought in advance about what is wrong with the world. It *is* arguably a mistake, on the other hand, *not* to have had done any such thinking. If there has been no forethought about injustice, if one waits until the last minute to even pose the question, one leaves oneself unprepared for the task of criticism, whether in the Arnoldian or the Foucauldian sense. Forethought does not "determine in advance how we interpret texts." It offers ethical guidance, yes, but it also leaves one open to surprise, self-correction, fresh hypotheses. It would be quite a serious ethical and professional lapse, on the other hand, to decide in advance, as Marcus and Best recommend, that in order to ensure that one will not search for particular predetermined treasures, one should *not* think about what is wrong with the world. As Best and Marcus concede, it is this prior commitment that "might easily be dismissed as politically quietist, too willing to accept things as they are."[20] They say nothing in the rest of the introduction that makes this characterization seem inexact.

"Surface reading" repudiates the questionable assumption that the primary text is committed to withholding its statements, thereby allowing the secondary text to say them as if for the first time. But the assumption that the primary text holds back seems less essential to Foucault's insight than the idea that it is inexhaustibly rich in secrets or treasures—that its very essence is statements that require preservation and repetition. What is decisive for Foucault is that the primary text be capable of producing an unlimited number of new statements. And if the deep truth of commentary is that the interpreter can rely absolutely on the primary text's immeasurable, quasi-theological abundance, then the element of constraint or control around which Foucault organized his discussion of "internal exclusion" seems much less crucial. Granted, "The Order of Discourse" is almost entirely concerned with the gentler, more productive side of power, the side that says an insidious yes rather than a prohibitive no. Granted, too, that Foucault's exposure of this less manifest side of power's operations was a genuinely significant contribution to the discipline's self-understanding. Still, commentary seems less guilty of exclusion than Foucault at first seems to want to claim—or more precisely, it seems guilty of little if any exclusion that is *objectionable*. You can't have a politics without a strong sense that something *is* objectionable. In other words, there is reason to think that what looks like a politics of commentary is less a political judgment than a neutral description.

Disciplinarity

If commentary is less political than it seems, it is also closer to another term (again announced as producing "internal exclusion") that is of obvious significance to literary critics: namely, the principle of "the discipline." Before getting to the discipline, Foucault considers "the author." His argument has become familiar: the author can be considered a retrospective construct, limiting what criticism can say about a given set of texts to what is consistent with their supposed common origin. The discipline, he then says, is "opposed"—a strong word—both to the principle of commentary and to the principle of the author. It is opposed to the author because its objects and methods, rules and definitions, are not tied to a given name, but are "a sort of anonymous system at the disposal of anyone who wants to or is able to use it."[21] The discipline is opposed to commentary because its aim is not to rediscover a meaning or repeat an identity but merely to make new statements. "For there to be a discipline, there must be the possibility of formulating new propositions, ad infinitum."[22] Note that the possibility of formulating new propositions is where we were led in our discussion of commentary above. Note too that each of these points—the capacity to make new statements and the availability of that capacity to anyone—makes the discipline sound both productive and democratically open. In other words, Foucault is not exposing a moral scandal. He is not offering the emancipation he seemed to have in mind when he framed this discussion in terms of "internal exclusion." And what follows is also short on scandal. In order to be acceptable to the discipline, propositions must fulfil certain conditions. Since errors are also an integral part of disciplinary discourse, a proposition need not be true in order to be acceptable to the discipline; but before a proposition can be judged disciplinarily true or false, it must "fulfil complex and heavy requirements."[23] Those requirement or preconditions make the discipline a "principle of control over the production of discourse," a matter of "policing"; any discipline "pushes back a whole teratology of discourse beyond its margins."[24]

For Foucault the discipline, like the dream of reason, produces monsters. He seems to assume that readers will root for the monsters: cheering on the entrapped victims of disciplinary constraint as they struggle for freedom. That is the scene we would have to envisage in order to assume that there is a politics at work here. We would have to identify with those rebellious things that, because of these principles of exclusion, can't be said, or with those who would like to say them. If there were no victims, there would be no politics. But Foucault does not trace unspeakable responses back to any particular constituency, as I suggested Williams does. He gives us no other motive to applaud these unnamed things that can't be said. And he needs one. Otherwise, common sense might well suppose that at least some of those extra-disciplinary statements are just stupid, inconsistent, irrelevant, wrong, or genuinely crazy—in short, undeserving of a place in the discipline. Can Foucault possibly want to argue that all statements are equally deserving of being included in any discussion, however open and undisciplined? Is he demanding equal time for creationists and flat earthers? Are we sure, in sum, that the logic of disciplinary expertise deserves to be described as tyranny or oppression? Next to the world's very real oppressions and the emancipations they call out for, the invocation of freedom here seems potentially irresponsible. Fake democracy—winning admission for all statements that the discipline might exclude—does the cause of real democracy no good at all.

"The Order of Discourse" is structured as a political allegory. On one side is an apparently innocuous but nevertheless oppressive order; on the other are all the things that this oppressive order makes it impossible to articulate. Escaping from the paradox of commentary looks, accordingly, like a kind of emancipation. Foucault does not hesitate to concede that it would be a costly emancipation, perhaps entailing even that we forfeit our sanity. He mentions, at one extreme of his dilemma, the belief expressed by a psychiatric patient that each and every passing shred of utterance must be clutched tight, preserved, examined again and again, for who knows? It may be infinitely rich in as yet uninterpreted meanings. For criticism, this cautionary figure of insanity has not seemed cautionary enough. Because of its origins in the Romantic reaction (never without reservations) against the Enlightenment, criticism has always had a quaintly open-minded attitude toward irrationality, and even toward out-and-out madness. Foucault's argument thus flatters some of the discipline's habitual prejudices, and it would have been unwise to bet on the discipline performing a sharp-eyed scrutiny of it. Under inspection, however, it reveals neither a coherent anti-commentary politics nor a coherent anti-disciplinary politics. In fact, it reveals no coherent politics of criticism at all.[25] What we find is an incisive analysis of a very real tension—a tension that recent impulses in the discipline have recognized, indirectly, by their very efforts to escape it. A tension, but perhaps not a contradiction—not, at any rate, if we do not consider it scandalous that a discipline should need both to generate new statements and, in order to guarantee the value of those statements, to exclude statements that are less valuable. This is, again, a description of disciplinarity, not a critique of it.

One valuable takeaway from Foucault's analysis is that it would be a mistake for critics to pursue what amounts to a literature-based identity politics. It would be a mistake, in other words, to seek a disciplinary rationale, whether promulgated to other disciplines or to the public at large, that centers on the supposedly unique properties of literature as its object of knowledge, and in particular on literature's supposedly unique insubordination to disciplinarity. As one form of primary text among others, all of them giving rise to secondary texts that must respect the same paradoxical imperatives, literature is not unique. It does not defy the rules of disciplinarity; on the contrary, it offers a perfect illustration of how those rules work.

I am thus to be discouraged, speaking as a literary critic, from indulging in the all-too-familiar form of humble brag: while you, of course, belong to a genuine discipline, I alas do not. But my "alas" implies that my discipline, not having a solid, distinct object, is really about everything and, unlike yours, can therefore claim credit for allowing the mind to roam free, undisciplined, with privileged access to a wisdom that defies disciplinary specialization. John Gross illustrates with admirable clarity this tempting but delusive rhetoric of anti-disciplinarity: "'Isn't there a certain basic antagonism between the very nature of the university and the very spirit of literature? . . . Think of the whole idea of regarding literature as a *discipline*. Literature . . . can be a hundred things—but a discipline is not one of them.'"[26] Gross argues, accordingly, against "experts and specialists" as well.[27] Criticism has often embraced the notion that it is the proper domain of the amateur. In the conflict of the faculties, not being a true discipline has been sold as an advantage, though perhaps not always profitably.

For all its proud claim to study an object that is uniquely devious and inscrutable, literature is much more similar to other objects of disciplinary knowledge than its commentators might want to think. "I chose sociology," Andrew Abbott writes in *The Chaos of Disciplines*, "because more than any other social science sociology would let me do what I pleased. If I went into sociology, I wouldn't have to make up my mind what to do."[28] All disciplines have to generate a potential infinity of new statements. All of them therefore require an object that, like literature, cannot be conclusively defined or definitively mastered. Literary critics often speak as if literature's difference from other discourses, its seemingly infinite potential to proliferate meanings, its autonomy vis-à-vis the demands of everyday accuracy and instrumentality, made it uniquely mysterious, eliciting critical interest because it refuses the rational laws governing non-aesthetic phenomena. But a side glance at other, contiguous objects of disciplinary knowledge—society (for sociology), culture (for anthropology), politics (for political science), rhetoric (for composition), or space (for geography)—quickly reveals that these other disciplines, too, are obliged to stake out and defend a large zone of inscrutability, if only in order to guarantee continuing work for the discipline's practitioners.[29] All disciplines seem to resemble literary criticism in the sense that they too exist in an unstable and precarious relation to a shifty object of knowledge that they can never fully possess or master, an object of knowledge that, like literature, sustains their work only by perpetually threatening to escape from their possession and undermine that work. Though critics like to think that they are blessed or cursed by the uniquely obscure and recalcitrant nature of what they work on, a wandering, undefinable object of uncertain borders is not in fact a deviation from some supposed disciplinary norm. That goes emphatically for "politics" as well, considered as the object of knowledge of political science; some of the confusion that attends invocations of that term result from its own productive ambiguity.

And yet the wandering and the inscrutability can never be unlimited or uncontrolled. Like the objects of other fields, literature must satisfy two opposing if not contradictory exigencies: (1) the mystery of distinctness, and (2), the impulse toward clarity, closure, and constraint that accompanies what Derek Attridge calls the "power to intervene in the ethical and political life of a community."[30] In order to show that they are not merely of interest to amateurs, eccentrics, and antiquarians, all disciplines must submit themselves to some criteria of urgency, ethical concern, public usefulness. As I have been saying, they must render, however implicitly, some account of their social significance.[31] In this minimal sense at least, they must have a politics. As a genre, disciplinary rationales do not inspire much confidence. One approaches them with a sense of duty and a sinking heart. But read with the buoyant misgivings of, say, Helen Small's authoritative *The Value of the Humanities*, the genre has something to offer those seeking a sense of political meaning and identity in intellectual work.

John Guillory, one of the figures of whom Small is least skeptical, opens an indirect but valuable way into what Attridge calls "the power to intervene in the ethical and political life of the community"—that is, the discipline's claim to matter. Writing in the midst of the culture wars of the 1980s and 1990s, Guillory argued that "the politicization of the humanities is an effect of the latter's marginalization and not the other way around."[32] In other words,

> [T]he transformation recognized in the discourse of the right as "the crisis of the humanities" represents not the self-immolation of these disciplines through a process of politicization but rather the effect of their marginaliza-tion over the long term in relation to other disciplines that have become more integral to the needs of what has come to be called "the professional-mana-gerial class."[33]

This analysis can be broken down into two linked and crucial propositions: (1) to make political claims for their work, as criticism and other humanities disciplines were doing then (and are now accused of doing again), was and is a way of asserting their significance vis-à-vis other disciplines, and (2) to assert their significance vis-à-vis other disciplines is a way of asserting their significance to society as a whole, a society that as Guillory says is increasingly subservient to the principle of profit and therefore increasingly indifferent to the humanities. Talking politics is an ineffectual protest against the sad fact that criticism no longer matters.

This point could be made in a tone of pure cynicism, as if to say: "Do not take any political claims made by critics seriously. They are nothing but the despairing cry of a discipline suffering from chronic marginaliza-tion and now in terminal decline. Claiming to be political is nothing but a way of claiming to be socially significant when your social significance is waning or nonexistent." But Guillory is not cynical, and I think he is right not to be. Claims to be political are a way of asserting social significance, which seems to me self-evidently true, and an important truth, though to state it is not necessarily to reject either set of claims. That such claims are made only when a discipline's social significance is waning seems more questionable. Claims to social significance are one form of disciplinary rationale, and (as I have argued elsewhere) disciplinary rationales, however uninspiring, are a normal, even inescapable part of professional existence. I will not address here the question of whether literary criticism's significance *is* waning, or is waning any faster than that of other disciplines that are similarly unimportant to society from the perspective of short-term profit. Instead, I want to pull out an element of Guillory's argument that I find especially enlightening: the idea that the social significance of criticism or the humanities is waning assumes, logically, that its significance used to be brighter or larger. If so, what significance did it once have? If a mode of critical being has been lost that no longer works, what was its secret when it *did* work?

Guillory does not answer these questions explicitly, but two answers can be extrapolated from his argument. The one he develops at greatest length is deduced rather cleverly from the sides taken by the key players in the culture wars—specifically, the fact that it was "the journalistic media that flushed the intellectuals from their university covert in the 1980s."[34] It was largely journalists who attacked academics for politicizing the humanities, thereby encouraging them to claim membership, justifiably or not, in the more honorable and more political category of intellectuals. Why journalists? In Habermas's eighteenth-century public sphere, Guillory reminds his reader, the boundaries between journalists and literary critics had not yet been drawn, and the two enjoyed a certain intimacy. The public sphere was "a domain of private citizens engaged in public discourse—a 'print culture' that had emancipated itself from domination by the church and the state but was not yet wholly subject to domination by the market."[35] It "assumed large political significance" because it allowed the new middle class to "identify itself as a class with common interests."[36] Not yet specialized into today's journalism, which is subdued to the logic of the market, and today's academy, which is relatively autonomous of the market but also cut off from any direct or major role in forming public opinion, the critics of the eighteenth-century public sphere were genuinely public and political. It is "nostalgia by social agents in both domains for the public sphere,"[37] or for that heroic role they played in it, that animates, Guillory says, much recent polemic:

> Hence the practices of journalism and of literary criticism can continue to
> confront each other as *mirrors* in which they see . . . an idealized image of

their former Enlightenment identity (their identity *with each other*), an image of their former function as autonomous critics of politics and culture.[38]

The problem with this argument is the heavily value-laden word "autonomous." Was autonomy something that the eighteenth century in fact offered either to proto-critics or to proto-journalists? Both sold their intellectual wares on the market. Then as now, the choice between selling your wares on the market and being unable to pay the rent counts as genuine autonomy only within the dream world of capitalist ideology. The fact that market relations have tightened their grip on both professions since the eighteenth century, making life dramatically harder for so many and provoking both journalists and academics to recall or invent a more independent past, does not redeem this nostalgic idealization. There was no earlier autonomy. The critic/journalists depended on the market; they were never truly autonomous.

Guillory is more plausible when he makes a very different argument. He says that these proto-critics allowed the new middle class to "identify itself as a class with common interests."[39] This is not a wild speculation. Literary history offers a plenitude of evidence that in the bourgeois public sphere of which Steele's *Tatler* and Addison's *Spectator* were "central institutions," as Terry Eagleton writes, the "major impulse" was "class consolidation, a codifying of the norms and regulating of the practices whereby the English bourgeoisie may negotiate an historic alliance with its social superiors."[40] To see the eighteenth-century critic/journalists as performing this function is again to concede that the proto-critics were *not* autonomous, but it is to make the same point from another angle.

What Guillory is saying, with reference to Gramsci's concept of the organic intellectual, is that they were not simply dependent on the market, as a replacement for patronage; they were organic to and thus supported by a rising class. Nothing could be further from pure autonomy. And for this same reason, it would be a mistake to see them as critics in the sense of being exclusively or fundamentally critical or oppositional. They were doing something constructive. They were teaching the emergent members of the middle class to contest the ruling class above them—in that sense they were of course "critics," or finders of fault. But they were also teaching the middle class how to become a governing class in their own right, even if that meant (as it did) discovering ideological common ground with the old aristocracy. In other words, their role was political in the old Aristotelian sense: they contributed, at a moment of democratic revolution, to the coherence of "a class with common interests," foremost among them a common *interest in becoming a governing class*. Becoming a governing class would entail finding a different way to govern.

I will have more to say below about the art of governing, a traditional and seemingly obsolescent view of politics. For now, let me say only that to put the art of governing back into the discussion of criticism and politics is one way of conceding, as the rejecters of critique would put it, that there is no criticism without positive attachments or belonging. However, it is also to translate "the attachments of others"—considered by the rejecters of critique as sacrosanct, a zone that would-be critics must be chastised for entering, analyzing, evaluating—into attachments *to* others. Attachments *to* others ought to be respectful but are not necessarily reverential. They can be expected to include antagonism as well as solidarity. They are not committed to leaving the beliefs and practices of others unchanged. Governing may indeed entail a commitment to change certain beliefs, like the belief that classroom discussion time should be devoted to discussing the superiority of the white race, and to outlaw certain practices, like the practice of meeting face to face in crowds, unmasked, during a pandemic. If I were committed to guaranteeing that no one's beliefs or practices would ever be changed, if I were committed to protecting those beliefs and practices from profane analysis and evaluation, I too would be very suspicious of any commitment to politics. But I would not want to be a critic.

When and Why Criticism Mattered

Let us return to Guillory's premise (which follows logically from his argument that criticism has become more marginal) that once upon a time, criticism used to be *less* marginal. If it used to enjoy greater social prestige, the prestige does not seem to have come solely from criticism's proud autonomy from church and state, but also from, for example, (1) the ideological backing of the free market, which propagates for both buyers and sellers the illusion that they are acting autonomously; and (2) its service to a class-in-formation, which, also relying on a notion of autonomy consistent with the market, was busy negotiating a more powerful position for itself vis-à-vis the older ruling class.

This slight revision of Guillory's argument is important because the role of developing the self-consciousness of an emergent class with common interests is more than merely an object of nostalgia. This is a role that criticism can still play, and perhaps has already been playing. What survives from the eighteenth century may be (in Guillory's caustic formulation) only "an imaginary or simulacral version" of the role played by critic/journalists in the eighteenth-century public sphere,[41] but there is no reason to conclude that, with the triumph of the middle class, that role has disappeared either as a potentiality or as a goal. When Gramsci looked back at what the revolutionary middle class had done to win, legitimize, and consolidate power, he was of course thinking not just of the past, but of the present and the future. He was seeking wisdom that would apply to those in revolt from below against what the rule of the middle class had become. Nothing stops us from doing the same with the story that Guillory tells, even if Guillory himself prefers not to. Indeed, that is roughly what I have already been doing. It is more or less the hypothesis I've been proposing about the new social movements of the 1960s, about how their social rise drew in a new set of critics (critics like Edward Said and Judith Butler, Terry Eagleton and John Guillory, to stick with figures on whom I have been drawing heavily) and how it helped effect a reorientation of criticism.

This reorientation did not amount to a working-class revolution. Class was not central to it. At a minimum, however, there is a compelling if imperfect parallel here that demands reflection: a parallel between the organic role that, in Guillory's telling, the critic/journalists of the eighteenth century played for the rising (middle-class) collectivity of their day and the relation that the historical and political critics of the past decades have had to collectivities stigmatized by race, gender, and sexuality, as well as class and other forms of collectivity.[42] In neither case does this entail a crude model of speaking for whole groups in some unrealistically and ineligibly direct way. It is enough to say that, as in the eighteenth century, these constituencies have made criticism more political by finding fault with the status quo (as Addison did with the licentious aristocracy), but also, or so I would argue, in the sense of teaching a new group of future leaders how they might eventually come to govern, which is to say how to imagine a society constituted very differently from the one they saw around them, and to win assent from others interested in the long-term project of bringing it into being.

Politics as the art of governing—this very old-fashioned sense of politics, seemingly of no more than historical interest in an era when progressives very properly focus on the plight of those who remain governed, and all too much governed—thus turns out to point toward the future. It is also surprisingly relevant to a second line of thinking about why criticism does or doesn't matter. Committed as he is to the premise of criticism's present marginality, Guillory is necessarily also committed to the premise that in the past it did have the prominence that it has now lost. Anchored as his argument is to that premise, Guillory seems strangely at sea as to whether criticism was ever socially central.

One interpretation, following the lead of a cynical common sense, would suggest that the study of the classics, which preceded the study of English literature up through the eighteenth century, was never in fact any more functional to its society than literary criticism is now. Knowledge of the classical languages was of course a marker of class status, but it was a random and empty marker. If the real purpose of a classical education was merely to distinguish the haves from the have-nots, the content of that education would be arbitrary and irrelevant. Greek and Latin could as easily have been replaced by any other difficult-to-obtain but non-useful knowledge. As it happens, this exact argument has been extended to modern education by Pierre Bourdieu, and in discussing the modern canon, Guillory follows Bourdieu. In *Cultural Capital: The Problem of Literary Canon Formation*, Guillory argues that adding women writers, people of color, and so on, to the canon—the offense that drew the ire of the right during the culture wars—was in fact a mere distraction, offering no real benefit to anyone. There are no real political stakes one way or the other, he insists, in the *content* of the canon. Like Bourdieu, he suggests that whatever gets taught will serve equally well as "cultural capital," that is, as a possession that will distinguish its privileged possessors from the great unwashed: "the left hand of the educational system—the dissemination of a supposedly national culture—remains ignorant of what the right hand is doing—the differential tracking of students according to class or the possession of cultural capital."[43] The real political issue, therefore, is not the content of literary education but unequal *access* to education, and unequal access to the credentials the university has the power to bestow. The working class refuses a politics of canon revision because it is indifferent to the prospect of a syllabus where working-class identity is more generously and fairly represented; what it really wants is not to change what is taught but to obtain access to what is taught, whatever we professors decide that is.[44]

Guillory's emphasis on access is necessary, and his final point seems plausible enough, if not necessarily faithful as an account of what any unrepresented or newly represented demographic might actually be thinking about the prospect of their culture's inclusion in the curriculum. Even from Guillory's own perspective, however, the shift to access does not harmonize well with the narrative of lost centrality. If the contents of literary education never really mattered to society at all, then they don't matter less now. If literary study was *never* useful, it could not well have become *less* useful. If on the other hand there was in fact some real usefulness to it, then it becomes more likely that the same could be said of the content of literary education today.

The hypothesis sends us back to the study of Greek and Latin. The critic/ journalists of the eighteenth century transmitted some of the knowledge that was then taught in universities (however they had acquired it) to the newly literate outside the university walls, including knowledge of literature. The modern concept of literature as distinctively creative and imaginative, as a subfield of aesthetics, was not yet in the ascendant, if indeed it had any pedagogical purchase at all. What literature meant at Oxford and Cambridge was still the classics, whether the texts taught were love lyrics or speeches ending with a reminder that Carthage still had not been destroyed. Guillory's narrative of criticism's decline from centrality to marginality would seem to commit him to disagreeing with Bourdieu here—to maintaining, in other words, that a classical education was not an arbitrary marker of social status but was genuinely functional to the society around it, and it enjoyed a certain authority for that reason, an authority that after all resembles that of science, law, and religion.

This is quite plausible. Latin gave authoritative access to the sacred scriptures and canonical interpretations of medieval Christianity. Learning Latin, and later Greek, prepared students for careers in the church (the clergy, Gramsci's paradigm of the traditional intellectuals, were feudalism's organic intellectuals) as well as, later, in the state, its own authority enduringly entangled with that of religion. Starting from that obvious linkage to power, we arrive back at the same argument we have already sketched out above. A classical education was not after all a random indicator of class status. It *was* genuinely functional. It taught the ruling class how to rule. It taught rhetoric.[45]

"Rhetoric," the term that then covered the formal study of how language worked, was explicitly not criticism in the sense of faultfinding or how to come up with an original interpretation of a great work; it was a practice aimed at producing the use of language with similar competence and for similar ends. A rhetorical education "culminated with imitative exercises in which the student produced speeches and poems in the manner of one of the great authorities," thereby demonstrating not an original point of view, but "mastery of standard techniques."[46] Studying the speeches of Pericles and Demosthenes, of Cicero and Seneca, meant learning about situations and choices that the leaders of empires had faced, but also learning to produce the same rhetorical effects in one's own writing or (more often) one's own speaking. This explains some of this pedagogy's detested rote-ness; like playing the piano, a practice requires practice. Like the study of the piano, the study of rhetoric had a practical goal: the ability to give a persuasive speech. And the ability to give a persuasive speech was an important part of the ability to lead, to win assent for one's preferred policies, which is to say to govern—and especially (Athens and Rome both being imperial capitals) to govern an empire. The point does not hold quite as well for the study of the lyrics of Sappho, but it could be stretched (desire as a threat to self-mastery) and not much stretching would be needed to include the court poet Horace or Caesar's *Gallic War*, required reading for all schoolboys.

The fact that rhetoric was functional to its society does not of course mean that the same holds for literature in the modern sense. The movement from the study of rhetoric to the study of literature, like the movement from the critic/journalist to the specialized academic, could be narrated as a loss of social mission or function. In the eighteenth century, Eagleton writes, criticism engaged with "the shape and destiny of a whole culture," and therefore could claim a "serious title to exist. Today, apart from its marginal role in reproducing the dominant social relations through the academies, it is almost entirely bereft of such a *raison d'être*."[47] Like Guillory's, this is a story about the loss of criticism's function, though it is a loss that is promisingly offset at the end of Eagleton's account by the then-recent rise of the women's movement, which allows Eagleton to imagine that criticism might be returning to its "traditional"—that is, political—role.[48]

Guillory omits the hortatory addendum. For him, criticism's traditional-political role has been lost forever—and good riddance to it. Humanists must be distinguished from the professional-managerial class, Guillory says, because the latter, given its place in the "management of the productive process," is involved in "the government of *others*."[49] Humanists are not, and presumably should not be. Not being involved in the governing of others, like these more functional knowledge workers, is why humanists have less power but instead enjoy greater "autonomy." It is this autonomy, their compensation for their powerlessness, that humanists should prize—and *do* prize, one might say, especially at those moments when they are instinctively skeptical of any real-world or extra-academic political commitments. At any rate, that is how both Immanuel Kant and Matthew Arnold instructed humanists to feel. Kant taught that the price of free thought inside the university was paid in obedience to authority outside it. Arnold taught that culture must be disinterested, which is to say, must separate itself off from the crude self-interest that defines the realm of politics. (Foucault's name also belongs on this short list of thinkers who were both discourse-founding and depoliticizing, as I shall argue below.)

The predictable recurrence of complaints that the cultural disciplines are (over)politicized is evidence that, structurally speaking, autonomy remains a fundamental disciplinary identification, though not the only one. The logic is clear. Any political position-taking would threaten to compromise criticism's autonomy. Autonomy has been an essential part of criticism's self-conception. Thus the refusal of political position-taking recurs again and again, today as during the culture wars of the 1980s and 1990s or with Lionel Trilling during the 1940s and 1950s. Like politics itself, resistance to politics seems hard-wired into the discipline.[50]

In terms of Guillory's narrative, however, this conclusion, while perhaps attractive, is also incoherent. If (unlike rhetoric) literary criticism was always resistant to claims to social significance, what social significance did it once have? How to explain why a discipline that was autonomous, which is to say independent of whatever society might have wanted from it, would ever have been more socially central than it is now? How can Guillory speak of criticism's marginalization, let alone speak of it with a jeremiad-like lament and an implicit demand to retrieve the centrality that has gone missing?

Guillory himself has already provided one answer: criticism in the eighteenth century found a vocation by doing the consciousness-raising work that an emergent class demanded of it.[51] My point about that proposition, and it is a large one, is that while we should not expect to uncover an identical sense of vocation in the discipline today, neither should we assume in advance that this *kind* of function has disappeared. Criticism's past shows us what kind of thing to look for in the present. We should look for transformations as well as similarities of structure. The same methodological point holds for other possible answers to the lost centrality question.

One such answer is that the teaching of vernacular literature was once more socially significant because it served the purposes of nationalism. This plausibly worked for literature, as for culture, in a period when what Francis Mulhern calls "the world-transforming power of nationalism" was at its height, but it plausibly no longer does in a period when (though nationalism has by no means disappeared) the world's most powerful nations have staked their preeminence on their place within global capitalism, thereby neglecting the educational and other needs of large sectors of their own populations.[52] Unlike the classics, English literature was, after all, *English* literature. In *The Social Mission of English Criticism, 1848–1932,* Chris Baldick stresses the moment of the Newbolt Report, after World War I, when the new literary studies benefited from "the conjunction of a new national pride and a new recognition of the importance of education," thus furthering "a national consciousness, based upon the native language and literature."[53] (Somehow national pride did not prevent English from staking a claim to Sophocles and Dante.) In *The University in Ruins,* Bill Readings also centers his narrative on criticism's link to the nation. He tells a story that, like Guillory's, begins from the premise that "the centrality of the traditional humanistic disciplines to the life of the University is no longer assured."[54] This is because "the notion of culture as the legitimating idea of the modern University has reached the end of its usefulness."[55] Readings's interpretation of why culture has reached the end of its usefulness then takes Baldick's a step further. The reason is (in the book's final words) "the end of the epoch of the nation-state."[56] The humanities served culture. As Baldick argues, culture served the nation. In the era of globalization, however, the nation supposedly no longer exists. Like Guillory, Readings sees criticism, now unmoored from the nation, drifting aimlessly. Unlike Guillory, he sees nothing worth going back to.

In other words, the former centrality or social significance of the humanities was, after all, real. When it was doing better, criticism was not autonomous; on the contrary, it was more prestigious because it had what Baldick calls a "social mission." But its mission was to serve the nation-state, on whose interests it depended. In the nineteenth century, when rhetorical education gave way to the study of literature in the vernacular and, little by little, to literature in the modern sense of the word, literary criticism did get some respect, but it did so because of its service to nationalism, imperialism, and class rule—in other words, for reasons that are no longer of much use to it. That's one way to read Gauri Viswanathan's pathbreaking *Masks of Conquest.*[57] The passing of the Charter Act of 1813, which renewed the charter of the East India Company, "enjoined England to undertake the education of the native subjects," and as Viswanathan notes ironically, this was "a responsibility which it did not officially bear even toward its own people."[58] In fact, "[t]he discipline of English literature was formally instituted in British schools only as late as 1871."[59] During these in-between decades, with Christian missionaries clamoring to get their fingers on Indian souls and the East India Company clinging to a policy of non-interference in Indian religion, it was possible to experiment with the study of English literature in India as a new secular branch of study that, without direct propaganda for Christianity or violation of Indian religious beliefs, would nevertheless mold the moral character of Indians according to the interests of their colonizers.[60] In short, "English literary study had its beginnings as a strategy of containment."[61]

There is another possible answer to the lost centrality question, and again it is violently undesirable. At home, the emergent rationale for literary studies in the same period aimed at saving the country from anarchy, and anarchy meant the unruly working class. In the words of David Lloyd and Paul Thomas, the expanding system of nineteenth-century education was intended to serve "as an instrument of social control directed specifically at the working classes."[62] "To trace this story," Lloyd and Thomas write in *Culture and the State*, "is to grasp the reasons for the continuing importance of cultural institutions to the liberal state, as means to its maintenance in being, its reproduction."[63] This is unacknowledged legislation with a vengeance. If "the place of culture in the formation of citizens and the legitimation of the state"[64] is the centrality that criticism has lost, it's not a centrality most members of the discipline would like to see criticism regain.

This seems like an impasse. Historically, criticism seemed to enjoy social centrality only when it served as an agent of power, self-interested and malevolent. On the whole, we critics no longer want to serve the power of a nation or an imperial metropolis or a ruling class. Many of us want only to be autonomous, which means that we do not want to serve power at all. If so, criticism seems destined to fade into even greater marginality, following the path of classics. It's hard to imagine any critic today who would call for criticism to win back its centrality by helping to suppress revolt in the (now unofficial) empire or to police movements like Black Lives Matter.

Centrality is no doubt an illusory goal. But some measure of the social significance assumed by these disciplinary narratives seems within reach, and even difficult to ignore. Let us return to Guillory's account of the eighteenth-century critic/journalist. As I suggested above, the most interesting of Guillory's explanations for the centrality of the eighteenth-century critic/journalist was the critic/journalist's role in helping the new middle class to identify "itself as a class with common interests."[65] For Lloyd and Thomas, writing of course about a later century, criticism's servicing of the interests of the middle class was aimed against the class below it; thus it cannot be recalled with anything like pride. For Guillory, on the contrary, the class aimed at was above, not below, and there is a strong whiff of heroism about the formative role criticism then played, the role of articulating an emergent class's common interests and collective self-consciousness.

More can be made of that heroism. As I noted, Guillory need not have treated the role of the eighteenth-century critic/journalist as a piece of vanished history. He might have seen it, following Gramsci, as a role that was still available, and perhaps still being enacted even now. (Implicitly, that is what Eagleton does when, interrupting a story that anticipates Guillory's, he refers to the emergent women's movement.) When Guillory insists on criticism's autonomy, thereby undermining his own argument about its lost centrality, he excludes the possibility that criticism might once again be organically linked, however weakly, to constituencies outside the university—antisexist, antiracist, antimilitarist, and anticapitalist constituencies, pro-environmental and health-care-for-all constituencies, and so on. Outside the university, for Guillory, there is only the wasteland of the cash nexus. The only choice for humanists is between joining the moneymaking disciplines (now, for example, including digital humanities) that are rewarded for aiding and abetting capitalism, thereby betraying their true selves, and standing up for the principles of their own intellectual autonomy and trying to extend those principles to others. For Guillory, collectivities outside the university might be grateful for a taste of our unique work autonomy, but it seems unimaginable that like us they might also be inclined to resist the rule of capital, or do so in a way that might permit an alliance or synergy with the content of work going on inside the university. That's why Guillory cannot imagine an "organic" academic of the present or the future, only of the past.

But an organic academic of the present should not be so hard to imagine. Symbolically, if not organizationally, we have already seen it. That's what the culture wars have always been about.

Starting from the generational hypothesis with which we began, the proposition on the table is whether, to what degree, and with what success critics today can be considered organic to the new social movements that took off in the 1960s and have persisted, with various transformations, through present-day movements against racism, police brutality, climate change, and so on. That is what criticism's right-wing critics have complained about, during the culture wars and since. For all the divisiveness both within the social movements and within criticism, I think the right-wing critics are largely right. If so, then what Guillory says about the critic/journalist's role in forming the eighteenth-century middle class seems absolutely relevant today—relevant, that is, to criticism's role in the forming (and dealing with resistance to the forming) of new political coalitions in the era initiated by Bernie Sanders, Alexandria Ocasio-Cortez, and Black Lives Matter.[66] Without the advantage of hindsight, we do not know as yet what collective consciousness is cohering, outside and inside the university. And we do not know, of course, what power it will and will not be able to exercise. These were open questions faced by Guillory's eighteenth-century critic/journalists, who were trying to define "common interests" for their very diverse readership and trying to bring practical coherence to a collectivity that had not yet fully emerged. It should not be surprising that things are no clearer today: diversity is even more pronounced, "common interests" are harder to agree on, and the question of class, common interests, and other solidarities extends its tremulous uncertainties well beyond the borders of the nation.

4 Aesthetics and the Governing of Others

I was drawing on the energy of sixties movements and the keenness
of their grievances and insights, trying to organize that ferment into a
comprehensive story and totalizing analysis.

  Richard Ohmann, English in America

Like That

I have been suggesting that "the energy of sixties movements and the keenness of their grievances and insights," to quote Richard Ohmann,[1] played a
major but neglected part in the development of criticism over the past half
century. Sometimes criticism has been written in direct solidarity—out of
the "rage and the sense of revelation" that, again in Ohmann's words, "flowed
directly from the 1960s insurgencies . . . [t]he civil-rights and black-power
movements, opposition to the Vietnam War, draft resistance, women's liberation, lesbian and gay rights, environmentalism, student power."[2] Sometimes
the relationship has involved less solidarity than curiosity, qualified agreement, or even indignant disagreement. Unsurprisingly, the links have often
been complex, as rippling with contradictions as the movements themselves.
But taking these complications into account, it seems clear: the 60s movements set a public agenda that criticism inside the university could not ignore
lest both criticism and the humanities forfeit such public significance as they
enjoyed. That has been the main hypothesis thus far about criticism's relation
to politics over the half century between 1970 and 2020.

  If this hypothesis has not seemed more obvious to observers, one reason
is Michel Foucault. As I have been suggesting, Foucault, though not himself
a literary critic, did more than any other thinker to gather the heritage of
the 1960s into a vision of what literary criticism is and does. In that sense he

was (and perhaps remains) the period's single most organic figure. Yet Foucault strenuously resisted the Gramscian model of the organic intellectual, a model that (extended from intellectuals to the university) sees academic work as holding itself accountable to extra-academic causes and constituencies. Nothing could be less congenial to him, therefore, than the positive sense of criticism to which, by analogy with the class-formative mission of the critic/journalists of the eighteenth century, I am proposing to attach him.

On the one hand, it would be odd if he did not resist this model. In Foucault, as in the average academic, you don't have to dig very deep in order to uncover a self-image of the intellectual as, above all else, autonomous. Autonomy is the distinguishing self-image not of the organic intellectuals, but of their opposite numbers, the traditional intellectuals—for Gramsci, servants of the pre-capitalist aristocracy. As Gramsci said, the "various categories of traditional intellectuals," foremost among them the clergy, "experience through an 'esprit de corps' their uninterrupted historical continuity and their special qualification," and they therefore "put themselves forward as autonomous and independent of the dominant social group."[3] (How the aristocratic model has adapted itself so successfully to capitalist society is a subject for the sociologists.)

On the other hand, Foucault's resistance to an organic linkage to the new social movements was also a *response* to those movements. In a 1972 discussion with Gilles Deleuze about what they had learned from 1968, he wrote, "The intellectual's role is no longer to place himself 'somewhat ahead and to the side' in order to express the stifled truth of the collectivity."[4] Deleuze puts it more bluntly: "Representation no longer exists."[5] This is by no means the only message that Deleuze and Foucault might have received from 1968. It also anticipates with uncanny accuracy the gathering right-wing critique of left-wing academics, as in Dinesh D'Souza's 1991 commentary on the "Western civilization" debate at Stanford: "If Rigoberta Menchu does not represent the actual peasants of Latin America, whom *does* she represent? The answer is that she embodies a projection of Marxist and feminist views onto South American Indian culture."[6] In this cynical view—itself quite representative across the political spectrum—the truth of the matter is self-interest; left-wing academics represent only themselves. Still, this skepticism about representation does reflect the 60s movements' suspicion of party politics, their sense of generalized opposition to the status quo, and their hesitation to risk the premature consolidation of diverse aims and impulses into a single critical platform, whoever might try to articulate it.[7] In this sense, Foucault is the theorist-leader who represents the 60s movements— while and by asserting that the principle of representation is dead.

Foucault's own idea of critique was a rigorously oppositional one. In other words, it was both intensely political and, in an important sense, apolitical. In his 1978 essay "What Is Critique?" he answers his title question as follows: critique is "the art of not being governed, or the art of not being governed like that and at this price."[8] Leading up to this formulation, and among other tentative accounts, he uses the same two words, first italicizing them: "How not to be governed *like that* . . . " The "*that*" in "*like that*" is a deictic. A deictic points at something (*deixis* is from the Greek *deiknumai* "to show"), but it declines to give that something a name, a set of coordinates on a conceptual grid, a classification. It thus restricts the referent of the words spoken to the momentary place and time of the speaker who is pointing—here, pointing at some mode of governing. Dependent on looking out from that location, the deictic refuses to make a proposition that would hold for anyone other than its own speaker, its own context. In this instance, Foucault's deictic defines "critique" as resistance to being governed, but as a resistance that, while pointing to what it doesn't want, will not say what it does want, why or in the name of what it is resisting whatever it *is* resisting.

Foucault's reason for this evasive phrasing is consistent with his other positions. To protest in the name of some principle that those who govern are violating (for example, the Enlightenment values of freedom and human dignity) would be to endorse that principle, that set of rules, that moral norm. But (so Foucault would say) one cannot endorse a norm without generalizing one's perspective to others and thus directing those others to join up or stand up and do likewise—without participating, that is, in the governing of those others. As Foucault had spent more than a decade instructing his readers, governing is what norms do.[9] He refuses norms because he refuses to take part in the governing of others. He will have nothing to do with the exercise of power.

The reason why Foucault is so intent on not exercising power is not self-evident. From a Nietzschean perspective (and Foucault's many acknowledged debts to Nietzsche invite such a perspective), this self-restraint could look like a life-denying squeamishness—like slave morality carried to a new, hyper-sensitive, self-defeating extreme. Nietzsche himself embraced what he called the "will to power." Foucault, trying to rewrite *The Genealogy of Morals* from the left, had the problem of reconciling the will to power (assuming he too embraced it, or some version of it) with a very un-Nietzschean concern for those whom power excluded or marginalized—in other words, a concern that informed and was informed by the 60s movements. Trying to juggle Nietzsche and the 60s movements left him in some difficulty. Is it possible to have nothing to do with power? If so, is it desirable? What is the price of abstaining from power for a thinker like Foucault who came to see himself, and was seen by others, as a paradigm of contemporary political commitment? And if critique is as Foucault defines it—the art of not being governed *like that*—then what politics does it inspire, or preclude, for the would-be critic or the would-be follower? These questions lead, perhaps unexpectedly, to aesthetics.

Within the literary criticism of the past half century, there has been a widespread suspicion of aesthetics, and that suspicion has been associated with the social movements of the 1960s.[10] Foucault, though personally involved in few of those movements, is probably the thinker most often blamed (or acclaimed) for the rejection of aesthetics and for the drive to politicize that follows from it.[11] Thus George Levine, in his introduction to *Aesthetics and Ideology*, concedes that "to a certain extent the Foucaultian critique is correct, and much literature works as a means of acculturation or politicization."[12] And Regina Gagnier, in her contribution to the same volume, takes Foucault's *Discipline and Punish* to represent the understanding of aesthetics "as a subtle tool of control."[13] These associations are obviously not ungrounded. But they don't do full justice to what remains most interesting either in the new social movements or in Foucault: the idea that, if one is committed to changing the world, some mode or degree of controlling, or governing, cannot *not* be an eligible option.

As Foucault's faithful readers will know, at the beginning of his career he was fascinated by the transgressiveness of the modernist avant-garde. He imagined literature not as a tool of control but on the contrary as a privileged *non-savoir*, a non-knowledge that (like critique for Kant) could expose the limits of what counted as knowledge, make visible the tools of control that operate through linguistic or epistemic categories. "Arts are meta-epistemic," as John Rajchman puts it, "allegories of the deep arrangements that make knowledge possible."[14] Thus Foucault gives literature, as Rajchman concludes, "a central position" in our culture.[15]

By 1977 Foucault had broken with this view, deciding that the fundamental arrangements in our history are not about language but about power. But in a final twist, aesthetics again becomes the keynote of Foucault's work in his last years—and it does so as an extension of his thinking about power. The so-called return to ethics, which scandalized admirers of Foucault's Nietzschean critique of the free moral subject, is also, as he declared, a turn to aesthetics. In an interview he gave on April 25, 1984, two months before his death, Foucault suggested that with the disappearance of "morality as obedience to a code of rules," a disappearance he welcomed, the alternative that was needed was an ethics of self-fashioning, or what he described as "an aesthetics of existence."[16] Here, as so often, the attraction of aesthetics is that, unlike moral conduct, it is understood to obey no concept, no law, no rules. It is defined as ungovernable. More to the point, one might also say that in having nothing to do with concepts, laws, or rules, *the aesthetic does not govern*.

This proposition may seem obvious. But there are reasons to doubt it. If the aesthetic *doesn't* govern, in a sense of that verb that needs to be specified, then why should anyone care about it? And if we *do* care about it, isn't that evidence that it *does* govern—that the patterned waves it sends through the murky turbulence of everyday life make a difference, however difficult that difference is to measure? Can aesthetics *avoid* governing, however mildly or benevolently? Those are crucial questions—for Foucault, but also for criticism that takes aesthetics as part of its object.

Foucault had been introduced to this set of questions by Nietzsche. Early in *On the Genealogy of Morals*, Nietzsche lays out an animal fable, the allegory of the birds of prey and the lambs. Birds of prey eat lambs. When they do so, they are following their nature. To defend themselves from being eaten, the lambs invent a proto-Christian "do unto others" morality: after all, they can tell the birds of prey, we don't eat you, do we? This morality may sound like simple justice, but the lambs are imposing on the birds of prey (whom the lambs now label "evil") a lamb-friendly philosophy. They endow the birds of prey with the "freedom" to be and do otherwise, an offering that is less generous than it seems, since it weighs down the birds of prey with the new and unforgiving responsibility of violating their nature. Getting the birds of prey to buy into this falsely universal ethics of good and evil allows the lambs to defend themselves from violence, but from the viewpoint of the birds of prey it is not a recipe for contentment. The moral of the story would seem to be that birds of prey, which is to say humans, should abandon this supposed ethical universal, along with the concept of freedom it presupposes, and go back to acting according to their particular species-nature—their identity.

This is the naturalist Nietzsche, arguing that it is the nature of the strong to dominate and that their nature or identity should be respected. It seems worth noting that, philosophically speaking, the origin of identity politics lies in Nietzsche's defense of the strong against the weak, not (as would later be assumed) in the defense of the weak against the strong.

But there is another Nietzsche, call him existentialist or constructivist, also well represented in the *Genealogy* and somewhat overrepresented among Nietzsche's recent champions, especially on the left. This Nietzsche undermines the very concept of identity or essential nature. This Nietzsche insists that there is no doer behind the deed, no essence that precedes existence: that the naturally carnivorous bird of prey is as much of a construct as the free subject, unhappy in its imposed vegetarianism. This Nietzsche, though no democrat, hesitates to turn the birds of prey loose again on the lambs. This Nietzsche wondered throughout his career whether some equivalent might be found for a bird of prey who could escape from the painful proto-Freudian repression imposed by universalist ethics, but could do so without leaving behind a bloody trail of lamb carcasses. Can one be a modern bird of prey (a Lord in Hegel's parable of the Lord and the Bondsman, which Nietzsche is here revising) without dominating others?

Nietzsche's best-known answer to this question was the so-called *Übermensch*, or overman. A lesser-known answer, laid out most explicitly in *The Will to Power*, was the artist. In the artist's mastery, the subject's freedom is rewritten not as a burdensome obligation to change, but as a desirable creativity—as the freedom that has to be assumed in order for the subject to produce itself rather than returning either to the mastery of others or to mastery *by* others. Artistic creativity seems to do no harm. It remains a question whether it does *anything*. Does it have the large public authority and forcefulness, for example, that Nietzsche seems to have invested in the word "myth"? Or, like poetry for Auden, does it "make nothing happen"? If it's the former, then the politics question is obviously still very much alive. (And if it's the latter, then why should anyone care about it—or pay those who teach and preserve it?) In progressive circles, Nietzsche's embrace of artistic creativity has been well received, and understandably so, though without confronting the conundrum: Is art a publicly compelling myth, or does it make nothing happen? Does the Nietzschean artist solve the problem of domination? Or is the problem merely displaced, taking up residence now inside aesthetics?

Inside aesthetics, the question is: Is *everyone* is supposed to be an artist? And if so, is it assumed that no one will pay attention to the art that the others are producing? This is not inconceivable (one thinks of certain creative writing courses and, for that matter, of the extreme, purist "difference" wing of certain identity movements), but it is so extreme in its individualism that the word "artist" would arguably no longer apply. Taking the word in its usual sense, as *not* applying to everyone, the assumption would be, on the contrary, that the production of art presupposes some sort of division of labor between artist and audience. And if all art presupposes someone else who is watching or listening, imitating or at least being moved to feel or act differently, then the analogy of the lambs and the birds of prey does not after all disappear. Something like mastery persists, converting aesthetics into the stage on which a new drama of political theory will have to be enacted: the drama of how to avoid, without slipping back into slave morality (which is what Nietzsche saw in democracy), the old will-to-power scenario of eating and being eaten, dominating and being dominated, governing and being governed, now rewritten as a scenario of producing art and receiving that art.

That drama peeks out shyly from behind Foucault's three-volume history of sexuality, where the theme of self-fashioning first emerges. In his research on ancient Greece, the status of other people is one of the underlying points at issue. It is rarely referred to directly, but it visibly troubles his thought. The Greeks may not see same-sex relations as sinful, as the Christians do, but don't they too impose ethical limits on, say, what an adult man can do to or with a young boy? When Foucault discovers in Greek ethics "the elaboration of one's own life as a personal work of art," he describes it as an attempt "to give one's own life a certain form in which one could recognize oneself, be recognized by others, and which even posterity might take as an example."[17]

To use one's freedom in order to give oneself a form that will be recognized by others, and will perhaps even be an example to the distant others of "posterity," is arguably not merely to govern oneself, but to govern others as well, if not necessarily (here we get into the meat of the question) in an unacceptably authoritarian way. As Simon During observes, in historical fact the point of those "techniques of self-mastery required by the Greek citizen" was "to master others," which for men meant—and all this was only for men— first of all, the members of their household, or women and children.[18] That example is no longer acceptable. But acceptability is a normative issue, and one Foucault doesn't want to contemplate. When he speaks of the "aesthetics of existence" in classical antiquity, he acknowledges that even conceived as a work of art, the Greek self always presumed the existence of interested onlookers. But when he invites his readers in the present (implicitly and off-handedly) to consider applying the project to their own lives, the onlookers and the eyes of posterity have vanished—as has the Hegelian problematic of equality and recognition by the Other. The spectators vanish because Foucault is worried that if an elaboration of one's own life as a work of art implies an audience, then it implies to some degree the governing of others.

From this viewpoint, Foucault's interest in self-fashioning looks like a last-ditch attempt to solve a problem that he had earlier hesitated even to articulate: How to acknowledge the Nietzschean will to power (which sponsors his critique of the free liberal subject) without accepting that if one dominates, someone else will be dominated? And that explains why for Foucault aesthetic self-fashioning is not just a late-life hobby but the paradigm for a new ethics. I cannot avoid dominating, Foucault admits. And I have treated dominating as a crime. But in aesthetic self-fashioning, I attempt to dominate no one but myself. If it's a crime, it's a victimless crime.

To my knowledge, literary critics have not found fault with Foucault's democratically inflected ventriloquizing of Nietzsche. But faultfinding cannot be avoided. How could self-domination do the job that is implicitly demanded of it, pouring all domination into or onto the self so that none is left over to subjugate anyone else? In order to believe that his aesthetic self-fashioning had no impact on the feelings or conduct of others, that it did not shape and form others as it shapes and forms the self—in short, it does not govern, if only in a mild and minor way—Foucault would have had to think he was invisible. He declared his desire to be anonymous. Far from being anonymous, however, he had become by the end of his life (what he had called in "What Is an Author?") a founder of discursivity. The founder of discursivity was not an "author" in Foucault's sense; he was not a retroactive construct intended to restrict the meanings associated with his name. He was a kind of super-author who produced, beyond merely a set of texts, "the possibilities and the rules for the formation of other texts."[19]

Like Marx and Freud, and for that matter somewhat like the primary text in his account of commentary, Foucault had "established an endless possibility of discourse"—a possibility that the present text is happily exploiting.[20] Like Marx and Freud, Foucault would continue to guide and command the speech-acts of subsequent generations, exerting power over others from beyond the grave. Few readers would want to complain that they have been abused by being subjected to this power. But that is just the sort of gentle, almost unnoticeable abuse that Foucault had specialized in diagnosing, and it is a prospect that in theory, at least, he resists.[21] In his last years he is still fighting to keep himself, his writing, and his project of aesthetic self-fashioning at a remove from the coercion that, in his view, defines power/knowledge—power/knowledge as "a mode of action upon the actions of others."[22] He yanks his self-fashioning out of the visual field of any potential spectator. It's a kind of indirect confession of guilt, as if he thought that for them to witness it would make him, and his receptive readers, more birds of prey tearing apart more lambs.[23]

Foucault's late attraction to aesthetics is almost the mirror image of the position with which he is more often associated: the labeling of aesthetics as a tool of political control, a means of governing. I am arguing here for a synthesis of these two propositions: (1) aesthetics need not be rejected and indeed ought properly to be accepted as alluring; and (2) this is so not because it is innocent of the exercise of power but because it *does* exercise power and is gifted or burdened with the existential seriousness of helping decide how life should be lived. I take these propositions from the rough overlap between Foucault and the new social movements, though neither proposition is perfectly represented in either.

Foucault: "Power Is Not Evil!"

On the events of May 1968, Foucault wrote:

> [T]he intellectual discovered that the masses no longer need him to gain knowledge: they know perfectly well, without illusion; they know far better than he and they are certainly capable of expressing themselves.[24]

Later in the interview he lists the collectivities to which he here ascribes impressive powers of undeluded knowledge and unimpeded self-expression: "women, prisoners, conscripted soldiers, hospital patients, and homosexuals."[25] The gesture of self-abnegation, both parts of it implausible (I *don't* know, but they *do* know), seems accurate only in its suggestion that Foucault's refusal to represent the groups he mentions is also a relationship with those groups, and even an intimate one. In refusing to represent them, he *is* representing them—representing, first and foremost, their suspicion of representation, but also the incompleteness of his own inventory of 60s constituencies. (His list of constituencies involved in May 1968 omits, to take one obvious example, students.)

This incompleteness is what Judith Butler memorably calls, in the conclusion to *Gender Trouble*, the "embarrassing 'etc.'"[26] Butler, who like Foucault would figure on anyone's short list of thinkers foundational both to the new social movements and to the criticism of the last three decades, writes as follows: "The theories of feminist identity that elaborate predicates of color, sexuality, ethnicity, class, and able-bodiedness invariably close with an embarrassed 'etc.' at the end of the list."[27] The et cetera—which she describes as exasperated, exhausted, and illimitable as well as embarrassed—marks the desire to turn all these diverse categories of disadvantage or oppression (along with categories that remain unnamed, like climate justice) into a coherent political subject. But it also marks the failure to do so—perhaps the impossibility of doing so. Foucault's impatience with politics is not just an impatience with conventional electoral politics. Asked in the same late interview whether the care of the self leads into "a new way of thinking about politics," he replies, with some irritation, "I admit that I have not got very far in this direction. . . . I don't like to reply to questions I haven't studied."[28] This is consistent with his refusal to represent the collectivities he names. And that refusal reflects not just their suspicion that, electorally or no, they will be badly represented again, as they have so often been in the past, but also his and their lack of confidence that at this historical moment it's possible to achieve even provisional closure to the list of who they are and what they want.[29] The new social movements were nothing if not political, and yet Foucault's impatience with politics is also theirs.

This ambivalence about politics is echoed by an ambivalence about aesthetics. Aesthetic value is often assumed to be something the new social movements are united against. Like the ethics of Nietzsche's lambs, aesthetics was and is widely understood to impose a false universality on all other species, who are asked to shed their un–lamb-like bodies, habits, and appetites in order to achieve a proper "taste." The grass-like is beautiful, the meat-like is not. Hence aesthetics, like morals, needs to be resisted on political grounds. This position is assumed to express the displeasure of various constituencies whose sense of taste and value is thereby excluded or marginalized. Demands for change in the university in the 60s and after, according to David Lloyd, were in fact inspired by the rejection of aesthetics, and the defenders of the institutional status quo responded in kind:

> The response of the professoriate was markedly aesthetic, circling around various expressions of distaste or disgust and driven by the sudden realization of being embodied—gendered and raced—in classrooms that had once guaranteed their abstraction and transparency as disinterested representatives of the ethical ends of the institution.[30]

Aesthetic judgment, whether inside or outside the classroom, demands that one's interests and embodied differences be checked at the door. This process of self-abstraction, which seems non-coercive and indeed supremely civilizing, in fact forces people whose gendered and racialized embodiment is important to them to undergo (in Lloyd's words) "a splitting that severs the corporealized human being from the formal subject of aesthetic judgment that is identified with the universal Subject of humanity."[31] The aesthetic sets a standard of universality, and judged by that standard women and minorities can only succeed by allowing their differences to be suppressed. The new classroom cannot afford to let that happen. The new pedagogy must be post-aesthetic.

But does this position faithfully reflect the demands of the new social movements? In a simple empirical sense, it does not. "Poetry Is Not a Luxury," Audre Lorde wrote in 1977. Poetry for Lorde is

> a revelatory distillation of experience . . . a vital necessity of our existence. It forms the quality of the light within which we predicate our hopes and dreams toward survival and change, first made into language, then into idea, then into more tangible action.[32]

The "we" Lorde is speaking of here is explicitly "women," and she is explicitly critical of "the sterile word play that, too often, the white fathers distorted the word *poetry* to mean."[33] But her case for the usefulness of poetry would clearly hold for other constituencies as well as women, and even for white fathers and sons who were capable of forsaking poetry as sterile wordplay and using it to move from language to idea to action. Like Raymond Williams, Lorde is not making a case against standards of aesthetic judgment; she is proposing a change in those standards so that they make room for the revelatory distilling of more kinds of experience. The nuance should not be lost.

In *The Difference Aesthetics Makes: On the Humanities After "Man,"* Kandice Chuh, who offers to speak for the new social movements in general, like Lloyd, holds Kant and the discipline of English responsible for the ways "the reigning humanism sorts people into the fit and unfit, the rational and the unreasonable, Man and other, Man and woman, and Human and racialized subject."[34] This makes aesthetics "integral to the production of . . . the racial and colonial order" and "sex-gender regulation," among other things.[35] The list, already impressive, then gets expanded to "imperialism and colonialism, White supremacy and capitalism, environmental devastation, patriarchy, and compulsory normativization of all kinds."[36] That is a lot of guilt to lay on aesthetics—and a lot of significance to credit aesthetics with, if only negative significance. But for Chuh, as for Lorde, aesthetics also allows the expression of "sensibilities that differ and dissent from liberal common sense."[37] As if in ignorance of the damning case she has just made, she goes on: if they are denied aesthetic value, "minoritized writings" will be seen merely "as political or anthropological documents rather than artistic creations. . . . Ethnic and women's literatures have . . . been conceptualized as important to study because of politics." Too little recognition has been given, therefore, to their "distinctively aesthetic qualities."[38] Today such double-edged arguments are less the exception than the rule, especially given the rising field of "world literature." More about this below.

Kant, Lloyd observes, classified those who were unwilling or unable to undertake the aesthetic passage toward universality as savages, irredeemable carnivores in a world where civilization and justice demand adherence to the moral code of the lambs. Assuming Lloyd is right, is this bit of Orientalism essential to Kant's thought, or is it what might be called an incidental vice, unfortunately representative of almost all European thinking in his time but perhaps not constitutive of it? (Not all vices, even very serious vices, can be assumed to be constitutive of the arguments in which they appear.) We know Kant held self-abstraction to be morally desirable for everyone, whatever their racial or ethnic origin. Lloyd's observation also fails to explain the oddly narrow focus, in *Under Representation: The Racial Regime of Aesthetics,* on race—race even to the exclusion of gender, which Lloyd notes above but which gets no mention in the book's index. The omission is not trivial. Racism was a major target of the movements of the 60s, but it was not the only target. From the perspective of 1968 and after, the problem with aesthetics, as Lloyd presents it, would seem to be the same for all those collectivities that Lloyd calls "minoritized"—collectivities that of course include women, though women are not a minority. It was not just race that, under the "regime" of aesthetics, would have to be checked at the door, or abstracted out of a student's aesthetic responses.

And to recall the plurality of new social movements is to arrive at a much more important point. Self-abstraction or self-scrutiny or self-doubt, as Lloyd describes it, would not just be the condition of speech for minorities speaking to a (white heteronormative male) majority. Self-abstraction would also be the condition of speech for the "minoritized" collectivities *if they were speaking only with each other*. A Black man speaking with a Black woman (about a literary text, or about a political issue) would have to be ready to step back from his maleness and ask what that text or issue looked like from the Black woman's point of view. A white woman speaking with a Black woman would have to be ready to step back from her whiteness and ask what it looked like from the Black woman's point of view. An educated person with disabilities speaking to a person without education but also without disabilities would have to be ready to consider their own class, race, gender, sexuality, level of education, and so on in relation to the class, race, gender, sexuality, and level of education of their interlocutor. And so on, and on, through the embarrassing and limitless et cetera.

The capacity to abstract from the self is not just a precondition of aesthetic judgment; it is also a precondition of politics, or at least of the sorts of political coalition that have been prized since the 60s. What has come to be called *intersectionality* (more on it in the next chapter) is sometimes thought of as an accumulation of injustices and vulnerabilities. In its crudest form, the logic seems to be that the larger your number, the greater your political credit. Intersectionality is a more valuable concept if it is considered as a list that mixes together vulnerabilities *and privileges*, credits and debits. A good example is Claudia Rankine's account of herself in *Citizen*, laid out in an interview with Lauren Berlant:

> "I made a conscious decision to inhabit my own subjectivity in this book in the sense that the middle-class life I live, with my highly educated, professional, and privileged friends, remains as the backdrop for whatever is being foregrounded. Everyone is having a good time together—doing what they do, buying what they can afford, going where they go—until they are not."[39]

If class, education, profession, and privileged friends have to be mentioned in a conversation about race, and not only because they will turn out not to matter enough to preserve the good times, then intersectionality is a political slogan that pledges its adherents to unceasing self-scrutiny.[40] Without accounting for privileges as well as vulnerabilities, one risks increasing rather than diminishing injustice. One also risks being politically ineffective. There can be single-issue movements, but a shared or coalitional movement is ruled out, and to that disadvantage is added the well-documented danger that even the plural movements will begin to splinter into still more and smaller and weaker movements, or factions. Self-abstraction is not properly cast as the villain of movement politics. The same would seem to hold, then, for aesthetics.

And in that event, much of the political case against aesthetics no longer looks persuasive. Consider, for example, Terry Eagleton's version of the argument. Unlike Lloyd, Eagleton does not object to self-abstraction as such. "In responding to an artifact, I place my own contingent aversions and appetencies in brackets, putting myself instead in everyone's place and thus judging from the standpoint of a universal subjectivity."[41] Since aesthetic response cannot be compelled and delivers disinterested pleasure, it results in a free and pleasurable experience of "non-coercive consensus."[42] Though aesthetics "discipline[s] and chastise[s] the self," by bracketing or abstracting out a spectrum of the self's interests and desires, "non-coercive consensus, providing the affective bonds which traverse the alienations of social life,"[43] promises a large compensation for this sacrifice. That sacrifice is not necessarily either gendered or racialized. Since what has to be abstracted out is above all what stands in the way of non-coercive consensus, there is no inherent reason why this discipline and chastisement would not have to fall more heavily on, say, the bearers of white male privilege, who do stand in the way of non-coercive consensus, than on the minoritized, who merely desire to be rights-bearing members of it. Would it be wrong to *want* to pressure the holders of privilege into some self-inspection, followed by some self-abstraction? If that is what aesthetics does, it does not seem politically counterintuitive. Indeed, it seems vastly preferable to leaving the privileged to scrutinize only what and when and where and if they feel like scrutinizing. Yes, pressure to scrutinize would be an exercise of power, but it would not be the moral equivalent of the stockade or the strappado.

Eagleton has no objection to the universality of this discipline. His objection is that this imaginative foretaste of human solidarity only reminds us of how scant and precarious actual solidarity is.[44] He also objects that it distracts from the political work of creating solidarity where genuine solidarity does not yet exist. Politics is a realm of interests, often necessarily colliding interests. Aesthetics pretends that it is possible and desirable to inhabit a realm of disinterestedness. In the Kantian tradition, Eagleton complains, the two realms are utterly separate from each other. Or as Lloyd puts it, in substituting for politics, aesthetics blocks the way to it.[45] We have just seen, however, that the complaint is unfounded. Politics requires interests, yes, but politics also requires the self-abstraction that the critics of aesthetics see, wrongly, only in aesthetics. At any rate, self-abstraction is certainly required by the intersectional politics of the new social movements.[46] And under present circumstances, we should be glad that there is more than one way in which pressure can be applied, and we should be prepared not to cede to complaints about that pressure. "We must make ourselves comfortable with the notion," Charles M. Blow writes in the midst of the spring 2020 protests in support of the BLM movement, "that for the privileged, equality will feel like oppression."[47]

As Hannah Arendt argued in her *Lectures on Kant's Political Philosophy*, delivered at the New School in 1970, Kant's thinking about the aesthetic in his third critique can be considered as the volume of political philosophy he never wrote. He never wrote an explicit book of political philosophy because, overwhelmingly concerned as he was with the moral individual, he saw the domain of politics as defined by gross self-interest, hence unlikely to yield the just society that was his goal.[48] Justice had to be freely chosen. It could not involve tutelage, or obedience to another. The *Critique of Judgment* gets written when, despairing that reason will be freely chosen, he pursues the hopeful insight that judgments of beauty are both absolutely free and yet also, miraculously, public-spirited. Aesthetic response seemed (to Arendt, if not necessarily to Kant) a more roundabout but also a more promising means to achieve the same end. It was disinterested—indifferent to the actual existence of the object found to be beautiful, separated off by the "as if" from any actual gain or loss. And yet it gave pleasure, and a pleasure that needed for mysterious reasons to be shared with others. This sharing, while each individual was free to judge as they liked, unconstrained by any universal rule or law, was a model of how the crooked timber of humanity might, while remaining crooked (as it seemed doomed to do), freely choose to be hammered together into a more just community, and hammered together without protesting against each blow of the hammer.[49]

It does not detract from the brilliance of this insight to add that, like other miracles, this one was too good to be true, at least in its pure form. Aesthetic judgment could not be perfectly free if it was also going to be public-spirited. If the point was to move in the direction of justice, then pressure would have to be applied—applied *by* others and *to* others. But the kind and degree of pressure applied in the sharing of aesthetic judgments were indeed distinct from the sorts of gross authoritarianism that Kant saw around him. Perhaps this was even a way of maximizing freedom, a way of coming as close as one could come to applying no pressure at all. But one cannot justify one's continuing admiration for Kant or (more important) Kant's continuing relevance to the practice of criticism without recognizing that the freedom of aesthetic judgment cannot be absolute. The place of politics in the practice of criticism cannot be understood unless one understands—the other side of the same point—that in aesthetic judgment pressure is and must be applied.

As the minoritized have pointed out, aesthetic judgment is never as free as Kant thought it was. What has not so often been pointed out is that it was never in the interest of the minoritized for the privileged majority to enjoy absolute freedom. In order for there to be significant change, force would have to be applied to that majority. This is the radical side of the concession to unfreedom that is more visible, and more complained of, on its conservative side. Kant famously argued in "What Is Enlightenment?" that freedom of thought (of which freedom of aesthetic response can be considered a subset) was guaranteed only as long as, in the practical domain, there was a guarantee of obedience to the authority of church and state. In the short term, that left authority in place. Objections to this political compromise were articulated early, well before racialized and gendered collectivities began pressing their claims in the 1960s. The same for Matthew Arnold's disinterested culture, a moralized version of Kantian aesthetics. This was (in Chris Baldick's words) "a pact of non-interference in practical affairs"[50]—in the formula of "The Function of Criticism at the Present Time," acceptance of "force till right is ready."

These surrenders to existing authority would seem to make both Kant and Arnold into fatally anti-political thinkers, leading the humanities into social irrelevance. But disinterestedness is not simply a political mistake. "Under any sustained cross-examination," Baldick concludes, in the wake of many such cross-examinations, "[Arnold's] 'disinterestedness' breaks down"— breaks down, one assumes, into real, irreducible interests, giving priority to those of the ruling class, little as Arnold liked that class.[51] "Arnold was trying to treat social classes," Baldick says, "as if they had no distinct interests."[52]

Common sense would reply that class interests (and other interests) are the indispensable building blocks of politics: no interests, no politics. Although politics needs interests, however, interests are not all it needs. What is intersectionality *but* a willingness to expose the taken-for-grantedness of class self-interest or class identity to the scrutiny called for, in a given political moment, by the practical desire for coalition with other collectivities? Self-scrutiny is a necessary habit for collectivities as well as for individuals. It is not just aesthetics that requires a willingness to suspend or step back from pre-given collective identities, including what passes for their natural and irreducible interests. The same holds for politics in the most practical and everyday sense of the word. Matthew Arnold's backing off from the laissez-faire impulse of nineteenth-century liberalism and his insistence on the positive role of public institutions, including the institutions of higher education, boost his claim to be considered an organic intellectual of the nineteenth century middle class while they also lift him above the culture wars context in our time and renew his interest as an anticipatory critic of neoliberalism.[53]

From Samuel Taylor Coleridge to Matthew Arnold and from I. A. Richards to the American New Critics, no operation has seemed more definitive of literature than the reconciling or harmonizing of apparently divergent views and interests. This appearance is a bit misleading. In practice, critical appreciations of literature have often looked elsewhere. As Jonathan Arac observed apropos of the call, during the culture wars, for critics to remember their commitment to beauty, well before the culture wars the interpretation of modern literature was already heavily invested in what is *not* beautiful or unified but rather unreconciled, fragmentary, excessive, shocking. Fredric Jameson speaks of "the canonization of a hitherto scandalous, ugly, dissonant, amoral, anti-social, bohemian high modernism."[54] And in any case, "the main line of academic and public discussion of literature in the English-speaking world since the nineteenth century has not been primarily or fundamentally aesthetic."[55] Public discussion of literature has been solidly moral and political—and that is one large reason why modern criticism, responsible to its time, has so highly valued the disunited and inharmonious.

Yet the paradigm of aesthetic reconciliation has not disappeared. Nor would one expect it to. As its harshest critics have agreed, the anti-instrumental aesthetic has never not been instrumentalized and instrumentalized for better as well as for worse. I have speculated that, despite the differences—academic versus public sphere, class versus non-class—there is a substantive parallel between the role of critic/journalists of the eighteenth century vis-à-vis the emergent middle class and the role of academic critics over the last decades vis-à-vis the new social movements and the society at which they aim. If there is any substance to this speculation, one would expect the mission of reconciling divergent perspectives and interests to have remained operative. One would also expect, therefore, a positive commitment to the aesthetic—not just to aesthetic effects of shock and discord, in other words, but also to artistic effects in which diverse perspectives are acknowledged and, to the extent possible, reconciled.

And that is what one finds, though not necessarily where one would expect to find it. Fredric Jameson has famously argued throughout this same period that Claude Levi-Strauss's formula for the analysis of myth, the imaginary resolution of real contradictions, applies not just to "primitive" societies but also to the work narrative does in modern class society. To describe it as the work of *ideology*, as Jameson and other Marxist critics sometimes do, is of course to deny that literature is unique or politically innocent, but it is also to affirm that literature is politically significant—and potentially significant for good as well as for ill. (For Jameson, ideology is not opposed to aesthetics.) And when collectivities other than classes are politically self-conscious and forceful, and the social contradictions that are being exposed have to do with, say, race, gender, and sexuality, it is not surprising that the same formula of imaginary resolution would apply to them.

According to David Lloyd and Paul Thomas, the work of reconciling and harmonizing divergent interests is performed by the state. Aesthetic culture, like the state, aims at "the mediation of conflicts among interests."[56] Or to put this in other terms: "reconnection, reconciliation, reunification, these being what the state is supposed to provide" and "*at the same time* what culture is supposed to provide."[57] Let us presume that this is correct. What follows from it? If one assumes, as Lloyd and Thomas do, that any work of reconciling and harmonizing divergent interests is politically undesirable, whether done by culture or the state, and that the state's desire to do this work serves only its own interest, then it will be clear that a Kantian aesthetic, whether racist in its essence (as Lloyd's single-author monograph argues) or incidentally or historically racist but not essentially so, is also politically undesirable. But that would only follow if it were also assumed that the state, invulnerable to pressure from below, was incapable of ever doing anything that was politically desirable. That seems historically counterintuitive, especially in light of what the civil rights and other mid–twentieth-century movements were able to force into legislation. What is it contrasted to? If the presumed alternative is a revolutionary transformation after which no separate interests will be left to reconcile or harmonize, then that conclusion seems less than self-evident. The exclusive focus on racism in *Under Representation* raises the same question. What about other genders and sexualities? What about other movements? What about other races? Assuming that movements against racism want to eradicate racism but do not want to eradicate racial identity, how can they possibly aim at an end to all separate interests? In a world of many races and many racisms, some sort of reconciliation or harmonizing of interests, aesthetic and political, can hardly be kept off the table. Like ideology—and that is Eagleton's term for aesthetics—the aesthetic work of reconciling divergent interests would seem to be a permanent feature of human society, after as well as before the revolution. It is by no means the only kind of work that critics do; much of that work is *not* political in this sense. But it *is* work, and political work, which is to say that it applies power against resistance.

Criticism's allergy to power, its tendency to recognize power only as something that is possessed and wielded by others and that critics would be wrong to claim, is worth more scrutiny than it has received. (One avenue well worth going down is Kant's concept of the sublime, which unlike the beautiful *is* an exercise of power, though it does not display the same inclination toward justice.) The simplest thing to say in this context is that culture, defined by its separation from power, will always make those who serve it seem *critical* of power, but will never make them want to *take* power. One happy exception, and a crucial one for my argument, is the role John Guillory attributes to his eighteenth-century critic/journalists, with its mission of identifying and cultivating a class's "common interests" so as to turn it into a governing class.

In presenting this as a valuable legacy for criticism today, both in politics and in aesthetics, I was proposing that the labor of reconciling divergent interests, which is both aesthetic and political, should be recast and revalued as part of the work of governing—a kind of labor that is not only done by others and is not only done at our expense, whoever we think we are. Learning to do such work (or to see this as a fit description of work we are already doing) is by no means a guarantee that criticism's lost social significance will be retrieved. What it offers at a minimum is a more positive but not inaccurate account of what criticism is today and of the critical generation that made it what it is.

What stands in the way of this argument is a problem to which I have already alluded. Let me spell it out. It is now generally acknowledged that the aesthetic exercises power. But this exercise of power is generally acknowledged *only as a bad thing.* That is an assumption that should give pause to those who think of themselves as progressive. The powerless may be righteous—and they may not. They may not even be powerless, as certain successful cancellations of the very powerful have proved. That's one moral that could be drawn from the parable of the birds of prey and the lambs: by their invention of ethics, the lambs did in fact acquire power over the birds of prey, even if that power is not their favored self-presentation.

Foucault is so central to my argument in part because, although he is a chief sponsor of this squeamishness about power, he also encourages an overcoming of that squeamishness, reflecting thereby that desire to see the world governed differently that is the other side of the 60s movements. Both are visible in the exemplary career of Ian Hunter. In his 1988 book *Culture and Government: The Emergence of Literary Education*, Hunter was inspired by Foucault to identify literary education with techniques of governmental supervision of the population.[58] Although modern pedagogy prides itself on being "fiercely anti-didactic," and all the more so when the subject is literature, in fact the opposite is true: the "aesthetic imperative is deployed to oversee the machinery of popular education."[59] Like other apparent reforms, modern literary pedagogy serves a new regime of domination. But Foucault himself worried that those who were applying his thought in this way had misunderstood his view of power. In one of the late interviews, he writes,

> We all know that power is not evil! For example, let us take sexual or amorous relationships. . . . And let us take, as another example, something that has often been rightly criticized—the pedagogical institution. I see nothing wrong in the practice of a person who, knowing more than the others in a specific game of truth, tells those others what to do.[60]

Hunter too reconsiders the over-eager abstention from telling people what to do. Eight years later, in a 1996 essay called "Literary Theory in Civil Life," he reminds his readers of the tradition by which literary education has functioned "as a cultural qualification for the exercise of political and administrative power."[61] His essay displays none of the usual horror at the exercise of power. Power is real, for Hunter, but it is not necessarily to be shunned.

It would be better for criticism, and better for society, Hunter suggests, if criticism were to reinvest in the notion of citizenship. By defining itself in terms of literariness or the aesthetic, criticism made the mistake of surrendering in advance this older claim to political significance. The aesthetic, like critique, is a practice of self-problematization. The habit of mistrusting experience encourages us to think we are or can be, if we separate ourselves off from ordinary social institutions, free of dogmatism. Worse, it discourages us from recognizing how much freedom is to be enjoyed, and made use of, within ordinary social institutions.

Hunter's proposal is thus for a return to the "rhetorical" tradition of training for governance or civil life that used to be associated with the classics—a training that does not insist on a prior distance from or hesitation before the existing institutions of civil life. In my view, this proposal is unduly dismissive of the citizenly value of self-scrutiny and the aesthetic recognizing and reconciling of divergent interests, both of which have figured prominently in my argument. As a question of timing, it may also be premature in the United States, where possibilities for liberal-minded people doing successful and self-fulfilling work in government bureaucracies do not seem quite as heartening as they have sometimes been in Hunter's Australia. But it remains useful to reflect, with Hunter, on the hypothesis that the freedom we have associated with critique is also to be found in the institutions we have seen solely as *targets* of critique, and that we have perhaps seen these institutions as lacking in freedom not because we have studied them but (at least to an appreciable extent) because we needed a foil to define the aesthetic against. There is of course a danger involved in abandoning an intellectual default setting of suspicion and critical distance, a predisposition that has perhaps deformed criticism's habitual judgments but has done so, so to speak, on the progressive side, by keeping a certain amount of intellectual energy automatically flowing in the direction of social change. Nothing in Hunter's hypothesis tells us how power should be used or when it should be resisted. Nothing in his program would prevent criticism from being refashioned into some sort of capitalism-friendly consumer advice or management training. On the other hand, our critiques of capitalism would certainly be more persuasive to outsiders if those critiques were no longer felt to be hard-wired into the premises of our discipline. And Hunter's respect for institutions provides ground for measuring generational/institutional accomplishment—given the discipline's anti-institutional bias and its horror of the supposed complacency of progressive linear time, the registering of accomplishments is not one of its salient virtues.

Varieties of Coercion

David Lloyd, looking back on the left's campaigns of the 60s in a book that argues that racism is at the very heart of aesthetics (and, counterintuitively, that aesthetics is at the very heart of racism), suggests that the situation of the 60s radicals was potentially revolutionary: "At that moment, the claims of minoritized subjects for redress and access to state institutions, and not least to the educational apparatus, threatened not so much a demographic adjustment as a complete transformation of those institutions."[62] Was a complete transformation in the cards? Was it called for? What would it have looked like? The closest thing to such a transformation in this place and time was the shift from literary studies in the direction of cultural studies. Cultural studies might be considered the hypothetical institutional embodiment of the 60s movements. Its rise as a new way to structure knowledge may seem anticlimactic; the rubric did not lead to the foundation of a host of new university departments. But cultural studies had a much larger impact on the publishing industry.

Was this a political defeat? The question has been controversial. According to Francis Mulhern, disappointment is not in order. The problem with Matthew Arnold, as Mulhern argued in *Culture/Metaculture*, extends through Raymond Williams and all the way to cultural studies. Cultural studies seems radical by virtue of its subject matter, which welcomes all the cultural objects and practices by which the ordinary lives of ordinary people are lived, thereby relegating literature (as a relatively elite field of interest) to a much smaller role than it had for traditional literary criticism. For Mulhern, however, this would not be a triumph worth celebrating. For cultural studies, like literary criticism, reposes on the foundation of "culture," and it too has been severely hampered in its proper political aspirations by dependence on this object of knowledge.

As I suggested above, the concept of culture endowed criticism with a spectacularly persistent discipline-wide hostility to capitalist modernity—a feat whose magnitude has not always been adequately appreciated. But it also inspired its devotees to reject with disgust two indispensable components of anticapitalist politics: (1) mass democracy and (2) political instrumentality.

Elitist and aestheticist, the concept of culture insidiously installed a depoliticizing tendency in the heart of the very discourse on which social critics have depended to define their presumed subversiveness. And it is still having the same effect on cultural studies, Mulhern argues. The cultural studies formula "everything is political" (which derives theoretically from culture's seemingly infinite expansiveness, and practically from feminism and the other new social movements) leaves nothing political in a usefully specifiable sense. Politics in this more precise, specialized sense is defined by action. "It is normally deliberative in character, governed by the question, What is to be *done*?"[63] Culture has been able to serve as a conceptual umbrella offering equal shelter to Marxists and to romantic reactionaries, along with other otherwise divergent groups and interests, because it refuses to divide along the definitive axis of political action. Politics must be divisive, or it ceases to be politics.

This argument leads, however, to a further qualification of demands for complete or revolutionary transformation. The institution from which Lloyd is demanding complete transformation and Mulhern is demanding united action is the university. Universities cannot aim at the goal of unity, least of all unity that passes the test of revolutionary action. Departments and disciplines lodged in universities are structurally obliged to do precisely what Mulhern accuses the concept of culture of doing: accommodating divergent values, identities, and interests, even seemingly incompatible ones, in a structure obliged to produce continuing controversy. (I would argue that political parties and movements do a version of the same thing—hence the strangebedfellows principle—though of course not to the same degree.) No scholarly discipline can be unanimous. It's not that the discipline *should* not, for ethical reasons, demand consensus, but that it literally *cannot* subsume internal differences without ceasing to function as a discipline at all. It is internal differences that generate new scholarly work.

These internal differences are of course not without limit. As Foucault demonstrates, they are directed into certain channels rather than others. In that sense, it is not nonsense to talk about particular disciplines having a distinctive political character, as criticism arguably has. But the formal need to allow for unending controversy, to provide space for and indeed provoke substantive argument, means that there are severe limits to the political force and focus that can be demanded of any discipline. Culture, which has done so much to make literary criticism's case for its social significance, has indeed limited the politics of critics working within its ambit even while giving many of them a politics (politics of a certain kind) in the first place. But if culture were to be replaced by some other term, like "discourse" or "signifying practices" or "political action," that term too would have to be limiting—not in precisely the same way, granted, but to more or less the same extent. Like culture, the new term would also have to allow for controversy. It would also have to explain to society, as culture did, why society should sponsor its study. And it would have to do so in a way that society could accept.

By these criteria, the candidacy of "political action" as an academic raison d'être is a non-starter. Universities cannot be treated as if they were pressure groups or political parties. Let us translate back into the more familiar term "advocacy": say, a pedagogy that would champion a particular political cause, organizing all readings and discussions on one side of that cause and demanding student adherence as a prerequisite for admission or successful completion. Advocacy of this hypothetical and perhaps extreme sort represents a version of political commitment that cannot recognize or adapt itself to the constraints of being located in a university department, constraints not all of which are open to renegotiation. Such advocacy therefore doesn't belong in a university department. The humanities, for all their encouragement of activism and revolutionary thought, cannot reasonably expect to rename themselves "activist studies" or "revolution studies."

That said, it is also important to recognize, again, the fact that institutions like disciplines and universities do exercise power, a fact that still tends to be greeted as a surprise, and an unwelcome one. The actual procedures by which intellectual authority is exercised in the academy tend to go unacknowledged, if only because they are embarrassingly out of sync with our squeaky-clean democratic self-image. We know, though we are not eager to say so, that the academy is not in fact a perfectly open, perfectly democratic space where all opinions can always be expressed and/or are offered equal time. Far from it. There exists a slow, obscure, but more or less efficacious process whereby certain opinions are little by little dismissed as indefensible and unworthy of any time at all on our overcrowded syllabi and conference programs. This involves neither the brutal extermination of the dissenters nor tolerant, helplessly uncritical cohabitation with them. What happens is that certain beliefs are sidelined and then silenced.

Sidelined? *Silenced?* Verbs like these are usually assumed to mark academic misdemeanors, if not capital crimes. But they stand for operations that I think most scholars would eventually be ready to endorse. Those who believe the world is flat have not been rounded up and done away with; they have merely lost the pre-argument about what arguments are worth spilling ink over, and thus they are no longer much heard from. The same for believers in the inherent superiority of men to women, or the coming corruption of the white race by immigrants from Asia, or the idea that the Palestinians exiled in 1948 left their homes voluntarily. These propositions have had their glory days; many scholars have held to them fiercely; a few lonely eccentrics still do. But now these ideas have been dishonored, and who can regret it? Is it a scandal that neither their proponents nor their critics can win funding from foundations? Is it a scandal that there is no "balance" where they are concerned? "We" are a functional consensus at least in the minimal sense that no one insists too loudly that we should waste our precious waking hours on these ideas anymore. It is to be hoped that divine intervention in the affairs of men will similarly subside as an active hypothesis both inside the academy and, above all, beyond it. If this happens, it will not have been as a result of the worst tyranny ever exercised by human beings over their fellows. In the academy disinterestedness remains a working rule, and despite much ideological discord there is considerable agreement concerning standards of argument and evidence. The same cannot be said everywhere.

Is the political power exercised within a largely self-regulating discipline like criticism any less coercive, any more democratic, than the power exercised elsewhere—say, in the democratically accountable nation-state? If so, why? As a more limited question of criticism and its politics, it is perhaps useful to distinguish between institutions of different scales and different purposes. No, the freedom that Kant attributes to the aesthetic is not absolute. But in the institutions that matter here, we do not take freedom as an absolute value. At least ideally, the literature classroom is a kind of Kantian microcosm to which students bring diverse interests, histories, and perspectives, baggage that is *not* checked at the door, and in which the discussion does the work of recognizing and reconciling and even perhaps harmonizing those interests, histories, and perspectives. But not all will get equal recognition. Some will end up being (as the saying goes) silenced or marginalized. For in the classroom, power, like knowledge, is unequally distributed. The instructor applies pressure—pressure in some directions and not in others. This is what movement toward genuine democracy requires. It is what happens in literature itself. We do not cry authoritarianism when a novel pushes its reader toward a particular resolution of the perspectives it has raised. We do not cry authoritarianism when an academic discipline curtails the freedom of racists, homophobes, and flat earthers to speak their minds and set agendas of debate for others. The same can hold of course for a curtailing of freedom that happens at the level of the state, or *should* happen—for example, by the government demanding that all citizens wear face masks or get vaccinated during a pandemic for the protection of their fellow citizens.

One objection that I anticipate to this argument is that, like the nation-state, aesthetic values like wholeness and harmony, conciliation and unity, were often rejected, and sometimes violently rejected, by the liberation movements of the 60s. You can see that rejection in Bill Readings's retelling of the familiar narrative of criticism's lost social significance. What has replaced criticism's previous national-cultural rationale, in Readings's view, is an abstract, content-neutral ideal of "excellence," which adapts the university to the exigencies of global capitalism via the quantifying language of corporate management.[64] Readings blasts the new rationale, though no more than it deserves. Yet on second glance, there is something questionable about his critique. Excellence, he says, offers the university a "unifying principle,"[65] and what it unifies is an otherwise unmanageably diverse assortment of intellectual enterprises, divided for example as scientific versus humanistic, and then subdivided endlessly. The problem is that Readings is opposed to unity as such. His charge against the unifying done by "excellence" could be directed with equal force against the earlier rationale: against "nation," "culture," "public" (society conceived as capable of collective self-representation), and "society" itself. All of these terms, whether national or post-national, are unities that impose themselves on a diversity of particulars. Readings's own preferred idea of the university is what he calls "the community of dissensus,"[66] which is to say a community that, however paradoxically, leaves diversity as is. It's as if Readings has developed an aesthetic of disunity in order to adapt to a disunited social landscape. In his view, the initial particulars of identity must be fixed and preserved, as if sacred and untouchable. All commonality between them must be forbidden. The usual name that is given to this position by its enemies is identity politics, and the usual source it is traced back to is the liberation movements of the 60s—the period that also produced (and it is no coincidence) the style of "theory" in which Readings writes. Representatives of the liberation movements and representatives of theory often did not get along with each other, but in retrospect it is possible to see the certain impulses of the latter, nevertheless, as an abstract crystallization of the former's demands. That is one reason why I have permitted myself to give Foucault, as theorist, the prominence here that I have.

But what are the demands of the 60s movements? Are they in fact demands that the particulars of each identity be fixed and preserved, as if sacred and untouchable? Obviously not, at least if the point is to form a single movement, or (in the epigraph to this chapter that I have taken from Richard Ohmann) "to organize that ferment into a comprehensive story and totalizing analysis." It is a mistake to confuse, as Readings does, a desired aesthetic with an imposed social landscape.

Global capitalism may or may not have put an end to the era of the national public, but in either case, Readings was already opposed to the very *idea* of a national public. By definition, publics put pressure on the diverse identities within them, attempting to impose at least some degree of reciprocal translation. This is something that the liberation movements of the 60s did with each other in trying to become a single movement, as I have been suggesting. Ethically and politically, intellectually and institutionally, this effort, with its failures and its successes, is in my view their real and lasting legacy. Readings's view is different. For him, the legacy of the 60s is a simple refusal of the project of reconciling divergent perspectives. The case can of course be made. But assuming it as he does, Readings cannot in good conscience mourn the loss of the idea of national culture or blame that loss on global capitalism. By Readings's logic, globalization continues at a transnational level the unifying work that the national public was already doing, *but it also undoes that work.* In that sense globalization is his ally. If it had not happened and if national publics still flourished, Readings would have been obligated by his own logic to resist those national publics just as strenuously as he resists globalization itself, and again in the name of the "incalculable otherness" of singular identities. By breaking down the nation-state and liberating its particular identities from bondage, globalization is doing his deconstructing for him and thus making his own pro-diversity point at the expense of the national culture. If global capitalism didn't already exist, Readings would have had to invent it.

Readings is right that disciplinary rationales must adapt themselves to the social landscape of their time. But he is wrong about our landscape. The nation-state is not defunct. If there was any silver lining in the COVID-19 pandemic, it is the demonstration that even in the face of a global virus, prompt, well-informed, decisive action by a national government, where it happened, was able to save many thousands of lives. The absence of competent centralized leadership, as in the United States, was responsible for hundreds of thousands of deaths. Those on the left as well as the right—whose propagating of anti-statism has contributed to the pervasive distrust of the state that triggered this avalanche of unnecessary fatality—are free to draw their own conclusions. Criticism did not play a decisive role in this disaster. But the assumption that the nation-state no longer exists—an assumption that is clearly premature, empirically speaking—has been an excuse for critics both to ignore the actual power that states still exercise and (continuing the parallel between state and culture) the actual power that critics too still exercise as cultural agents.[67]

It is true that the social movements of the 60s and after had a special interest in politics at the transnational or planetary scale, as has the generation that inherited so much from them. During the culture wars of the 90s, critics from the right aimed much of their anger at the generation's supposedly exaggerated empathy for the victims of European colonialism in the past and American militarism in the present. Richard Rorty, ambivalent about the 60s, accused the movement of failing politically because of its lack of patriotism. So did a once-enthusiastic 60s radical like Todd Gitlin. These criticisms are a backhanded acknowledgement that the internationalist legacy was successfully passed on—as one sees in the simple fact that recent scholarly common sense values so highly a comparativist and transnational view of its object of knowledge.

It is less clear, however, what politics if any follows from that geographical or cosmopolitan expansion of the object of knowledge. To the extent that globalization has reshaped the cultural landscape, as Readings argues, how have criticism's choices been redefined? Has criticism quietly made itself a part of a new left internationalism, now that the old socialist internationalism has collapsed along with the world's communist parties? If there is such a thing as a critical cosmopolitics, an uneasy hybrid of solidarities that are neither those of party politics nor those of private humanitarianism, what does it look like? Where does it stand on the feud (if that's the right word) between a long-established but perhaps fading "postcolonial studies" and an emergent but perhaps somewhat depoliticized "world literature"? Has it inherited the ambivalence and irresolution of the 60s movements themselves? Within today's cultural politics, which doesn't take national borders as a natural limit on its scholarly curiosity, are the sides again defined—as they seemed to be at the national scale—as an empowered universalism versus a disempowered but protesting particularism? On those occasions when it is named rather than silently assumed, universalism is generally complained of as an illegitimate means for the governing of others. But if the discipline of criticism is a means for the governing of others, and not the holier-than-thou refuge from interest and governance that it has sometimes liked to think itself, then it would seem to follow that the universal, too, needs to be reconsidered.

5   Grievances

*What is the obligation of white intellectuals to *their* people?*
Hortense J. Spillers

How did Native American criticism enter the academy? In telling that story, the editors of the volume *Reasoning Together: The Native Critics Collective* begin with a series of historical coincidences:

> From the late 1960s to the end of the 1980s, more federal legislation affecting Indian country was passed than during any comparable period in U.S. history. Within that same period literary studies were in an upheaval over the question as to what constitutes literature, which books should be considered the proper objects of study, how they should be read, and the very ability of language itself to effectively name the world.[1]

Two pages later, the introduction again juxtaposes legislation affecting Native Americans with innovation in criticism:

> In 1978, the same year French philosopher Michel Foucault's landmark study, *The History of Sexuality*, is published in the United States in its English translation, American Indians are granted religious freedom . . . when Congress passes the American Indian Religious Freedom Act (AIRFA), which promises to "protect and preserve for American Indians their inherent right of freedom to believe, express and exercise their traditional religions."[2]

"In the same year as Foucault's study is published and AIRFA becomes law," the editors go on, "Congress passes the Indian Child Welfare Act, which gives tribal courts jurisdiction over Native children living on reservations. Now the tribes will make the decisions as to whether the children will be removed from their families."[3]

What should be made of these coincidences? Between the late 1960s and the end of the 1980s, big things were happening in literary criticism, and big things were also happening in Indian affairs. But how were these things connected to each other, if indeed they were? How much did the political self-assertion of Native Americans, inspired in part by the civil rights movement, have to do with Foucault, the history of sexuality, and the upheaval in literary studies?

From the perspective of literary studies, one place where the two trajectories clearly converged was on the question of "which books should be considered the proper objects of study"—in a more loaded vocabulary, what cultural heritage is worth preserving. Variants of this question have been asked for as long as books have been studied, and most if not all of the answers could certainly be considered political in at least some sense of that word. But in this period the politics is right up front. A new set of answers arrives (in Native American studies, for example, the proposition that the community's oral traditions as well as recent Native American authors should be taught). That new set of texts arrives, in general, by way of direct political action, and action on the part of a new set of political agents: activists representing women and minorities. But the new discipline of Native American studies is not established without difficulty.

From academia's perspective, the difficulty is not hard to understand: politics, including politics of the sort that gets bills passed, was seen by many academics as trespassing where it emphatically did not belong. As laid out in the plan for "Native American Studies as an Academic Discipline" at the First Convocation of American Indian Scholars in March 1970 at Princeton University, the aims of the incipient discipline included defending Indigenous control of their lands and Indigenous rights and ultimately reforming US Indian policy.[4] These aims might well seem threatening in themselves, but they also collided with the assumption, held by a considerable proportion of faculty members, that the kinds and standards of knowledge produced in the university should be decided by the university alone. Any outside influence counted as a violation of the university's autonomy. The sense of threat would be more immediate for legislators and university trustees who benefit materially from ownership or control of what had been Indigenous lands and resources.

In 1966, when members of the as-yet unnamed American Indian Movement (which in 1973 would go on to participate in the armed standoff at

Wounded Knee) submitted a report requesting that the University of Minnesota reach out to the surrounding Native American community, they found that they could not get a satisfactory hearing until they had that community vociferously behind them. According to the university's own website, "University administrators did not lend their support for the report until political pressures forced them to respond to the demands of a growing American Indian student population and the radical activism of the Twin Cities' American Indian community."[5] It was only thanks to "political pressures," in other words, that the nation's first department of American Indian Studies was brought into being in 1969.

Versions of this story were repeated around the country. There were petitions and demonstrations in the streets. Thanks in large part to this agitation, new programs and departments came into being, and with them different kinds of attention to more inclusive sets of texts. Teachers in old departments, often newly exposed to and charmed by those texts, freely chose to make adjustments to their reading lists and research agendas. Multiply the breakthrough at the University of Minnesota by the many organizations of women and minorities that were simultaneously pushing for greater academic representation, whether in ethnic studies programs or women's studies programs or within traditional departments, and you get a snapshot of a nationwide struggle that would go on for decades, always available for use by controversy-seeking journalists. The so-called canon wars would pit those holding fast to the great tradition— or the core curriculum, or E. D. Hirsch's cultural literacy, each seen as neutral and universal (or *national* and universal, as paradoxically proposed by Hirsch)—against rebels clamoring for the inclusion of culture produced by women and minorities and insisting that the canon itself, which largely excluded them, has never not been the product of "political pressures."[6]

There is no need here to dwell on the specifics. Though the hostilities never officially ended, this is now ancient history. And by now it should be obvious who won. Take down from the shelf a random stack of recent volumes of the *Publication of the Modern Language Association* (*PMLA*) and skim each table of contents, and what will you find in the discipline's flagship journal, fifty years later? A nine-essay section devoted to *There There*, the debut novel of the Native American writer Tommy Orange (May 2020), another nine-essay special section devoted to disability in Jennifer Egan's *Manhattan Beach* (March 2019), as well as pieces on the Nobel Prize–winning

Indigenous activist Rigoberta Menchu (March 2020), on the troubled translation of Indigenous languages into Spanish (March 2019), on the relatability of
queer poet Frank O'Hara (October 2019), on "reading Jewish" (January 2019),
and on the slogan "Black Lives Matter" (January 2020). None of these essays
could be presumptively classified, to use the Old Guard's indignant terminol-
ogy, as "grievance studies." (Their relation to grievance depends not on the
materials chosen, but on what the authors do with those materials and how
you feel about what they do.) But there is no doubt that groups with a grievance are now much better represented in the discipline than they were a half
century ago. To be more precise, they are participating in the university's governance. What began as a rebellion is now an administration.[7]

To return, then, to our initial question: What does criticism's new small-d
democratic administration have to do with the fate of American democracy
in general? This is not the place for a full discussion of the consequences for
society as a whole of what happens inside the university. That would require a
separate book. But to address what has happened in criticism is to take at least
a baby step in that direction. Assuming that it was indeed "political pressures"
intruding on the academy that put criticism's new government in power, do
the critics so empowered retain a special relationship with the constituencies
that empowered them? Do they offer anything in return? Do these constituencies render the authority of their representatives, such as it is, more legitimate? Or is there reason to doubt whether they do in fact continue to represent those who made possible their entry into the academy? What do they *do*
in the academy other than what the academy wants them to do, whatever that
may be? Would they be better described, to use a 60s phrase, as coopted?[8]

Those who have observed that class was never as high on 60s agendas
as race, gender, and sexuality will also have noticed that, during this push
toward greater equality of representation, economic inequality increased
massively. Seen from this angle, the institutionalization of the 60s movements
is likely to count as a pyrrhic victory, if it counts as a victory at all. One out-
look on the canon wars, which we have already encountered, would maintain
accordingly that the only truly important measure of progress would have
been the achieving by the economically disadvantaged of something that thus
far they have been unequivocally denied: greater access to the socially valued
credentials that higher education bestows, however the content of those credentials is defined. The implication is that the content of the canon is politically irrelevant and that in demanding curricular representation, women and

minorities have been misled, distracted from their real interests, most likely by an overinvestment in matters of social symbolism that are finally inconsequential. If one steps back from a university-based perspective to take in the full social landscape, curricular victories certainly do not seem worth gloating over, even if economic equality is not one's sole concern. As Elizabeth Cook-Lynn notes in introducing the issue of *Wicazo Sa Review* in which her history of Native American Studies appears, "The assault by white America upon Native Indians goes forward, it seems, which is not good news for those who want to believe that racism is declining in our good land."[9]

Responses come to mind, but they are not very satisfying. Yes, the juxtaposition by the Native Critics Collective of better representation in the academy with better representation at the level of federal policy hints that significant democratic processes are operating in both domains, and perhaps conjointly, even if there has been more success in one than in the other and neither has had a decisive triumph. The legislative achievements referred to above—there are more than I listed, including a federally funded mandate for instruction in Indigenous languages—have had practical effects for Native American life. The same holds for academic achievements. It is certain that their effects are never felt *only* in the academy. Although the situation of Native Americans in the United States is no cause for celebration, those academic achievements demand to be given their due. Yet it remains hard to know how much *is* due.

Edward Said and the Organic Intellectual

I have referred above to the journalist-driven narrative that presents the channeling of the political energies of the 1960s into the university as something between a betrayal and a bad joke. This narrative has its adherents within the university, but for insiders the more frequent response to a yoking of their present academic employment to the 60s movements would probably be expressions of suspicion (is this really the case?) and (assuming it *is* the case) a pained signaling of unease and ambivalence.

One prime site of ambivalence is the concept of the *organic intellectual*. As applied to academics, who might not otherwise seem to deserve the honor of being called intellectuals at all, Gramsci's term has suggested that in this instance the honor is in fact deserved. It's deserved because of the academic's bonds with a constituency outside the academy. Such a constituency would have to be one of a multiethnic, multigender, and nonheteronormative collection of constituencies that (like the working class for Gramsci) are supposed to be in the process of overcoming entrenched hostility and fighting their way upward or inward. Because they are embattled, they could theoretically be helped in their struggle by the cultural work of those who emerged from or attached themselves to those constituencies. The suggestion is by no means self-evident. In "Romancing the Organic Intellectual," Aimee Carrillo Rowe hesitates to affirm it, and the reason she gives is the confusion that comes of inhabiting multiple identities. She describes herself as a "middle-class Chicana; indigenous-identified Xicana; queer, single mother, living in a multigenerational home; teacher, student, scholar; post-structuralist U.S. third world feminist."[10] Her relation to the concept of the organic intellectual has therefore been a "romance," but a "vexed" romance."[11]

> While Gramsci productively signals the ideological force our "connection" to home communities exerts over knowledge production, his account doesn't provide an intersectional lens to untangle how multiple, cross-cutting connectivities become vexed through our labor as intellectuals. On the one hand, academics who seek to hold themselves accountable to colonized and marginalized groups often find themselves . . . inhabiting "alien (if not hostile) territory." Not only do our radical (be)longings become vexed vis-à-vis the academy, but the production of our labor as intellectuals may also alienate us from home communities: rising class status, assimilation, and institutionalization often strain those ties. The organic intellectual is forged not only through belonging to a social class but also through the thick-hot-molten force—the push-pull, in-out, here-there dance—of a radical in-betweenness that arises through our affective ties to multiple and often contradictory sites of power.[12]

A similar set of reservations leads Hortense Spillers, writing in response to invocations of the organic intellectual by Cornel West, to break up with "organicity" once and for all.[13] In a classic essay, Spillers sets herself the task of comparing the situation of African Americans in the mid-90s with their situation in the mid-60s, when Harold Cruse was writing his *Crisis of the Negro Intellectual*. What has happened since then? She begins: "Although African American intellectuals as a class have gained greater access to organs of public opinion and dissemination . . . " There follows a sequence of more "although" clauses ("although we can boast today a considerably larger black middle and upper-middle class"). The sequence goes on; and by allowing it to go on, Spillers almost seems to be indulging the idea that there has in fact been significant progress since the 60s. But her list of middle-class Black achievements since the 60s, inside the academy and out, bumps down hard at the same spot where Cook-Lynn does: "the news concerning the African American life-world generally is quite grim."[14] Is this conclusion an unavoidable acknowledgment of grim social facts? Does it chiefly express, in excess of those facts, Spillers's personal modesty? Perhaps it also reflects a *disciplinary* modesty, a collective tilt toward self-castigation. Spillers mentions "guilt over one's relative success" next to "profound delusion about one's capacity to lead the masses (of which, one supposes, it is certain that she is not herself one!")[15]

But what is most objectively disabling about the concept in Spillers's view is its fictitious idea of "the community" to which the organic intellectual supposedly remains or should remain bound. For Cruse, this community is a putative African American nation. Spillers doubts that such a nation has ever existed:

> The "organic intellectual" that we have imagined after Antonio Gramsci locates a romantic, liberated figure . . . who never really fructified and who remains a symptom of nostalgic yearning, looking back on a childhood perfected through the lens of distance and distortion.[16]

The community to which you imagine yourself linked is really just your idealized memory of your past, to which you *cannot* be bound in a way that has anything practical to do with the achievement of social justice in the changed circumstances of the present. To this Spillers adds, in a characteristically explosive footnote, a series of questions as to why the Gramscian model should be permitted to lay a responsibility on African American academics from which white academics are somehow exempt:

> What is the obligation of white intellectuals to their people? And why is the question never posed in that way, linking the white intellectual subject to "race"/ethnicity, since there seems to be incredible need for someone to tend this field? Or did 1968 take care of that?[17]

These questions sound like they don't expect answers. But they do not defy all possible rejoinders. My hypothesis here is that an effort to answer the first—that is, to affirm that non-Black intellectuals too have an obligation to "*their* people," and to specify the logic behind this obligation and clarify the possible expansiveness of "*their*"—might point toward a reconciliation of sorts with the Gramscian model, considered as an aspirational account of what teachers of the humanities might want to accomplish, and feel capable of accomplishing, not as citizens but (unfairly) merely in the course of their professional duties. Pushing harder, as Spillers urges, on the question of what the ferment in the university might have been organic *to*, and insisting very properly that we cannot be content to posit either a singular, delimited African American community or any version of community that places no responsibility on whites (or straight white males), we might find ourselves taking the revised, post-60s notion of the organic intellectual away from an exclusive or primary identification with identity and placing it on firmer ground.

The Norton Anthology of Theory and Criticism (2001), a much-visited monument to the institutionalization of the 60s and one possible bookend to Bate's *Criticism: The Major Texts*, thirty years earlier, makes the organic intellectual an emblem of that institutionalization.[18] In the introduction to its Gramsci section, the Norton editors describe the concept as follows:

> [O]rganic intellectuals rise out of membership in social groups (or classes) that have an antagonistic relationship to established institutions and official power. They "articulate" those groups' needs and aspirations, which have frequently gone unexpressed. The organic intellectual does not simply parrot preexisting group beliefs or demands but brings to the level of public speech what has not been officially recognized. While a given group does have certain tendencies, the process of articulation itself will shape it.[19]

In a characteristic post-60s move, class is here relativized; it is assumed that the organic intellectual can also be organic to collectivities other than classes.[20] What the organic intellectual does for and to those other collectivities, however, corresponds perfectly to the class-formative role that John Guillory observes, as we have seen, in his account of the critic/journalists of the eighteenth century: not merely reflecting or broadcasting the group's preexisting claims and values, but actively helping to articulate the group's consciousness, adapting that consciousness to the forces and opportunities it is facing, teaching it to exert and not merely contest power. The term comes up again in the Norton's selection from Stuart Hall (1932–2014), to whom the Norton might have offered some of the credit for this relativizing and to whom the term "organic intellectual" could plausibly be applied. But the only example of the organic intellectual the anthology offers, according to the index, is Edward W. Said (1935–2003). "In some sense," the editors write, "Edward Said fulfills the definition of an 'organic intellectual'—to use the phrase of the Italian Marxist philosopher Antonio Gramsci, one of Said's intellectual heroes—developing his criticism of Western representations of Arab culture and his advocacy for the rights of Palestinians out of his personal roots."[21]

There is a problem here, and its name is "personal roots." Personal roots were an attractive and perhaps inevitable way of putting Said's then-audacious positions across to a reading public that was and is especially timid in those areas, like US policy in the Middle East, where Said was most passionately engaged. For that public, Said's criticism of Western representations of Arab culture and his advocacy for the rights of his fellow Palestinians will perhaps make the most sense, or incur the least hostility, if seen through the mollifying lens of his familial and geographical background. After all, your identity is something you are stuck with, not something you choose. It is what it is. Yet to suggest that his roots offer a satisfactory explanation of Said's commitments, as the Norton does, is to give a very misleading idea of what it means to call him, or anyone, an organic intellectual. Roots talk makes it seem impossible to maintain that critics as such—most of whom had very different roots and many of whom did not "have" roots at all in the sense of being unmistakably and pejoratively marked—might also be considered organic. The implication is that, once the category is expanded, race and ethnicity are substitutes for class—in other words, you had to be a Palestinian, or the equivalent thereof. You did not qualify unless you belonged by birth to an embattled or disadvantaged racial or ethnic minority. This is much too simple.

"As he remarked in an interview," the editors add, qualifying their heavy reliance on Said's identity, "he has always experienced his identity as complicated. . . .": true, but the complications mentioned—for example, that Said was trained "as a Western scholar educated in the British tradition"[22]—did not pertain merely to Said as an individual, or indeed to his personal attachment to the British literary tradition. The complications are a natural consequence of the multiplicity of identities that defined the 60s movements. And if they make the "romance" with the organic intellectual so "vexed," as Carrillo Rowe puts it, they also keep the romance alive. They do so by being irreducible to any one identity, any one set of injustices and disadvantages.

Consider how Carrillo Rowe makes the term "organic intellectual" intersect with the word "intersectional." Carrillo Rowe's list of identities includes being middle class and being educated. It includes being educated in the United States, and being educated in poststructuralism, which presumably

stands in here for the paradox that the most advanced, obscure, and prestigious ideas the imperial metropolis has to offer are also the most subversive
of the metropolis's authority. She is very clear about this when she speaks of
"affective ties to multiple and often contradictory sites of power." The term
"intersectionality" is sometimes understood to imply adding further forms of
oppression to an existing set of oppressions, the point being that an increase
in quantity turns into a new and distinct quality of oppressiveness. But that
is not what Carrillo Rowe seems to mean by it, and it is certainly not what
she is doing when she juxtaposes, for example, her Indigeneity with her status as an educated member of the middle class. She is also adding forms of
privilege. And whether or not she explicitly presents them as such, we should
understand these forms of privilege as informing as well as complicating her
"radical (be)longings." The parenthetical neologism makes a useful point.
Longings, however radical they may be, cannot be separated off entirely from
the comforts or the empoweredness of belonging.

Intersectionality is a direct legacy of the long 1960s. The term was coined
by legal scholar Kimberlé Crenshaw in 1989, but as Keeanga-Yamahtta Taylor
observes, it was the Combahee River Collective, formed in 1974, that articulated "the analysis that animates the meaning of intersectionality, the idea
that multiple oppressions reinforce each other to create new categories of suffering."[23] As noted above, the idea "the multiple oppressions reinforce each
other" is one major way in which the word is used. It also seems to be what
Barbara Smith, one of the CRC's members, has in mind, looking back:

> "What we were saying is that we have a right as people who are not just female,
> who are not solely Black, who are not just lesbians, who are not just working
> class, or workers—that we are people who embody all of these identities, and
> we have a right to build and define political theory and practice based upon
> that reality."[24]

But the crucial twist, which gives emotional substance to the abstract phrase
"political theory and practice," comes almost as an afterthought.

> "We didn't mean that if you're not like us, you're nothing. We were not saying
> that we didn't care about anybody who wasn't exactly like us . . . it would be
> really boring only to do political work with people who are exactly like me."[25]

The list of identities is most interesting and most useful, in other words, if
it's seen as an invitation to do political work with people who are not exactly

like oneself—people whose lists of politically pertinent identifying factors might well be shorter or just wildly different. From this perspective, the listing of multiple identities is not a way of accumulating further points so that the most legitimate political agent becomes the one who scores highest in an oppression derby. It can involve subtraction as well as addition: for example, the way the privilege of having benefited from higher education might take something away from the total quantity of oppression carried by person X in spite of person X being, say, Black and female. Other additions and subtractions are of course possible, but the general rule is not a matter of arithmetic: no one form of oppression, no one form of identity, can be granted absolute political authority. There are no winners; there is no oppression derby. Properly understood, intersectionality would therefore involve both a mobilizing of oppression and a *relativizing* of oppression. And in the concept's post-60s articulation, the same is true for the organicity of the organic intellectual. The formula is not solidarity with the suffering of one's own.

Edward Said is not usually thought of as a 60s person. The student protests at Columbia in 1968 and 1969 were not formative experiences for him; by then he was already in his mid-thirties and a faculty member. In 1968, as it happens, when antiwar protests broke out and students occupied Columbia's administration buildings, he was on a research fellowship in Illinois. When he got back to New York, according to biographer Timothy Brennan, he "was one of only a handful of professors . . . to support the national student strike, sponsored by Students for a Democratic Society (SDS), against the elections that year, agreeing not to hold classes on campus in solidarity. His take on the college Left, however, was complicated."[26] Expressing various "gripes with the student protesters,"[27] Said defended the autonomy of the university. "He took the position of many other faculty that despite the obvious justice of the students' demands, intellectual life should not be disrupted."[28]

As noted earlier, two of the things Said valued most highly in Jonathan Swift, the subject of a book he planned (the plan got him the fellowship to the University of Illinois) but never completed, were Swift's willingness to expend his combative energies on the controversies of his moment without worrying about what posterity would or would not understand of his writings once his enemies were dead and the battles forgotten, and his horror at organized violence, a consistent and politically inconvenient antimilitarism. Both appreciations encourage us to place Said's criticism in the combative context of the 1960s. If the 1960s were the period of "theory," of which Said was an early advocate, they were also the period of outrage against American militarism in Vietnam and elsewhere. Said was "transfixed," the biography tells us, by Noam Chomsky's essay "The Responsibility of Intellectuals," a passionate protest against American foreign aggression that came out in *The New York Review of Books* in 1967.[29]

Said's enthusiasm for that essay led to personal friendship as well as political solidarity between the two men; Chomsky was the first person to read the initial draft of *Orientalism*. Chomsky's essay, which has been described as the period's most influential piece of antiwar writing, offered a theory of the intellectual that emerged from, and commented on, the protest movements of the 60s. Commentators on those movements, Chomsky writes, were puzzled by the question of what motivated them, "what has made students and junior faculty 'go left' . . . amid general prosperity and under liberal, welfare state administrations. . . . Since these young people are well off, have good futures, etc.," Chomsky says, paraphrasing Irving Kristol, "their protest must be irrational. It must be the result of boredom, of too much security, or something of this sort."[30] In short, the protesters are privileged. Chomsky ignores the question of their motivation, but he does not ignore or deny the privilege. On the contrary, he makes their privileges definitive of who they are and—more important—he makes them intrinsic to their responsibilities.

> Intellectuals are in a position to expose the lies of governments, to analyze actions according to their causes and motives and often hidden intentions. In the Western world at least, they have the power that comes from political liberty, from access to information and freedom of expression. For a privileged minority, Western democracy provides the leisure, the facilities, and the training to seek the truth.[31]

The responsibility of the intellectual is a direct function of "the unique privileges that intellectuals enjoy."[32]

The "unique privileges that intellectuals enjoy" come from being "in position," as Chomsky puts it, or from a certain mode of belonging—to the West, to the United States, to the university, all entities that possess power and pass it on to their members. Belonging was antithetical to Said's own theory of the intellectual. For Said, the intellectual was supposed to speak unwelcome truths to power, not to share in power. Belonging anywhere was a symptom of fatal compromise with empowered institutions. In his theoretical statements, Said championed, instead, the detached and unhoused exile, the heroically independent outsider, the oppositional voice of unceasing and unsparing scrutiny. In *Representations of the Intellectual*, he mentions Gramsci's concept of the organic intellectual, but he presents it, misleadingly, as a critical diagnosis of how intellectuals sell out to powerful institutions:

> [G]roups of individuals are aligned with institutions and derive power and authority from those institutions. As the institutions either rise or fall in ascendancy, so too do their organic intellectuals, to use Antonio Gramsci's serviceable phrase for them.[33]

This is a very partial interpretation. Positive ideas of serving, being accountable to, and helping to shape a constituency, ideas that correspond to the lesson Gramsci is usually understood to be deriving from the experience of other classes and offering as a model to aspiring intellectuals of the working class, have no place in Said's theory. Said cites Chomsky's essay of protest against the Vietnam War twenty-five years earlier, but when he does so he celebrates his friend as an amateur bravely taking on the credentialed, sold-out experts. This is not wrong. But nothing is said about how, for Chomsky, the intellectuals' privileges are bestowed by their institutional belonging and their responsibilities follow from their privileges.

It is Chomsky's implicit theory of the intellectual, however—his linking of the antiwar protests of the 1960s to the relative prosperity of the United States in that moment and to an insider's epistemological privileges in a time of war—that better fits Said's own extraordinary practice as an intellectual and the example it continues to set. With his privileged perch at Columbia—not to mention his comfortable family background, his classical tastes in music, and his high-end Anglophile clothing—it was inevitable that Said would be charged with elitism.

From Chomsky's perspective, which is to say from the perspective of the Vietnam War and the protests against it, this charge loses much of its sting. What is referred to as elitism would have to be seen rather as preconditions of intellectual responsibility: on the one hand, epistemological privilege, on the other, a necessary acceptance of the limits of democracy in the presence of military aggression. After all, what authority could democracy claim over the bombing in Southeast Asia? Those on whom the bombs were falling had not been consulted; they had not been offered an opportunity to vote on whether or not they should be bombed. Then as now, the relevant unit of democracy did not extend beyond the borders of the aggressor nation. But in order for democracy to be entitled to pronounce authoritatively on the subject, the potential victims of the bombing would have to enjoy full voting rights. Within the aggressor nation, military violence against distant others might well have received overwhelming electoral endorsement. But what was that endorsement worth? As mentioned above, the commitment to antimilitarism, coming out of Said's early indignation at war in Vietnam and renewed periodically by new American bombings and invasions in the Middle East and elsewhere, was nourished throughout Said's life by American military, economic, and diplomatic support for Israeli aggression against the Palestinians. *None of this military violence was unpopular in the United States.* None of it could be described, within the framework of American democracy, as undemocratic. In resisting American or Israeli militarism, Said could not depend on support from an upswelling of Orwellian "decency" on the part of the "common man"—this is surely one reason why Said had no time for Orwell. (And why he did make time for a strong appreciation of Swift, despite Swift's conservative politics.) Nor could he depend on the American working class, however unjustly and disproportionately that class was called upon to put itself in harm's way.

The legitimation of literary studies, now concentrating its energies on collectivities both smaller and larger than the nation, may eventually depend on stretching the public's understanding of democracy so that those other forms of belonging begin to be seen as legitimate—as legitimate and as natural as the culture of the nation once seemed.

Chomsky does not quite say that you don't get antimilitarism, or solidarity with US militarism's remote third-world victims, without a certain degree of education and prosperity—that is, without a certain privilege. But that is the implication. The uncomfortable idea can be entertained without pretending that the antiwar left or the draft-age students who were its foot soldiers were somehow definitive of the 60s protest movements. They weren't. The antiwar movement was merely one movement among others. Equally distorting, however, would be any account of 60s protest that, excluding antimilitarism (or the anticolonial and environmental movements), would present the identity constituencies (race, gender, sexuality, disability, and so on) as representative. Such a picture would be distorting in particular with regard to the concept of the organic intellectual. If that concept takes for granted, in the Norton anthology's words, an "antagonistic relationship to established institutions," it cannot be rescued for the post-60s era merely by demanding, say, that whiteness, straightness, and maleness should also be considered marked constituencies. Those categories have lost some of their privileged unmarkedness, and that's a good thing. But whiteness, straightness, and maleness don't explain antagonism to established institutions, and without that antagonism the concept is blind. Identity is not enough to give it proper vision. In Said's case, as I have described it, the antagonism—which of course is shared by many who are not male or straight or white—has to do with military aggression. In other cases, it might be provoked by the destruction of the environment and the complicity of established institutions with that destruction. If the concept of the organic intellectual can maintain its usefulness, it's by extending its reach beyond matters of identity.

To return to Hortense Spillers: it must be assumed that responsibility does not fall exclusively on Black intellectuals to concern themselves with the interests of a Black constituency. There are enough interests to go around, many of them overlapping different identity classifications and "their" peoples. As Said, Chomsky, and the Vietnam-era protests suggest, organic intellectuals don't require a personal relation to a specifiable identity. The concept of the organic intellectual can flourish, well past its Gramscian heyday, without identity serving as a sole, definitive post-60s replacement for class.

Grievance and Governance

Said's well-to-do background and high-end training were sometimes taken to explain his loyalty to the Western canon. But as Brennan suggests, class background works just as well as an explanation for the opposite position: the puzzling anti-Westernism expressed by many of the postcolonial critics who followed in *Orientalism*'s wake. Non-European scholars "from South Asia, Latin America, and the Middle East," Brennan says, many of whom "migrated to the metropolitan university in part because of the openings Said had created" in the new field of postcolonial studies, were "often from well-to-do families with political connections."[34] Though this was also Said's socio-economic profile, he did not share in the postcolonial elite's "general loathing for a Western entity dubbed 'modernity.'"[35]

Rather than asking why Said did not share that loathing, it seems more interesting to ask why there has been so much loathing in the first place? By making a blanket condemnation of the West (where most had been trained) or the Enlightenment (which provided most of their intellectual tools, including a critique of colonialism), third-world elites distracted attention from their materially privileged, quasi-aristocratic status in their countries of origin. This enabled them to stake a claim to represent those countries as undivided wholes. Divisions between landowners (often their own families) and the peasants who worked their lands, for example, could be conveniently forgotten, as if the nation's rich and poor were somehow magically united against the West by virtue of a national essence. The implication was that the rich too had a grievance, and an equal grievance. Third-world elites also strengthened their claim to represent anticolonial resistance by assuming (just as deceptively) that this resistance was otherwise entirely absent from the (white) metropolis. Thus the metropolis needed people like them; it had no anticolonial critics of its own.[36] Such claims would look flagrantly absurd, or worse, if much attention was paid to the claimants' class or caste origins back home, or for that matter if their subaltern compatriots back home were asked how they might feel about obtaining, say, human rights or modern plumbing or welfare safety nets or other benefits, however precarious, of the loathed Western modernity. This diagnosis of elite non-Western identity politics is already there in the "Pitfalls of National Consciousness" chapter of Frantz Fanon's *The Wretched of the Earth*.[37] One thing Said was telling the anti-modernity critics—when, like Fanon, he gave his qualified approval to the term "humanism"—was that they were much less representative than they claimed to be.

If the legacy of the 60s is understood first and foremost as identity politics, Brennan's analysis of postcolonial criticism, which takes identity politics as a function of class position, becomes a backhanded swipe at the 60s. Grounds of complaint exist. The charge of elitism is not unfounded. The argument I make above comes uncomfortably close to a version of *noblesse oblige*. Yet that charge would not discredit the legacy of the 60s, even in a time of ruination when to many the ebullience of that decade must seem almost incomprehensible. It's true that class was not at the top of the 60s agenda. (When Spillers asks whether 1968 "took care" of the question of what obligation white intellectuals have to their own people, she seems to be hinting that this question came off the agenda because the movements of that year alienated the white working class. Whatever the answer, Spillers gives an accurate sense of how the social landscape looked.) Nor was class central to the founding texts of postcolonial criticism.

By the third decade of the twenty-first century, however, class is very much on the agenda of postcolonial critics. Gayatri Chakravorty Spivak, who since the 1980s has been heroically highlighting the non-European critic's class and caste privilege, is no longer so isolated in that indispensable enterprise. The need to work an interrogation of systemic inequality into the routine of cultural interpretation may not be universally acknowledged, but it *is* acknowledged; such interpretation has become a highly valued practice among those who deal with non-European texts, a solid part of the discipline's common sense. According to Google Ngram, references to B. R. Ambedkar, fearless critic of the Indian caste system and champion of the so-called untouchables (Dalits), did not take off until more than a decade after his death in 1956, and the most dramatic spike in citations occurred after 2010. This is not hard proof, but it is certainly suggestive of what impressionistically seems to be in the air: as academic interest in the world outside Europe moves beyond its formative focus on European colonialism, highly educated critics from countries outside Europe and North America are coming to pay serious attention to the system that makes those critics themselves *un*representative of their countries of origin.[38]

It is tempting to conclude, therefore, that the most pertinent legacy of the 60s movements in the university is not the content of those movements, but rather a dynamic of democratic inclusiveness that has transcended the limits of those movements (including their relative hostility to the white working class) and gradually forced class onto criticism's to-do list.[39] Whether this is the logic that resuscitated class or not—other explanations are possible, including financial crises and the devastating collapse of the academic job market—it raises the same question raised by the rumblings of change within postcolonial studies as it threatens to mutate into world literature or into a field as yet unnamed: the question of the interests and purposes of the university, considered not as a passive recipient of outsider grievances but as an active agent.

Let us assume that the true legacy of the 1960s is not, after all, the university's surrender to the demands of formerly marginalized constituencies for greater representation. Let us assume further that, like Said, those constituencies did not demand the blowing up of a Western tradition seen as fatally sexist, racist, and so on. It would seem to follow that what criticism inherits from the 60s movements is a series of unresolved debates and, to the extent that those debates have been resolved, creative compromises in which both grieving identities and the discipline's own practices have been, and continue to be, reinvented. The reinventions would include the discipline's recent recovery of interest in class. The extent to which this process is a model for similar processes outside the university is hard to estimate; what seems undeniable is that it is a part of those wider processes and, based on the publicity these issues receive, is recognized as such. And it is certain that the university must be considered an active agent in those processes.

The academy's choices have never been limited to surrendering to outside political pressures or else defending its institutional autonomy. To think of the university as ever entirely self-sufficient or self-governing is to idealize a much more checkered history. The founding of institutions like Stanford University or the University of Chicago did not rely on the world's cleanest money. With regard to the humanities at least, it would seem more accurate to propose that the university is a site where contesting claims to representation are adjudicated, and contesting versions of collectivity are fashioned, scrutinized, and tested out. By its participation in this activity, moreover, the university would be laying an implicit claim for its own significance to the society around it. This proposition would explain one sense in which academics can legitimately be thought of as doing what Gramsci expected of organic intellectuals: they do not merely convey or reflect the values of their constituencies, but actively help to shape them in relation to the values and constituencies around them. If Gramsci remains relevant in this context, we could say that yes, this is part of the larger and longer process by which a new constellation of constituencies and movements learns how to cohere so as to eventually (one hopes) govern and govern differently—a process that of course can't yet be verified, as it obviously remains very unfinished.

Does it sound absurdly idealistic to maintain that, rather than merely reflecting passively the values of the society around it, the university also works to shape those values by bringing them to fuller articulation? If so, the same point can be made in much less idealistic terms. It seems obvious enough that teaching the imperial history of Rome, once upon a time, and asking students to imitate the rhetorical tropes and strategies of the Roman governing class, served to teach the future officers of the British empire useful lessons about how to rule. (As I argue above, this is a strong counterargument against the Bourdieu-inspired position that the contents of education are arbitrary and that all that really matters is the credentials conferred and the restricting of the numbers of those who receive them.) But if we have no trouble seeing the apparatus of education as a tool of the ruling class, it should not be so very hard to see that same apparatus as an object whose usage might at certain moments be disputed between those who rule and those who aspire to replace them, even if those who might seem most motivated to replace them do not tend to recognize themselves in that aspiration.

In 1970, the claim of the humanities to social significance still rested mainly on the function of preserving and transmitting the cultural heritage of the nation or the West. (Then as now, the West was not always clearly distinguished from the nation.) This function is both literally and metaphorically conservative. Gramsci assigns it to the traditional intellectuals, not the organic intellectuals. When it begins to be widely accepted (partly because of the academy's new demographics) that the West systematically maligned and mistreated the peoples of the non-West, as argued in Said's *Orientalism* in 1978, that claim to social significance comes to look unreliable.

One might have expected, then, that the goal of preserving and transmitting the cultural heritage would be thrown out and replaced. That didn't happen. Why not? For one thing, it is unclear what might have replaced that claim to social significance. It could hardly be replaced by, say, a chorus of complaints about the West's bad behavior. However justified and important such complaints might be, no quantity of them would add up to another, better claim to social significance, especially in the society they were complaining about. For another thing, work in postcolonial studies fell with shocking ease into a familiar scenario: it too was all about the preservation and transmission of culture, if now a collection of different cultures. For postcolonial scholars trained within literary studies, it was hard *not* to assume that a (native) culture has been violated (by European colonialism) and is thereby threatened with extinction. This scenario duplicates the already existing, exclusively Western narrative on which literature departments were largely founded: the narrative according to which history is in the process of destroying the European cultural heritage, which unless rescued will disappear without a trace, leaving modern citizens wandering in a consumerist, value-deprived, tech-obsessed wasteland. What better rationale for the existence of a cadre of intellectuals charged with preserving and transmitting the cultural heritage than this view of the linear, destructive power of history? Substituting "colonialism" or "the West" for "history" in general (not a difficult substitution), the same rationale works equally well for non-European intellectuals. And for scholars of ethnic studies, of course. They too have cultural heritages to rescue or protect, whether from the mainstream's neglect and marginalization or on the contrary from absorption and obliteration. They too have an obligation to preserve and transmit.

But what exactly were they supposed to preserve and transmit?

To judge from the anxieties that accompanied the founding of the subfield of Jewish American literature, this question is not as straightforward as it might seem. As Benjamin Schreier shows in *The Rise and Fall of Jewish American Literature: Ethnic Studies and the Challenge of Identity*, observers worried that the successful assimilation of American Jews into the American mainstream in the decades after World War II would mean the impossibility of identifying Jewish American literature as a legitimate field.[40] They had assumed the field would take as its object the culture of Yiddish-speaking, eastern European immigrants. But as the hardships of the immigrant experience receded from the consciousness of American Jews along with an identity primarily derived from the Yiddish language and Orthodox Judaism, uncertainty as to what Jewish American literature was supposed to be about became pressing and uncomfortable. Would the field be closed down? Should it be? It would be unwise to assume that only budget-conscious administrators consider the possibility that a field might have lost its rationale. Commenting on Kenneth W. Warren's *What Was African American Literature?*, Schreier notes a parallel: each field, supposedly erected on the foundation of a firm and self-evident identity, is in fact precarious, and the reason is that the ground beneath it is subject to seismic historical shifts. Warren argues, Schreier says,

> that what we now know as "African American literature" was a postemancipation phenomenon, taking shape in the context of a "challenge to the enforcement and justification of racial subordination and exploitation represented by Jim Crow," and that its "coherence," since "the legal demise of Jim Crow," has "eroded."[41]

For Warren, appeals to "African traditions or the experience of slavery and the Middle Passage" to make up for this missing coherence are mere symptoms of the field's crisis, not a cure for it.[42] Warren concludes, with some asperity, that "African American literature as a distinct entity would seem to be at an end."[43] Once you accept that "African American literature is not a transhistorical entity," the field is, in both senses, without an object.[44]

Schreier is more positive about his field than Warren is about his: "rather than a nihilistic dead end for scholarship," he says, the "critical knowledge" he brings should be seen as "an invitation to imagine an alternative future for Jewish studies liberated from the reactionary restrictions of ethnologic,"[45] or liberated from being "about" Jewish Americans. If the field can abandon its commitment to aboutness, it can and should survive. But one is obliged to wonder whether the field *deserves* to survive if it is not doing the socially valued work of representation. Does every field, once established, deserve to survive forever? Warren certainly doesn't think so. Why does any object of knowledge deserve a field of its own? Why do certain people and certain objects of interest *get* fields, while others don't? What gives a field the right to exist in the first place? It may seem irresponsible even to pose such questions, given the visible eagerness of the university's money people to seize upon any and all excuses to defund, consolidate, and even dissolve existing humanities fields. And yet we cannot expect to offer a better account of an existing field unless we can speak to the primal question of why *any* field deserves to exist, a question that cannot be properly addressed unless it is assumed that they may *not* deserve to exist. And this is especially true, if also especially treacherous, in the case of those highly precarious, perpetually underfunded fields, as in ethnic studies, that only came into existence in the last half century.

The details of Warren's argument seem open to question. Despite the legal transformation that brought the Jim Crow era to an end, the majority of the African American population continued (and continues) to experience systemic racialized inequality, and this continuity—mass incarceration, police brutality, unequal monetary incomes, unequal inherited wealth, unequal health outcomes, and so on—arguably overrides the change in legal status, important as that was. If the collective experience is still there, it's too soon to decommission the field. That said, however, Warren's argument remains a valuable guide to ethnic studies in general. If Jewish American literature, say, made sense as a field during the period of immigration (fueled by anti-Semitism) and assimilation (both blocked and shaped by anti-Semitism), and if African American literature made sense during the period of Jim Crow (or, in my view, beyond it), it would seem to follow that the key lies in something that those two periods have in common and that offers, or offered, the two fields a similar means of legitimation.

The most obvious common factor is something like (on this subject it is hard not to speak crudely) the representation of hardship, a collective experience of suffering and injustice. If the threat of (or call for) the field's disappearance comes from the withdrawal of that factor—legalization in the case of African American studies, assimilation in the case of Jewish American literature—then one can speculate that there is a general principle at work here. The case for the field's existence does not rest, as one might think, merely on collective ethnic experience *as such*. That would make it a specialization for specialization's sake, an empty formality. The case depends on the representation (call it the preservation and transmission) of a collective ethnic experience, but more precisely a collective experience that violates democratic norms or rules, demands to be factored into a democracy's self-understanding, and therefore makes an urgent claim on that democracy's attention.

This is more than a case for specialization. It is more than a story of diversity denied and then recognized. To found a field on diversity as such (now the empty slogan of the corporations) is not to give it a firm foundation. A field like Native American studies does not emerge because of brute political pressure alone, exerted from a certain demographic and surrendered to by the university. The story must be told, from the opposite end, as the university's embrace and application of a principle that the humanities need not disavow: democracy's own imperative to recognize and understand the experience of collective suffering and injustice, an undertaking in which the university has a special role to play.

If the content of the cultural heritage is not a unique ethnic identity but a historical experience of collective suffering and injustice (much of it probably shared with other groups and other fields); and if *that* is what keeps the field in the business of cultural preservation and transmission; and if it is the fear of losing that claim to the country's attention that shakes the field's raison d'être to its core, then one conclusion that follows is that the case for the study of the national culture laid out by Bill Readings (discussed in the last chapter) is not dead after all. It survives on at least two and perhaps three different scales. First, each ethnicity functions as a mini-nation, making its own version of the case for the preservation and transmission of a cultural heritage. Aboutness has not been phased out; it still works for subnational collectivities. That case is by no means rendered inoperative by globalization, as Readings suggests; on the contrary, it continues to justify the study of culture in much the same terms as the nation-state did, but on a smaller scale.[46]

But second, this rationale also gets a new lease on life at the scale of the nation, as before. The incorporation of ethnic studies offers evidence that the modern nation-state has dealt successfully (or less successfully) with the injustices of its past by welcoming (or not) better representation for its victims. This evidence could of course also strengthen that state and boost the nationalism that goes with it, now reconceived as a proudly multicultural but perhaps no less militarily aggressive project. Aside from the obvious fear that ethnic and racial minorities would see what is distinctive about them absorbed into a larger identity and thus erased or deactivated, there is also the perceived danger that a national policy of multiculturalism will serve the purposes of what Schreier calls "an expansive Americanism."[47] That perception seems to be behind the angry rejection of "liberal" multiculturalism, for example by the would-be founders of another recent subfield, critical ethnic studies.[48] I leave aside for the moment the possibility, alluded to by Schreier, that so-called pan-ethnicities might extend this set of concerns from the subnational and the national to an international scale.

The point here is not to decide whether ethnic studies as a collective enterprise is too patriotic or on the contrary not patriotic enough. The point is that in staging this controversy, the discipline as a whole has been asking socially useful questions: socially useful to existing democracy, for those who think existing democracy can be reformed; and socially useful to those who identify with ethnic studies, whose participation in the controversy can be translated, in Gramscian terms, as preparation for the future role of governing a democracy that might well be quite different from the one we have.

6 The Historical and the Transhistorical

In his celebrated riff on Klee's painting *Angelus Novus*, Walter Benjamin imagines the angel of history:

> His face is turned toward the past. Where we perceive a chain of events, he sees one single catastrophe, which keeps piling wreckage on wreckage and hurls it in front of his feet. The angel would like to stay, awaken the dead, and make whole what has been smashed. But a storm is blowing from Paradise; it has got caught in his wings with such force that the angel can no longer close them. This storm irresistibly propels him into the future to which his back is turned, while the pile of debris before him grows skyward. This storm is what we call progress.[1]

Over the last half century, no single passage has better captured Anglophone criticism's attitude toward history. (Its incompatibility with Fredric Jameson's less poetic but also much quoted "Always historicize!" seems to have gone unnoticed.) According to Google Ngram, usage of the phrase "angel of history" has risen precipitously since 1980, and it keeps rising. Invocations of Benjamin's angel tend to feel like political position-takings, and not just because Benjamin, arguably the most brilliant and influential left-wing critic of the twentieth century, would fall victim to the fascist storm around him soon after writing that famous paragraph. And yet his reading of Klee is a problem for anyone committed to the proposition that criticism is or should be a political activity. For progressives, politics has to be about changing our collective situation for the better. It is not a coincidence that the word "progressive" has progress in it. Nor should that be an embarrassment. What could a progressive politics be that did not in some way seek collective change for the better—seek progress, that is, considered not as an article of faith but simply as a nonnegotiable object of aspiration? Critics who quote Benjamin, however, tend to dismiss progress as naïve, complacent, illusory.

There are reasonable grounds for this dismissal. Anyone who takes progress as an object of aspiration will also look for evidence that progress has actually occurred; if it has never happened in the past, why believe it is possible in the future? Any such evidence can always be met with countervailing evidence of ways in which change has been unsatisfactory, or worse. Yet that countering move is suspiciously automatic, and its predictability suggests that not all of the grounds for rejecting progress have been fully thought through. One, already discussed, is built into the infrastructure of disciplinary specialization: criticism's founding assumption that the cultural heritage is threatened—threatened by the movement of history or soulless techno-rationality or merely the passage of time; the precise cause can be left undetermined. If it is threatened, it must be rescued.

By assuming that culture must be rescued from history, critics bestow on themselves the heroic role of rescuers. Their desire is nothing less than the angel's desire "to awaken the dead," and the desire becomes a mandate. At the level of what might be called its deep unconscious, then, or to the extent that it has one, the operational truth of the discipline is anti-progressive, and this despite the explicit politics of its members, which more often than not (and by virtue of the same assumption that history is going in the wrong direction!) are demonstrably progressive. Too often the result tends to be political judgments that are predictably and uninspiringly negative. (Here my argument overlaps briefly but uncomfortably with that of the "limits of critique" school.) Critics do not seem anxious enough that they will be perceived as playing holier than thou. Speaking in the name of unrealized virtue, they feel authorized to see as blameworthy whatever *has* been realized. In one sense or another, of course, history always *is* blameworthy. But the discipline is not putting its time to good use by repeating the point over and over, allowing it to take over the framing of statements that, with a minor shift in emphasis, might have something more interesting to report. The result is not merely the dismissal of progress as a self-satisfied triumphalist meta-narrative, but hostility or indifference toward any putative achievement, however minor, that someone has had the temerity to claim as a step forward. In this sense, criticism and politics, which the influence of the 60s seemed to join so fully and so controversially, have not always pulled in the same direction.

Benjamin's view of history is messianic/catastrophist: its assumption is that history is so grotesquely awful that we can only be redeemed from it by the coming of a messiah, a force from outside and above history. In the English-speaking world, this historical vision is itself a phenomenon of this period; the Klee passage, though written in early 1940, wasn't translated into English until the fateful year 1968. I have already associated the 60s movements with another, equally distinctive attitude to the past: the so-called historicist/contextualist paradigm. More on this below. In the meantime, I have to speculate about how the discipline has been able to pledge itself both to that paradigm—call it, accentuating its internal tension, progressive pluralism—and to a Benjaminian common sense about history as an unmitigated catastrophe. In at least two respects—the pluralism of perspectives and the orientation toward a more desirable future—progressive pluralism looks like the antithesis of the "one single catastrophe" witnessed by Benjamin's angel. Yet in practice the two have managed a sort of strategic compromise. They have tended to converge in the shared affect of melancholy. From the vantage point of the new ethnic studies, the "one single catastrophe" can be understood to sum up a vast, almost infinite collection of individual catastrophes, each moment of suffering and injustice demanding to be remembered in its particularity. Like Benjamin's angel, this memory project has its back turned to the future. Progress, which had seemed intrinsic to the project of ethnic studies, now disappears. Consider the minority melancholy that pervades the critical ethnic studies project, outlined above, or Roderick Ferguson's Foucauldian take, which presents the fields of ethnic studies as "'a new form of biopower organized around the affirmation, recognition, and legitimacy of minoritized life.'"[2] From this angle, what looks like democratic reform is really just another mode of domination. (With Foucault, isn't it always?) Ferguson's Foucauldianism gives an individual twist to a structure of feeling that is much more broadly shared: the unhappy assurance that the institutional recognition of ethnic minorities must be what the institution wants, and what the dark powers behind the institution want, rather than what the minorities themselves ever wanted. Though many of their members will recall that once upon a time they did want something much like what they got, if also more of it than that, and that they had to overcome serious resistance in order to get it.

Optimism is conventionally accorded to the will, not to the intellect. The astute will always come up with good reasons to support the more melancholic view. In the third decade of the twenty-first century, young people may well feel they are living on the precarious scree slope of Benjamin's pile of wreckage, trying to keep their balance as the debris tumbles down around them and the mountain grows ever skyward, while they also watch earlier generations, blessed with employment and health care, who can afford to direct their attention elsewhere. The apocalyptic imagination of planetary destruction in Lars von Trier's 2011 film *Melancholia* finds an obvious justification in the context of global warming, which makes the colliding-planets premise seem less outlandish. Melancholy joins up with queer theory in Lee Edelman's influential *No Future*. For Edelman, the future is inescapably imagined in heteronormative terms:

> [P]olitics, however radical the means by which specific constituencies attempt to produce a more desirable social order, remains, at its core, conservative insofar as it works to affirm a structure, to authenticate social order, which it then intends to transmit to the future in the form of its inner Child. That Child remains the perpetual horizon of every acknowledged politics, the fantasmatic beneficiary of every political intervention.[3]

If what we act for is the children, then better not to act at all. This entails a refusal of

> history as linear narrative (the poor man's teleology) in which meaning succeeds in revealing itself—as itself—through time. Far from partaking of this narrative movement toward a viable political future, far from perpetuating the fantasy of meaning's eventual realization, the queer comes to figure the bar to every realization of futurity, the resistance to every social structure or form.[4]

Afropessimism is another notable example of a 60s-descended critical school structured around a melancholic refusal of progress past, present, or to come.[5]

Yes, we know we are living in the shadow of systemic racism, climate change, and other calamities. But before we critics signed on to excruciating but necessary self-periodizations like the Anthropocene and the Capitalocene, criticism's default position was already melancholic. It's as if at its founding the discipline had collectively pledged to preserve in perpetuity an archive of irreducible and incurable trauma. Denunciations of what is called liberal multiculturalism, whether in queer theory or in ethnic studies, are no doubt justified in suspecting the motives of liberal capitalism, or neoliberalism, in dividing austerity's potentially rebellious electorate into siloed, non-communicating identities.

But the cross-field pervasiveness and the somewhat ritualistic tone of these denunciations suggest a more obscure logic, and one that does not depend on a (properly jaundiced) view of racism, homophobia, or capitalist ideology since the 1970s. How could a collective affirmation and recognition of minorities possibly represent progress, the logic seems to go, when each racial, ethnic, or sexual minority has its own unique identity, unique experience of oppression, and unique demands? And each follows its own unique trajectory? Lisa Lowe argues paradigmatically that "differences of nation, language, religion, gender, race, and class" make it absurd to imagine an "individual moving in a linear fashion through a single, stable social totality."[6] If history is made up of differences, each of those different identities itself potentially subdivided into further differences, then there is no way of measuring linear movement in any direction, let alone of gathering up the distinct histories into something like a collective history.

Minority melancholy is clearly its own thing. And yet, as I have been suggesting, the melancholy of difference also fits comfortably within the already established melancholy of the critical mainstream, the professionally energizing melancholy of the critic/rescuer. It might be explained, that is, as the outcome of the compromise that an ethnic minority makes when, after winning a series of exhausting battles in its campaign for more democratic representation, it finds itself at last having achieved a foothold in the academy and then, rather than celebrating a victory, adopts, perhaps against its better judgment, the melancholy that was already the discipline's house style. By this compromise ethnic studies gains a convenient appearance of academic disinterestedness. That is not a negligible advantage. What it sacrifices, on the other hand, is the political energy that got it into the academy in the first place. It loses a sense of political direction that might make sense of—that is, provide a meaningful goal for—the collective experience and cultural heritage that ethnic studies exists, at least in part, to preserve and transmit.

The previous chapter began with the Native Critics Collective's suggestion that, in the period from the 1960s through the 1980s, the victories that Native Americans won for themselves inside the academy were roughly matched by political progress outside the academy, at the level of federal legislation.

Something is lost, for ethnic studies and for criticism in general, when this side of the 60s legacy is forgotten.[7]

Awakening the Dead

For critics, Benjamin's image of accelerating human unhappiness is not itself an unhappy image. Its melancholy, as remarked above, is also empowering. It presents critics as capable of doing, after their fashion, what even the superhuman powers of the angel cannot manage. The angel cannot awaken the dead or make whole what has been smashed. But metaphorically speaking, critics *do* awaken the dead. Within the same limits, it is arguable that their interpretations also make whole what has been smashed. Those are the goals that make sense of Benjamin's own paradigm of proper historical-critical labor: perceiving that a particular moment of the past makes a "constellation" with a particular moment of extreme urgency in the present.

That said, there are further reasons for being less than perfectly satisfied with the "angel of history" paradigm. For one thing, the notion of history as a melancholy pile of ruins is self-contradictory. Ruins are only melancholy, indeed they are only ruins, if they were once whole—whole buildings, whole artifacts, whole ways of life. If there was nothing attractive or imposing or comfortable about them before they were ruins, there would be nothing to lament in their ruination—indeed, they could not be properly described as ruins at all. The idea of the ruin presupposes that something unruined was once there and has now been destroyed. But there is no provision in Benjamin's figure of history for the process of creating that not-yet-ruin, no provision for making or building. The metaphor to which he most often appeals, in the section of *Illuminations* where the reading of Klee appears, is explosion: "to Robespierre ancient Rome was a past charged with the time of the now which he blasted out of the continuum of history."[8] In general, the task of revolutionaries is "to make the continuum of history explode." The historical materialist takes cognizance of "a revolutionary chance in the fight for the oppressed past . . . in order to blast a specific era out of the homogeneous course of history—blasting a specific life out of the era or a specific work out of the lifework."[9]

What critical routine can be imagined emerging from all this blasting? If criticism is a sort of construction site, its theoretical purpose would be the production of some entity that is not a ruin. But here no construction is going on. Everyone is blasting away, but no one is building anything. When and how would anyone *have* built anything? There is no space for the coming into existence of those living wholes that history will then turn into lifeless ruins, no pattern for the wholeness that the critic is supposed to be dedicated to restoring. The only location where wholeness can be found is presumed to be the past, and that is one reason why feelings about the past run so high. As a philosophy of history, however, this is incoherent. More precisely, it makes the past incoherent, but disguises that it is doing so by simultaneously treating the past reverentially, as a species of the sacred.

"I began with the desire to speak with the dead." This is the opening of Stephen Greenblatt's *Shakespearean Negotiations: The Circulation of Social Energy in Renaissance England*. That book was the flagship of the New Historicism, the single most influential contribution of the 60s movements to the study of literary history. Its first sentences reveal one distinctive way in which the 60s made their peace with the ground rules of the discipline.[10] This desire to speak with the dead, Greenblatt goes on, "is a familiar, if unvoiced, motive in literary studies, a motive organized, professionalized, buried beneath layers of bureaucratic decorum: literature professors are salaried, middle-class shamans."[11] All critics want to speak with the dead, in other words, though not all are honest enough to admit it. Going back into the first-person, Greenblatt inadvertently speaks on behalf of his intellectual generation:

> If I never believed that the dead could hear me, and if I knew that the dead could not speak, I was nonetheless certain that I could re-create a conversation with them. Even when I came to understand that in my most intense moments of straining to listen all I could hear was my own voice, even then I did not abandon my desire.[12]

"All I could hear was my own voice." The more reverential Greenblatt gets toward the dead, as if following the angel's impulse to bring them back to life, the more the dead seem to be in danger of retreating into silence, leaving the critic free in the present, under cover of modesty, to say and do what they please with their memory. Here what might be called Greenblatt's pastism—a quasi-religious fetishism of the past for its own sake—morphs paradoxically into presentism.[13] Something important about the past is suddenly gone.

Catherine Gallagher, fellow founder with Greenblatt of the New Historicism, makes explicit the connection between New Historicist presentism and the New Left movements of the 1960s. "American radicalism of the sixties and early seventies bred just those preoccupations that have tended to separate new historicist from Marxist critics in the eighties," she writes, and it's the new historicists who "preserve, rather than react against, many of the characteristic tendencies of New Left thought."[14] The first of these is that "the intellectual activist herself did not claim to stand or speak for some other oppressed group."[15] This modest disclaimer—Marxists claim illegitimately to speak for oppressed groups, but we properly claim less for ourselves—is not precisely what Greenblatt implies when he says that "all I could hear was my own voice," but it reveals a significant linkage. When "the logic of representation" collapses between critic and constituency, the critic's confidence in their ability to hear the voices of the past collapses along with it, and all the critic can be sure of hearing is their own voice.[16] The modesty is therefore misleading. Appearances to the contrary, the desire to speak with the dead leaves those who are alive cut off from those who are not, and cut off as well from the oppressed as such, whether dead or alive. With no accountability in any direction, the desire to speak with the dead leaves the live critic, however modest, alone and very much in charge.

It might be objected that this is just the way things are. Existentially, the past is gone. Are we not alone in the present tense and therefore, as the saying goes, in charge of our own fate, and in charge of nothing *but* our own fate? Well, yes and no. Nietzsche was right that history cannot be asked to serve as a secular substitute for a missing god. Speaking as members of the not-yet-dead, however, we should perhaps be permitted to suggest other ways, less reverential in appearance, in which certain of the dead's aspirations (our own aspirations, not so long from now) might continue to make themselves heard without any supernatural assistance. Does a materialist have to believe that collective aspirations share the mortal fate of individual bodies?

Greenblatt's criticism, in this book and elsewhere, of course respects the particularity of the dead he chooses to discuss, but his general statement does not. Why does he want to speak with the dead? Simply because they *are* dead. To him that seems reason enough. It's not a particular dead person or persons with whom he wants to make contact; it's not because there is some special connection between the unresolved present of this particular critic and the unresolved past of these particular lost lives—for example, a shared collective injustice or aspiration. The principle would be the same, the desire to speak would be the same, for anyone and everyone, simply because they are no longer there. Some of the dead are dead merely because their lives ended centuries ago. But some of the dead are presumably dead because they were killed. Despite the time that has gone by and the fact that by now they would be dead anyway, indignation at the manner and motives of their killing would not be inappropriate. Nor would it be inappropriate to draw political conclusions from that indignation. Greenblatt flattens out all these deaths, leaving no place for selective and creative compassion, selective and creative fellow-feeling, selective and creative indignation. Reverence like this, which creates an all-inclusive category of "the dead" while eliminating, for example, specifically political motives for speech between certain members of the dead and certain members of the living, seems doomed to end in irreverence.

Irreverence is not an empty threat. Among the many disrespectful descriptions of critics and criticism, one of the most irreverent comes in Jean-Paul Sartre's *What Is Literature?*—a strong case for literature's political destiny. For Sartre, critics are "cemetery watchmen." They watch over the silent, unmoving works of dead writers. It is not a noble calling:

> [M]ost critics are men who have not had much luck and who, just about the time they were growing desperate, found a quiet little job as cemetery watchmen. God knows whether cemeteries are peaceful; none of them are more cheerful than a library. The dead are there; the only thing they have done is write. They have long since been washed clean of the sin of living. . . . The trouble makers have disappeared; all that remains are the little coffins that are stacked on shelves along the walls like urns in a columbarium.[17]

If reverence depoliticizes the dead, Sartre's irreverence depoliticizes them even further. For Sartre, politics is everything, but it belongs completely to the present—to *engagement*. Writing is political if and only if it is engaged, which is to say committed to taking action. Action belongs to the present. And if so, then dead writers are really dead, as dead as the causes that they may or may not have embraced when alive. As time goes on and those causes recede from view, they become deader and deader. The assumption is that politics has no connection with the past. The past is irrelevant. For all practical purposes, or at least for political purposes, the past is meaningless.

Meaninglessness as Routine

HAMM: Clov!
CLOV: Yes.

HAMM: What's happening?
CLOV: Something is taking its course. [*Pause.*]
HAMM: Clov!
CLOV: [*Impatiently.*] What is it?
HAMM: We're not beginning to . . . to . . . mean something?
CLOV: Mean something! You and I, mean something! [*Brief laugh.*] Ah that's a good one!

The suggestion that some not insignificant portion of the discipline could take as a postulate that the past is meaningless does seem worth a brief laugh. Long before the 1960s, criticism was dominated by philology, a form of history. During the period of the New Criticism as well (when not everyone was a New Critic), criticism was proud of its historical curiosity and rigor. There may never have been a time when criticism did not identify itself, if pressed, as the place lay readers could go to find the historical knowledge that would help settle disputes over a text's meaning. That identification persists, and it's a good thing for the profession's standing that it does. At the level of routine, it continues to be assumed that texts *have* meaning even if we critics cannot confidently assert the same about what we spend our time doing with them. You and I, mean something! Ah that's a good one.

Meaninglessness will also seem like overreach in the sense that it's unclear what it's opposed to. The terms that would be capable of defining it by saying what it's not, like meaning and meaningful, seem quite elusive themselves. And yet useful distinctions can be made. In *The Meaning of Life*, Terry Eagleton proposes that people who wail "My life is meaningless" do not mean that it makes no sense, like gibberish, but "that their lives lack *significance*. And to lack significance means to lack point, substance, purpose, quality, value, and direction. Such people mean not that they cannot comprehend life, but that they have nothing to live for."[18] In other words, you can have purpose and value without a guarantee of comprehensibility. That follows from the position that if "life has no given meaning," then "individuals are free "to make what sense of it they may. If our lives have meaning, it is something with which we manage to invest them, not something with which they come ready equipped."[19]

Eagleton explains, "the meaning of life is not prefabricated but constructed"; this constructionism is "the conventional wisdom," but he does not wholeheartedly endorse it.[20] One way to step back from it would be to step back as well from the assumption that comprehensibility is too much to ask for. Eagleton is not an enemy of the comprehensible. Often what is meant by saying that history has meaning, he says, is that it displays "a significant pattern"—that is, a comprehensible pattern: "The cosmos may not have been consciously designed, and it is almost certainly not struggling to say anything, but it is not just chaotic either."[21] At the risk of sounding old-fashioned, one can speculate that the way back to "point, substance, purpose, quality, value, and direction" may start off from something as simple as (1) affirming that history may be comprehensible (in the sense of revealing significant patterns) and (2) denying the premise that it *must* be chaotic. That premise is not self-evident.

What does it mean to say that criticism has committed itself to meaninglessness? By adopting the "conventional wisdom" that meaning is a construct, it has quietly bought into the assumption that the cosmos *is* chaotic. It is only because we assume history to be a chaos of meaningless particulars that we can also assume we are free to impose on those particulars fictions, myths, meanings of our own. To quote the political theorist Bonnie Honig, one can measure the strength of one's will by one's ability "to do without meaning in things," that is, by the extent to which "one can endure to live in a meaningless world *because one organizes a small portion of it oneself.*"[22] Nothing is more characteristic of the critical common sense of recent decades than statements of the form "X is a construct."[23] And nothing does more to weaponize that common sense, to make it political. As Ian Hacking notes in *The Social Construction of What?* social constructionism was one of the most aggressively targeted topics in the culture wars—this because (not inevitably, but in practice) it was taken as a powerful way to conduct politics: "most people who use the social construction idea enthusiastically want to criticize, change, or destroy some X that they dislike in the established order of things."[24] On the first page Hacking lists alphabetically some things that are said to be socially constructed, beginning with authorship, brotherhood, and the child viewer of television and ending with women refugees, youth homelessness, and Zulu nationalism. The key items however, along with "reality," are probably gender and homosexuality, keywords of the 60s movements. It is those movements that provided the political energy that took up and pushed social constructionism in the academy. They made into cross-disciplinary common sense the proposition that identity categories based on sexuality, race, gender, and so on are constructs rather than natural kinds. This is the spontaneous philosophy of the new social movements, justifying the effort of their members to escape from identities that have been stigmatized or otherwise disadvantaged and to reinvent themselves as something else. It's a stirring call to action. This is another sense in which Foucault is the period's central philosopher: nominalism, a crude but useful summary of his many lessons, means simply that the world has been badly named and that renaming it will make a big difference.

The impulses behind constructionism exceed both its theory (French poststructuralism) and its major constituency (the new social movements). Writing in 1983, Terry Eagleton still had to italicize *construct*; the term had not yet fully arrived:

> Literature, in the sense of a set of works of assured and unalterable value, distinguished by certain shared inherent properties, does not exist. . . . the so-called "literary canon," the unquestioned "great tradition" of the "national; literature," has to be recognized as a *construct*, fashioned by particular people for particular reasons at a certain time. There is no such thing as a literary work or tradition which is valuable *in itself,* regardless of what anyone might have said or come to say about it.[25]

In contextualizing canon and tradition, Eagleton is making a case in favor of history: the case that something that appears eternal and ahistorical, and whose authority rests on that appearance, is in fact invented or constructed by particular historical interests and agents. He asserts that history is more, not less meaningful. How do we get from here to the apparently opposite proposition that "X is a construct" renders history meaningless?

The difficulty with "X is a construct" is that by positing the freedom to construct differently, this proposition steps away again from the project of historical contextualization with which it began. To say that authoritative and injurious categories under which people suffer have been historically constructed is not to say that those who suffer under those categories are free to change them. How free they are depends on the agents, forces, and interests that did the constructing and that now maintain those categories in place. In order to know the state of those forces, interests, and agents, one would have to look—to appreciate the state of play, the configuration of existing forces and agents on the ground, the historical situation. But the strong version of "X is a construct" denies access to that information. It erects a wall of playful skepticism. If you respond to "X is a social construct" by asking about this entity, "society," that did the putative constructing, the answer is that society too is a construct. If you ask what constructed society, or constructed it in such a way as to lead to X, you get the same answer: whatever it is, it too is a construct. The regress is the same for "culture" as the constructor in "X is a cultural construct." If culture too is a construct, then what constructed culture? And what constructed that? The regress is potentially infinite.

Irritating as it may be, the threat of infinite regress makes a certain sense in its own historical context. It looks like a diplomatic resolution of the dilemma created by the plurality of the 60s movements. A representative of any of those movements might claim that their form of oppression was primary, the cause of other forms of oppression. If so, then they were also entitled to claim that their movement deserved precedence over the others, deserved the right to set the collective agenda, what comes first and what comes next. The usual suspect here was class, which notoriously had been invoked on the Old Left in order to push gender further down the agenda (the time isn't ripe, wait your turn). But the rhetorical template was also available to be mobilized by representatives of gender themselves, and for that matter race, sexuality, the antiwar movement, the environmental movement, and indeed any other form of politicized grievance. The most elegant solution to this dilemma was to decide in advance that there would be no causal precedence, and indeed (in the academy, at any rate) that there would be no *discussion* of causal precedence. Thus no one could be offended.

But this move achieves civility only by jettisoning causality—not just causal priority, but causality as such. It makes history meaningless by creating a series of no-fly zones for historical explanation. It's not that there were things that remained unexplained, but that there were things whose causality *should not* be investigated. In Foucault, for example, the rules of the game stipulate that one must not seek any explanation for how and why one regime of domination transitions into another. Any such explanation would risk reinstating the forces, interests, and agents (like classes and capitalism) that Foucault was trying to unseat. In the foremost work of contemporary political theory addressed to the new social movements, *Hegemony and Socialist Strategy: Towards a Radical Democratic Politics*, by Ernesto Laclau and Chantal Mouffe, there is similarly no accounting for which movements might successfully join up in a coalitional politics with which other movements, and which on the contrary could not expect to form a successful coalition. There is a programmatic refusal to fill in the historical gaps of explanation that would be needed.[26] In general, this refusal protects the autonomy of politics from the competing claims of history, but within politics the logic is the same: any answers to these questions would risk favoring certain movements and modes of oppression over others. As was pointed out from the beginning, Laclau and Mouffe put "socialist strategy" in their title but are silent on why they assume the diverse movements they discuss would join together in any movement at all, let alone one that could be described as socialist. These are spots of historical meaninglessness, empty not by accident but by design, not merely unexplored but off limits to exploration.

In the 1980 essay "The Value of Narrativity in the Representation of Reality," Hayden White seems to suggest that it would be better to present meaningless things as they are—that is, to do without historical narrative altogether.[27] All narrative moralizes, White says. It moralizes by its closure (which we only recognize because it coincides with moral values we have internalized) and it moralizes because it is organized around a single center or subject. It would be better not to moralize. It would be better to forsake the deceptions of narrative in favor of, say, medieval annals, which have neither organizing subject nor final closure but simply list events in chronological order, each one an incomprehensible singularity unconnected in any way to the events around it. For example:

709. Hard winter. Duke Gottfried died.
710. Hard year and deficient in crops
711.
712. Flood everywhere
713.
714. Pippin, Mayor of the Palace, died
715. 716. 717.
718. Charles devastated against the Saxon with great destruction
719.

And so on. The list resists the temptation to end with "732. Charles fought against the Saracens at Poitiers on a Saturday."[28] We are not told the outcome of the battle, which would later come to be called the Battle of Tours and recognized as a decisive turning point in the struggle over Europe between Christianity and Islam. What we are told is that it happened on a Saturday. The day of the week is not helpful information. The list is full of gaps but empty of explanations. It has no subject to gather together its multitude of particulars. It has no order other than the chronological. One might say that the annals form accepts the true chaos of things.

But are we sure that the world in fact comes to us as a chaos of meaningless particulars, unordered except by the arbitrary acts of imagination we impose on it? How do we think we know that? Wallace Stevens, in his poem "The Plain Sense of Things," has a pertinent line: "Yet the absence of imagination had / Itself to be imagined." There are no doubt many ways of reading this line, but one of them, certainly, is that we cannot take for granted the initial chaos that we posit as a sort of raw material, sitting and waiting for imagination to work it up. This supposed chaos of particulars is not the plain sense of things, not a bedrock reality whose existence is beyond question. If interrogation is what we do, then it too has to be interrogated. It is as much a "construct" as any other construct. And perhaps it's time for it to get the same scrutiny as other constructs.

The case for actual, cumulative progress in the era of the Anthropocene is more than this argument needs or will offer. It seems enough to question the scholarly common sense that throws up insuperable obstacles even to starting that conversation. Yes, there is a job crisis. Yes, there is global warming. Yes, racism and sexism and homophobia and transphobia are bitter, systemic, continuing realities. But these facts have been serving as excuses for persisting in a melancholic posture toward history that has other origins and is sustained by other logics. It suits us to believe that history needs us to organize it because it has no organizing principles of its own. But we would understand the job crisis and the global warming crisis better if we did not see them as unconnected catastrophes, like the debris that piles up in front of Benjamin's angel of history. Maybe it's time for Benjamin's angel to be retired as the figure of what otherwise secular academics hold most sacred. If we could see those catastrophes as part of an overarching historical narrative that is not just imagined, we might also find ourselves capable of seeing something other than catastrophe and ruin.

History Versus Fun

Putting texts into historical contexts has always been one of modern criticism's most respected resources. As remarked above, historical criticism is noticeably absent from the series of current critical approaches that are so entertainingly parodied in Frederick Crews's *The Pooh Perplex*—unless perhaps one counts D. W. Robertson's religious medievalism. Contextualization in the form of religious, political, and biographical background was standard practice. It was unavailable for ridicule.

But in the wake of the 1960s, contextualization (now associated with Jameson's "Always historicize!") would come to mean something distinct. The new element becomes visible amid the sudden flurry of objections to it. Both are laid out with admirable clarity in *Trojan Horses: Saving the Classics from Conservatives* by the classicist Page duBois.[29] In the culture wars, duBois argues, conservatives, like Ronald Reagan's education secretary William Bennett, were relying on

> a cartoon version of ancient Greece to authorize their platform for contemporary America. They present a simplistic, ahistorical view of human nature, and find it everywhere. . . . Such thinking distorts, freezes, and idolizes ancient culture, representing our own time as simple repetition of a past these contemporary writers invent, often ignoring the inevitable differences produced in more than twenty-five hundred years of historical change.[30]

The key phrase here is "inevitable differences." The differences, produced by historical change, are the object of the protests. The conservatives do not want to recognize, duBois goes on, that ancient Greek culture itself "changed dramatically, even over the three centuries of the classical period," and the changes since then have of course been much more dramatic. What the conservatives want is "timeless truths . . . exemplifying the moral virtues of conservative twenty-first century America."[31] Apart from these particular virtues and truths, such as they are, conservatives also want timelessness as such, and that is what they feel they are being wrongfully denied. They want history without differences.

One of duBois's examples is Donald Kagan, a historian and classicist who was reportedly converted to conservatism in 1969 while watching in horror as armed students at Cornell demonstrated in favor of creating a program in Black studies. Kagan writes about the Peloponnesian War as if the cut-and-thrust narrative of battles between Athens and Sparta offered direct advice to Pentagon strategists facing down threats to America's global power. The intervening centuries have changed the technology of war, but for Kagan they have changed nothing essential. Violence is eternal, and so therefore is military history—as well as (here you get the implicit political moral) the need to assure your country's survival, which is to say its imperial hegemony, by whatever means necessary. You can be sure that enemies will always pop up. Kagan believes in "the unchanging nature of human society, its essential propensity to violence and war"; DuBois finds the same belief in "human universals" in others,[32] like Victor David Hanson and John Heath, authors of the culture wars polemic *Who Killed Homer? The Demise of Classical Education and the Recovery of Greek Wisdom*. For them too, "Human nature is constant over time and place"; they therefore reject "linear history."[33]

Note that unlike Benjamin, duBois does *not* reject linear history. It is linear history, and only linear history, that is responsible for the significant differences she badly wants us to recognize. On the other hand, she does reject "narrative" history like Kagan's, and this although one might say that narrative history is more fun than linear history. For in narrative history "events [are] recounted as if they themselves had meaning and needed no interpretation, as if they were all equivalent, *as if there were no epochal differences*"[34] (my italics). Differences cut down on the fun. For those who are trying to weaponize the classics, duBois concludes, "There is a belief in the human condition, in human nature, which is never historicized, but seen as absolute and enduring."[35] To historicize, by contrast, means to take account of what is not absolute and enduring. For duBois and her critical generation, time is defined as bringing change that is morally significant. This understanding of time rules out a universal human nature, which is to say any moral judgment that would consider itself valid for all times and places. To accept the sovereignty of time, as against timelessness, is to acknowledge the inevitability of "epochal differences" that *make* a difference. Time is thus a secularizer, fearsomely powerful even though it also seems innocently unobtrusive, working behind the scenes to disqualify the eternal, and with it a great deal of what is taken to be religious truth. What is at stake here is nothing less than the possibility that scholarship can be secular.

DuBois is not speaking quite the same language as fellow classicist Dan-el Padilla Peralta, whose challenge to racism in the discipline created an uproar that spilled over into the *New York Times*.[36] In both cases, however, the logic, which is essential to the legacy of the 60s movements, needs to be underlined. "Difference" here has a double meaning. To pay attention to "inevitable differences" *in time* is also to pay attention to *social* differences, the differences of subordinated groups. The historico-epistemological point has a sociopolitical foundation. And it follows that to pay proper attention to the fate of subordinated groups is to inhabit "linear history," a history that not only registers subordination in its scholarship but is also animated by the desire to make a positive difference in the welfare and status of those subordinated groups. Linear history is inextricable from plural and distinct struggles for something like democratic representation, struggles which make it both possible and necessary to measure political progress.

It's the emphatic insistence on "epochal differences" that distinguishes history in the wake of the 60s from history as it was earlier practiced. Historical contextualization—for example, in the form of the rich biographical background that Walter Jackson Bate appended to the writing of Johnson and Keats—did not necessarily imply "epochal differences." Now, however, it does. One might say that in this new understanding, history has been (further) secularized; the eternal has been banished. And this is an effect of political mobilization. To repeat: there is a logical link between (temporal) difference as a watchword of the new history and (cultural) difference as a slogan of the 60s movements. The radicals of 1968 insisted that, when the moment of interpretation came, attention should be paid to race, gender, sexuality, colonialism, and other collective experiences of injury that could be expected to shape one's perspective on the world. Representatives of those collective experiences had begun to speak up. But if present victims of historically inflicted injury have the right to interpret and evaluate texts from their particular angle, then it can hardly be denied that the analogous contexts are pertinent to the texts of the past.

Moving into the 70s and 80s, it became obvious to much or most of the discipline that to read a work of past literature without asking what sort of society the work emerged from was as reprehensible, in its way, as ignoring those who were suffering injustice all around you. (This is how, for better or worse, close reading—or certain forms of it—came to seem at least insensitive, if not arrogantly universalistic, and little by little went out of fashion.) There was an increase in the number of equally valid histories that had to be accounted for. At the same time, however, and with more than a touch of paradox, to pay attention to the fate of subordinated groups was to launch oneself into what duBois calls "linear history," that is, a history that not only registered the subordination of those groups but was also animated by the desire to take the ongoing destiny of those groups into account. It would be sad if the humanities were to resist claiming this legacy of the 60s movements, preferring a constitutional melancholy (better suited to the legacy of Matthew Arnold) over the commitment to a genuinely progressive history.

The commitment to "difference" in the double sense is indeed, as Joseph North charges in his discussion of the "historicist/contextualist paradigm," a program well suited to academic scholarship. To say that it has been highly productive would be an understatement. On the other hand, as a subject, the persistent and seemingly insurmountable subordination of so many of the dead has its narrative disadvantages. It is not conducive to costume dramas or rousing bestsellers in which (pleasant surprise!) the people of the past turn out to be fundamentally just like us: the literate, largely middle-class, relatively comfortable readers of books. That's a downer. Let us note in passing, however, that all the fun was never on the side of the Donald Kagans who cast historical differences away in order to give their readers the "you are there" thrill of immediate battlefield presence. Behind the innocent-sounding title of the influential Hobsbawm and Ranger volume *The Invention of Tradition* lurked a political target that was and of course still is pertinent: nationalism, and the claims of modern nations to be "rooted in the remotest antiquity, and the opposite of constructed, namely human communities so 'natural' as to require no definition other than self-assertion."[37]

I have mentioned how constructionism, the notion that seemingly natural and eternal traditions and categories are in fact historically (socially, culturally) constructed, became in these years not merely an immensely rewarding premise of historical research, leading to the exposure of many other inventions, but also an anti-authoritarian element in educated common sense, a common sense for which the new generation of post-60s academics may not have assumed full responsibility (as noted above, it had its problems) but that they did successfully convey to their students, however unintentionally. In doing so, they also conveyed a pleasurable and even inspiring message: the world could be constructed differently. If the idea that the world is essentially unchanging was a crowd-pleaser, there was also some crowd-pleasing in the idea that the world was always changing and was open to further transformation (as we are ourselves) by actions still to come—which is true, even if the constructionists tended to say little or nothing about the structures and forces constraining those actions.

That said, the populist appeal to timelessness, or ahistorical fun, has not gone away, and it should be kept in mind when considering more recent critics of historical contextualization, who are also trying to undo the legacy of the 60s. It hardly needs saying that none of them is a principled reactionary in the style of Donald Kagan (who argued that defense spending was too low) or William Bennett (who, while publishing the popular *Book of Virtues*, once tried out the genocidal "thought experiment" of reducing the country's crime rate by aborting every Black baby). Joseph North attacks the "historicist/

contextualist paradigm" from the left, demanding less scholarship and more direct political intervention against neoliberalism.

Still, some of today's resemblances to the rhetoric of the extreme right thirty years ago are striking. "After a long period of historically oriented scholarship," Rita Felski writes, attacking context in the name of fun, "scholars of literature are returning to aesthetics, beauty, and form. Are we not missing something crucial, they ask, when we treat works of art as nothing more than virtual symptoms of a historical moment, as moribund matter immured in the past?"[38] This is a belligerent fantasy. There *was* no "long period" in which literary criticism treated works of art as "moribund matter immured in the past." How could there have been, when the discipline's single most consistent principle is that the works of the past that we choose to read still manage to communicate with us? The figure of the historical critic who supposedly sees "nothing" in literature but a disease that reveals itself in its "symptoms," who sees literature as "moribund matter," or as death itself, is of a piece with the imaginary intellectuals whom Vice President Spiro Agnew nastily figured as "nattering nabobs of negativism," and not just because of the catchy alliteration. It is perhaps an exaggeration to equate Felski's portrait of the critic as a monster of pure negativism, living only to accuse the past of its unenlightened and lifeless pastness, with, say, the right's use of potent stereotypes like the Black welfare queen or the paroled repeat-offender rapist, but the echoes of political correctness–baiting are unmistakable— as is, more surprisingly, her inclination to align herself with actual "family values" positions, beginning with "love."[39] Tell the folks that love, country, and religion are being spat upon, and a taxpayer revolt against the funding of the humanities is already stirring.

Given Felski's dog whistle rhetoric, it is not remarkable to find more anger-inducing populism built into the pop sociology that frames her case. Her heroes are ordinary readers. Her chosen targets are not just academic experts, but academic experts of the left, for it is only the left that can be accused of hypocrisy: How can they possibly claim to be both on the left and yet also a credentialed, knowledgeable elite?[40] These left-elite readers lean so hard on their knowledge of historical differences, Felski suggests, not because such knowledge is of any real value to anyone, but because it shores up their false sense of superiority to ordinary readers. The moral of this sociological sketch is clear: it would be better if academic critics stopped thinking of themselves as leftists and left ordinary readers alone. Who needs the profession, anyway?

What a waste of taxpayer money. Ordinary readers should be free to take pleasure from literature that speaks directly to their own lives in the present, unobstructed by the scholarly insistence on "epochal differences," just as Kagan's readers can take unmediated pleasure in the honor and loyalty, obedience and ferocity, courage and cruelty of combatants in the Peloponnesian War. Virtues and vices are what they always were. Violence is violence. Love is love. Death is death. Beauty is beauty. The experts are killjoys. Reading is more fun without them. You, ordinary reader, already know all you need to know.

Intellectually irresponsible as this neo-populism is, it would be equally irresponsible simply to treat it with a dose or two of its own mockery and leave the matter there. Populism always speaks to real feelings, if undigested and often misdirected ones, and those feelings are not restricted to laypeople. Impatience with experts and elites, for example, is a gut-level emotion that also arises from *within* critical expertise. On the one hand, timelessness is escapism, a form of magic or miracle that gives pleasure in part because it is felt to suspend or defy explanation. Professional explainers may have their word to say about that pleasure, but their role is certainly not to stand in the way of anyone's enjoyment. On the other hand, however, as noted above, a certain defiance of time is hard-wired into the discipline, which *would not exist* without the premise that the literature of the distant past continues to speak to present readers, if only with the help of good translators. Translation works. If history brought nothing *but* differences, it would be even harder than it already is to answer the "so what?" question, to make the case that the discipline deserves to exist, or deserves an existence separate from history departments (which no doubt have their own version of the "so what?" question).

From this vantage point, it is to be expected both that critics would sometimes make proclamations against the weight of what duBois calls "linear time" and that they would invoke the ideological support of nonprofessional readers, would-be representatives of the greater public to which professional rationales are addressed. Like nonprofessional readers, they will be drawn to the proposition that differences don't really matter, and they may well say so in a style that can be called populist. Thus, the medievalist Carolyn Dinshaw begins her book *How Soon Is Now?* with a lighthearted but highly respectful account of fun-loving New Yorkers enjoying a holiday at the Cloisters dressed up like monks and other medieval figures. Playing dress up: Isn't that what criticism is really about? "I suspect that amateurs have something to teach the experts . . . that some kind of desire for the past motivates all our work, regardless of how sharp-edged our researches eventually become."[41] If they are honest, in other words, critics of past literature would admit that they *want* time to disappear. Time is not on their side.

The classics are not timeless. They do not transmit a set of intrinsic morals or meanings or even aesthetic forms that have "passed the test of time"; they have been appreciated (or denigrated) in different ways in different epochs and for varying historical reasons. This argument has been articulated with exemplary philosophical rigor by Barbara Herrnstein Smith in her book *Contingencies of Value*.[42] "The endurance of a classic canonical author such as Homer, then, owes not to the alleged transcultural or universal value of his works but, on the contrary, to the continuity of their circulation in a particular culture."[43] It is our culture, for its own shifting reasons, that has kept Homer in circulation. Are Smith and her colleagues the villains of the story, then, the solution to the mystery of who killed Homer? Obviously not, since in this version Homer lives on. But the serious question of *as what* he lives on, the question of the quality of his afterlife, has not been squarely addressed or even posed. And to do so requires getting beyond the premise that the history of the classics, or history itself, is *all* differences.

"I think we should still read the dead," Page duBois writes, "among them those Greeks who not only invented philosophy and democracy and the jury system, but also kept slaves and excluded women from political life."[44] But *why* should we read the dead? What is it that keeps the slavery and the misogyny from culminating in the conclusion that reading the classics is a bad idea, as the Padilla Peralta hubbub and the elimination of the classics department at Howard University inevitably suggested? Having made such a strong polemical case for "epochal differences" in order to combat conservative and pop culture uses of, say, "the ancient gods and goddesses as timeless paradigms of human character,"[45] duBois doesn't stop to reflect for very long on the other side of the question or on what better, historically informed uses of the gods and goddesses might be. "One of the great rewards of reading history," she writes,

> is the realization that things have not in fact always been the way they are now, that people in other times and places have organized human societies, of whatever size, differently. If we allow ourselves to be open to the myriad

lost possibilities of historical human cultures, we amplify our present often limited sense of human potential.[46]

Here she again speaks as if history were made up of nothing but differences. Then, in the next sentence, she shifts her ground a bit, reconceiving these differences as a kind of sameness: as unrealized potentialities of which present readers may wish to avail themselves, which is to say as close enough to present readers so as to count as options for them. It's an anthropological or difference-centered case for the classics. What we get from "our inheritance from the ancient dead" is a set of additions to "our repertory of human possibility."[47] Sameness, which had already been implicitly invoked via philosophy and democracy, achievements in which the present remains actively interested, comes back here, but very quietly and only as a possibility to be realized, perhaps, in the future. The contrary of difference, whatever the right word for that might be, has not quite been filled in. Felski, whose colorful propaganda is of little conceptual help on this question, does supply the familiar verbiage from which one has to start: "the puzzle of how texts resonate across time," "the present-day relevance rather than the historical resonance of Shakespeare's plays," "the question of why past texts matter and how they speak to us now."[48]

The best answer I can think of can be found in Fredric Jameson's *The Political Unconscious*. Jameson's alternative to the classics as conveying eternal truths is a cultural history with continuities as well as differences built in—continuities that help explain why the dilemmas of Achilles and Antigone continue to speak to dilemmas today without fitting them perfectly, and that also do as much as the differences to express the desires of the constituencies of difference. Proposing to retrieve the cultural past by placing it within "a single great collective story," a story in which many different actors have been trying in different ways, times, and places to wrest a domain of freedom from the domain of necessity, Jameson offers a version of "context" that does not reduce history to difference but also recognizes what one hardly dares to call sameness.

Great? Fredric Jameson on the Human Adventure

The title of this section refers to a once-famous passage in Fredric Jameson's 1981 book *The Political Unconscious*. Jameson is talking about the essential *mystery* of the cultural past, which, like Tiresias drinking the blood, is momentarily returned to life and warmth and allowed once more to speak, and to deliver its long-forgotten message in surroundings utterly alien to it. This mystery can be reenacted only if the human adventure is one.[49]

Only the oneness of the human adventure can bring back to life for us

such long-dead issues as the seasonal alternation of the economy of a primitive tribe, the passionate disputes about the nature of the Trinity, the conflicting models of the *polis* or the universal Empire, or, apparently closer to us in time, the dusty parliamentary and journalistic polemics of the nineteenth-century nation-states. These matters can recover their original urgency for us only if they are retold within the unity of a single great collective story.[50]

Jameson goes on to describe the world's single great collective story as "the collective struggle to wrest a realm of Freedom from a realm of Necessity."[51] I imagine that formulation will raise hackles, assuming there are any hackles not already raised by the idea of the "human adventure" as "one"—not just the unifying civilizational stories of emancipation and enlightenment, the two meta-narratives that in 1981 Jean-François Lyotard had just declared over and done with, but *any* story of humanity taken to be single and collective.

But the most interesting of these adjectives is perhaps the unassuming word "great," a term that does not get much attention and indeed rarely shows up even in the index of works arguing in favor of the Great Books. What *is* greatness?[52] The question mark I've added to it is intended to acknowledge that the question goes deep and generates doubts that Jameson himself gives signs of sharing. My argument, however, will be that the single great collective story nevertheless offers an attractive answer to the thorny and long-delayed question of "why past texts matter and how they speak to us now"—in other words, that is a way of historicizing transhistorical sameness.

Jameson's *Allegory and Ideology* (2020), which returns after nearly four decades to the central theme of *The Political Unconscious*, features chapters on Dante, Spenser, Shakespeare, and Goethe. On the surface, its subject is the unreformed curriculum of the Great Books. All the books are by dead white males. No apologies are made for the neglected differences of gender, sexuality, race, and so on that over these decades have made both the traditional canon and the singleness of the human adventure seem less and less plausible. As it turns out, however, difference is what the book is really about. "How do we know," Jameson asks, "that the emotion Homer attributed to this or that hero or heroine (and which has been dutifully translated into its alleged equivalent in English) is anything like what we feel today?"[53] It seems clear that differences between the past and the present, registered as the impossibility of knowing for sure whether the basic emotions are universal, stand in here for the constituencies of difference, the collectivities of the 60s movements. Given so much unknowability, can there be a common ground of shared feeling, shared dilemmas? Jameson reframes the question of whether the dead can still speak to the present as part of an effort to renegotiate a mutually acceptable coalition with the 60s movements, and vice versa. His proposed solution is history itself as he reconceives it, history as combining difference (the emotions have a history) with enough sameness so as to string the differences together, meaningfully and even emotionally, in a shared struggle.

Freedom and necessity, however, look like ahistorical universals. Can Jameson make this work? Here as earlier, difference seems subversive of such universals. As the reference to Tiresias in the underworld suggests, *The Political Unconscious* already assumed that the "long-dead issues" of the cultural past are, in fact, dead: otherwise, they would not need to be reanimated. But their deadness is not the result of mere forgetfulness. I take it as a roundabout way of acknowledging the possibility that the past is not alive for us politically—that the past as seen from the present is fundamentally different, fundamentally amoral. To put this another way, it's the possibility that the passage of time has an inexorably subversive effect on that *taking of sides* without which a political view of the human adventure seems less credible. Taking sides for something and against something is an inescapable gesture of politics.

Does this gesture apply to the cultural past? We have seen Sartre denying that it did, at least in the case of past writers. But about history as such he was less sure. When Lévi-Strauss launched a frontal assault on Sartre in chapter nine of *La Pensée sauvage* in 1962, his point was the absurdity of thinking, as Sartre appears to, that history is a narrative with heroes and villains in which, at any given moment, the modern spectator can and must choose a side. Jameson's writing shows over and over again a dramatic ambivalence as to whether taking sides is politically necessary or, on the contrary, whether the impulse to take sides is an undialectical concession to a childishly unhistorical Kantian moralism.[54] Jameson's fascination with the so-called Greimas square can perhaps be best explained in this context: starting out with a stark binary of opposites, good and evil being the paradigm, the Greimas square generates further, complicating alternatives, showing that the initial situation can never be reduced to the simplicities of good and evil or any comparable binary. Hence taking sides comes to look like a kind of category mistake. If so, Jameson might need to reformulate his single great collective story, taking the emphasis off the binary of freedom and necessity and playing up the deep ambiguity of "great."

Will readers today accept that the truth of these lost issues and conflicts was in fact the desire of some for greater freedom and a reluctance by others to let them have it? Jameson's relatively upbeat proposition is haunted by another, much darker vision, one in which, despite the incalculable violence and suffering involved, perhaps no good aims were served so the taking of sides made no sense. In this vision all the efforts and sacrifices were for nothing, or nothing that now makes those sacrifices seem worth making—where what we call "great" is great, like the conquests of Alexander, which seem to have left something like 500,000 people dead, conquests of which we do not now approve *and would not or should not have approved then.* Under inspection, how many passionate popular mobilizations of the past will come to look like the activism of white supremacists in America (a self-described victimized minority) or the anti-refugee wave that has swept the European Union since 2015? Jameson seems to share with Perry Anderson a wariness about provoking activism in causes that will later turn out not to have been politically coherent or worth the effort, even if people could successfully be moved to shed blood over them, including their own. To say that what we need is a single *great* collective story, in other words, is perhaps to say that the single collective story would have to be filled with greatness in the darkly amoral, Alexander-the-Great sense of greatness, a sense from which present approval is often missing. That is, it would have to build using chaotic and even nihilistic materials that are determined by difference that resists assimilation to any universal principle, including the struggle for freedom, that defy any moral or political identification that would lift them out of the violent realm of necessity.

From the point of view of changing the world, salvaging the greatness of the cultural past might appear quite ancillary. Those familiar with Marxist traditions of criticism will recognize in Jameson's concern for the cultural past his longstanding fidelity to Georg Lukács, a revolutionary who nonetheless had his own peculiar commitment to the past. As opposed to the "make it new" literary activism of a Brecht, Lukács of course puts his faith in history. One might open up some space between Jameson and Lukács by asking whether he too has faith, or by asking whether faith or belief as we understand them are things we can do without. Lukács believed in capital "R" Revolution, just as Brecht believed in action—believed, presumably, that action was not just a good in itself, but was or could be politically coherent. On the Lukács/Jameson side, perhaps one should say the belief is at least that the world *has* been changed, even if one is not entirely sure that it has been changed in a politically desirable or coherent way. That belief would not need History with a capital "H," meaning confidence in Revolution. What it would need is compulsive, repeated inspections of the record of the past in order to verify its always somewhat doubted coherence. You would look to the record of the past in order to decide whether or not history is all actions, some of them "great" actions, but actions *without* coherence—to verify whether history has moved forward, or just moved. To put this more positively, Jameson's willingness to entertain doubt is the other side of his political commitment to difference.

The second chapter of *Allegory and Ideology* starts with a long, mysterious description of a laboratory, a laboratory that turns into a Plato-like parable not so much about knowledge itself as about knowledge of history:

> It is a vast and ill-lit basement, intersected by pipes of all sizes, of various materials, in various states of deterioration, without obvious passageways and obstructed by tanks and storage containers of all sizes, each one of which, pipes and tanks alike, sporting dials and glass panels of equal variety whose registers, clocks, meters, thermometric pressure gauges, numerical scales, quadrants, warning lights, and calibrations are in constant surveillance by the innumerable historians in their white coats and checkboards, jostling one another as they jockey for a look or a sneer at their neighbors.[55]

The passage is not finished, but I pause here: if it is "historians" who are watching over all these tanks and storage containers and so on, then the subject would seem to be, again, the single great collective story, though presented from a different angle. Here history is inspected from the viewpoint of the present, by looking at those inspectors who are inspecting it. The implication is, I think, that the differences that might threaten to dissolve the great collective story's singleness may or may not be a fact about history itself; what is on display is differences in how we examine history: the different kinds of measurement, the different materials measured, and the rivalry between the measurers, who look or "sneer" competitively at their neighbors. Perhaps the point is that if we can mock differences of present perspective, we will have less of a problem with differences that are, so to speak, really there, whatever the perspective on them.

The passage continues without a break:

> No one knows how many kinds of measurements are in play here, nor even the antiquity of some of the devices, each of which registers the variable rates of different indicators, such as water pressure, temperature, instability, consumption, luxury goods, life expectancy, annual film production, salinity, ideology, average weight, average heat, church attendance, guns per family, and the rate of extinction of species.[56]

Putting salinity next to ideology is rather a nice move: you think at first that Jameson is playing up and then breaking the materialism of the metaphor's "laboratory" frame ("water pressure," "temperature," and so on), and then you remember that "salinity" may be an indicator of the imminent "extinction of species," hence very much on the same plane after all as ideology and guns per family. Climate change, which has given a boost in plausibility to the singleness and collectiveness of the human adventure, if not to its adventurousness, has also given a boost to the materialism on which the singleness side depends for its major support.

The paragraph finishes like this:

> Those who have concluded that these tasks are meaningless sit against the wall in various states of fatigue, others race frantically back and forth to invent a master statistic that might encompass all these random findings, while still others concentrate stubbornly on their own calculations and substitute their own algorithms which may or may not have any relationship to those of their neighbors.[57]

The possibility of meaninglessness is named, and there is no immediate riposte to it. In the next paragraph, Jameson comments that none of these instruments

> registers History directly, of course; it exists somewhere outside this basement or laboratory, and all the dials seem to record it in one way or another. You could certainly call it an absent cause (or an untotalizable totality) if you think it exists; but no one has ever seen anything but the gauges and their needles, the numbers and their rise and fall, which vary wildly and require

separate monitors. Despite this, there persist the occasional joint cooperative efforts along with the most unsubstantiated generalizations and a tacit conviction if not a mutual agreement that there must be something or other out there.[58]

Much depends here on how you read Jameson's tone, itself known to defy even very sensitive instruments. If you think he is simply being sarcastic, you may not register much if any variation from the 1981 passage about the single great collective story. On the other hand, those who are racing "frantically back and forth to invent a master statistic that might encompass all these random findings" do not sound like avatars of a single great collective story by which Jameson would happily choose to be represented. In this tongue-in-cheek version of Plato's Cave, the conclusion that "there must be something or other out there" does not inspire confidence in the sort of achievable unity of past and present that Jameson had seemed to be claiming four decades ago.

There are various other places in *Allegory and Ideology* where Jameson seems to sound a retreat from the single great collective story. For example:

> In an age in which heterogeneity and difference are the watchwords, unity and unification are suspect operations, as they may well deserve to be; but for that very reason they deserve to be acknowledged as categories in their own right, which also exercise the attraction of a certain security and domestication.[59]

This sentence has not one but two vacillations: first, from unity being suspect to unity needing to be acknowledged, and then from unity needing to be acknowledged to unity's attractiveness in terms of "security and domestication." Security and domestication do not sound like conventional left-wing virtues. They sound like signs of a desire to escape from politics.

After these vacillations, Jameson arrives at what I take to be the heart of his position. He says that "unification" reifies, turning processes into objects. Speaking at his most dialectical, but also in the name of a certain common sense, Jameson argues that turning processes into objects is not just (as in Hegel) a good thing—it's essential. The chapter focusing on the emotions, where he talks about the birth of self-consciousness, is quite Hegelian in this sense: to have or to be a self at all, he argues there, requires learning to see oneself as an object, as an Other, in that sense as reified. It is only by seeing oneself as a thing that one becomes able to scrutinize oneself. Among the other things it is, reification is also a bearer of self-consciousness. Though he flirts with the nominalist or "X is a construct" idea that the real history of the emotions is the history of their naming, Jameson's most reliable commitment is to a Hegelian-Marxist version of constructivism that sees objectification as a historical accomplishment, something that has happened, takes up space, persists, is built on. From this angle, history is something like the sum total of these objectifications, reified activity pushing forward in the midst of prior reifications. In other words, reification is essential to "progress," a word that Jameson refuses to disavow. He is willing to sound quite impious, by the standards of the contemporary left, in his defense of progress. He warns for example that Benjamin's now canonical "denunciation of 'progress' (whether bourgeois or social democratic) [has] become a crippling limitation on some properly constructivist socialism."[60]

Constructivism, whether qualified as "socialist" or not, is the word Jameson seems to have settled on, at least provisionally, to represent the fusion of difference and sameness that permits him to speak of a single great collective story as the way to save the cultural past. It's a position somewhere between, on the one hand, orthodox dialectical materialism, and on the other hand, the various structuralist and poststructuralist thinkers he has managed over the years to assimilate or at least engage with. If the first position asserts almost confidently that the arc of history bends toward justice, the second translates into common sense as "everything is narrative," the (largely unavowable) assumption being that, since the end of history is unknowable, there is an infinity of possible narratives—or at least as many as there are constituencies—and (as Hayden White suggests) that we are free to choose among them.

This might be thought of as the difference-friendly common sense. Jameson's longtime dialogue with White reflects his efforts both to acknowledge and to pull free from it. He does so by arguing that allegory is a model of dialectics in that it preserves what it allegorizes. "[S]o even a reading of Christian allegory will seek to preserve the substance of the original or literal text"; an allegorical reading of a text will not charge that a literal reading is false, but only that it omits the text's "prophetic dimension," hence sinking back into what Jameson calls "mere chronicle."[61] For White, as readers of his "Value of Narrativity" essay will remember, chronicle is *preferable* to what we think of as history, since it does not offer to the events recounted the illusion of a resolution. And annals—no resolution, but also no subject around which the events are organized—are even truer to reality than chronicle. In naming the "prophetic dimension" as something that should be restored to history proper, something without which "mere chronicle" is impoverished, Jameson is putting his money on a reality that is not open to any and all imaginative projections, but has been molded by collective intentionality, however slowly and imperfectly, and given a meaningful synthetic direction.

By underlining the term "ideology," Jameson also argues against White that narrative, which for him *is* ideology, is materially constrained, meaning that we are constrained in choosing *which* narrative we existentially prefer— it's not a free choice. Unlike "everything is narrative," this constructivism assumes that narrative, which is a product of human activity, is constrained *in the same way* that all human activity is constrained. Thus to call something a narrative is not to celebrate its unique existential or quasi-aesthetic freedom, and to call something ideology is not to denigrate its *lack* of such freedom. We are back in the vicinity of Marxist orthodoxy—making history, but not under circumstances of our own choosing. The story of the wresting of a realm of freedom from the realm of necessity condemns us to spending much more time than we might have wished in the company of a very dark necessity.

In the *Iliad*, which is shot through with dark necessity, what interests Jameson is those very early readers who, in an attempt to overcome the sheer gruesomeness of Homer's "interminable hand-to-hand combats," turned the "senseless slaughter" into scenes of education in which the real clash was between personified passions.[62] Translating corporal slaughter into a dialogue of antagonistic emotions, these critics could be seen as wriggling away from the domain of violent necessity and positing a domain in which some small quantity of freedom has been achieved.

Think of it as an example of what Jameson's program for literary history might look like. In that period violence arguably *was* necessity. A world in which violence was not a perpetual threat was as yet unimaginable. It was therefore necessary to prepare oneself to meet violence with violence. In such a world, the concept of atrocity could not exist. The Latin word "atrox," from which "atrocity" derives, meant "cruel," but it was not originally a pejorative. How could it be, when your survival might depend on your being thought of as cruel? It's no surprise, then, that in classical antiquity the imagined freedom to abstain from violence is rarely visible. Yet that is one form of greatness that Jameson and others have found in Homer.

Another stirring example is Thucydides's account of the dialogue between the representatives of imperial Athens and the representatives of the island of Melos, shortly before the Athenians massacred all the male inhabitants of Melos (a scene that Thucydides refrains from showing) and enslaved the women and children. The Athenians, arguing that the Melians should surrender, tell them that they are surrendering to necessity, *ananke*. The necessity is for the Athenians to defend their empire: if they let the Melians off, their other colonies will defy their authority as well. They argue, famously, that the powerful will always do everything they can, and the weak will suffer what they must. Yet it is not clear that Thucydides agrees with them. He offers his readers the counterexample of Mytilini, where the Athenians faced much the same situation but at the last minute decided against ethnic cleansing. Even for the former general Thucydides, Athens was apparently free to behave otherwise and could therefore be held accountable. This thought has bothered some of his readers so much that they speculate he may have been a secret Spartan sympathizer.

The closer one's attention to violence, the more plausible becomes a single great collective story, even if the dark ambiguity of greatness can never be ignored. In early modern Europe, Saladin was admired, though he was a Muslim who had fought fiercely and successfully against the Christian Crusaders, not so much for his chivalry but for his ability to mete out violence effectively. Ditto for Tamarlane or Timur, the Turco-Mongol conqueror Christopher Marlowe called Tamburlaine the Great.[63] As long as a world without violence remained impossible to imagine, it was hard not to attach greatness to those, like Timur or Alexander, who showed a noteworthy aptitude for it, whatever side they were on. One might have assumed that such figures, even without the numbers of Christian deaths for which they were responsible, would have been treated simply as religious and civilizational others. The fact that they were looked upon with considerable admiration seems evidence that achievements in the domain of violence were respected independently of other judgments, and respected so much that the respect could override ideological motives for repudiating them as monsters. Cruelty became questionable, and the concept of atrocity came into being, only when it could be recast as violence that was separated from necessity; violence (which of course never ceased) might at least theoretically be understood and was at least potentially open to control by human actions. In other words, there has been a tilt in the balance between necessity and freedom. If one follows literary representations of violence, whether canonical (like Homer and Thucydides, Caesar and Josephus, Las Casas and Montaigne) or non-canonical, a certain progress from necessity to freedom seems more than a random optimistic or humanistic projection.[64]

Jameson's account of the development of modern self-consciousness, part and parcel of his history of the emotions, is not triumphalist: it unfolds under the worst social conditions and is never unmarked by them. Yet for Jameson it nevertheless belongs to a metanarrative of both emancipation and enlightenment. In the Greek *polis,* for example, anger has no binary opposite. The place of that missing opposite is filled by the absence of all emotion, Stoicism's *apatheia* or *ataraxia,* which will later be pathologized as melancholy. For Jameson, who might be seen as making a dialectical case for melancholy, the absence of emotion is not a pathology at all, but rather a desire for utopian serenity that cannot be satisfied within the suffocating and non-stop emotions of the *polis.* Where, he asks, can the desire be gratified? Where can one find a peace beyond anger, which is to say beyond politics? Politics is depicted as a desire to get beyond politics. Even the most politicized can perhaps see the point of this redescription.

Here the argument goes back, conveniently, to those "conflicting models of the *polis* and the universal Empire" that Jameson had mentioned in the "single great collective story" passage in 1981. His point is that both allegory and emotion undergo a hugely significant shift at the moment of transition from the Greek city-state to a Christianizing Roman empire. Allegory is a way of dealing, within an empire, with "radical cultural differences as it seeks to reconcile Judaic, Roman, and many other mentalities."[65] In other words, it is a mode of coexistence—an unequal mode, of course, as one would expect from an empire, but deserving of a historical respect that is more than merely antiquarian. Christianity, universalizing itself within the empire, becomes for Jameson something like a mode of imperial surveillance, introducing sin and guilt as it demands that otherness be internalized. Greek virtues are thus paired with new, made-up vices. As this happens, the subjects of empire are forced to bend to the imperative of self-scrutiny. A new self-consciousness thus comes into being, and it does so as an effect of Roman imperialism. It's the central allegory of the book.

Imperialism is of course an especially alienating context in which to place the history of the emotions, which (as we've seen) both ordinary readers and some scholars hesitate to think of as historical at all. Yet empire generates welcome opportunities for indifference or *apatheia* that were not available within smaller social structures. It is obviously no utopia. History here does not look much like a series of intentional acts, still less acts informed by *good* intentions. On the other hand, it seems clear that Jameson, quietly polemicizing against Nietzsche and Foucault, is doing a make-over of their militantly Greek-positive version of the Greek-to-Christian transition, and is doing so precisely so as to *credit* early Christianity with good intentions. As part of the empire, Christianity was conquering as well as converting those it intended to liberate. Nevertheless, the intention to liberate was not illusory. It was consequential. And the realizing of good intentions, even in small part, counts as some of that "point, substance, purpose, quality, value, and direction" that stand between us and meaninglessness.

What does it mean for Jameson to give his allegorical method an origin in the ideology of empire? On one level, it means only that he agrees with Benjamin: there is no document of civilization that is not at the same time a document of barbarism. The readings of Dante, Shakespeare, Spenser, and Goethe that follow are in effect replays of this ambivalent dynamic, all of them about the emergence of self-consciousness within a power-laden society that is anything but utopian. They take greatness in the dark, amoral sense and write it back into the greatness of the Great Books—and this does not diminish the greatness of those books. Why should one be surprised, after all, either that the capacity to envision world history as a single great collective story has depended on the brutal and expansive power unleashed by imperialism or, on the other hand, that the "greatness" of this vision—a vision now available of course from the center of *American* empire—can be refunctioned so as to wring from this terrible spectacle a certain quantity of hope for the future? But the example also goes deeper into the question of the transhistorical. Dipping back into history's struggles to wrest a realm of freedom from the realm of necessity, one should reconcile oneself to a prolonged intimacy with the sort of amoral "greatness" that accompanies the reign of necessity. There is more of that sharp-taloned necessity on view than there is of freedom, faintly fluttering within it. Those looking for cheap consolation should look elsewhere.

Over the past half century, the assumption that history is or can be composed only of differences—or perhaps more precisely, that the thing to do, in any given case of interpretation, is to assert the existence of difference—has had behind it an understandable emotional force. In literary studies at least, it has seemed indispensable. The force was with us. Without it, what chance did one have of confronting the inertia of a massively entrenched mode of criticism that seemed to have no doubts about its universal legitimacy or adequacy? The value of the knowledge gained by bringing in previously silenced perspectives and relativizing universal judgments may be, in truth, inestimable. At any rate, this is not the place to try to estimate it.

Yet much of the past would also be silenced if there were no recognition of historical sameness. That recognition has always played a major part in literature's classroom pedagogy. But there is no doubt that it has been somewhat under-recognized there, and that it has been frankly neglected both in scholarship and in theory. It is time to state plainly, then, that you can't have the past if all you can notice is differences. A history composed of nothing but differences would not be historical at all. It would not correspond to the empirical facts or offer a plausible explanation of those facts, many of them similar across differences of time and place. An obvious example, once again, is violence. Many societies that are otherwise quite different from one another in culture and scale have in common the fact that they depend materially on plunder (like the Vikings) and tribute (like the Athenians). The rhythms of violence demanded by plunder and tribute are different, but both forms of social organization make violence inescapable and create a moral vision in which that inescapability is largely taken for granted. That fact helps explain what the Athenians did on Melos. And it also offers one reason—a reason that has nothing to do with any theologically inflected sense of the eternal—why contemporary Americans, who benefit immeasurably from the influx of surplus value siphoned off and shunted their way by the international division of labor, continue to discover uncanny echoes of their emotions and dilemmas in the culture of ancient Athens. The transhistorical *is* historical.

Jameson's is of course not the only model for preserving the cultural heritage. It has the salient virtue, however, of revivifying large portions of that heritage that otherwise would almost certainly be considered dead. But if it is extraordinarily voracious, like traditional arguments in favor of the canon it also has the virtue of selectivity, a focus on the struggles of freedom and necessity that sets it apart from the promiscuous and unconvincing reverence offered to the dead as such. To propose to revive everything is to propose to revive nothing at all. There's not enough life to go around. At the same time, as I have tried to suggest, the inconspicuous adjective "great" in Jameson's "single great collective story" opens the door to a great deal of meaninglessness—the meaninglessness of history as nothing but differences, which is hard to tell apart from the revolutionary position that it would be better to let it all go and, if it were only possible, to start over.

Those who are most concerned about the preservation and transmission of the cultural heritage are not always equally concerned to change the world. Those who are most concerned to change the world are not always equally interested in preserving and transmitting the cultural heritage. Either group could plausibly accuse Jameson of selling out to the other side. Those who refuse to take sides on this issue, however—and the discipline arguably has an interest in not letting go of either—can perhaps say that Jameson, like other representatives of his generation, has been in the business of trying to construct a usable past meant to serve a coalition of the future that will want, eventually, to govern, but (as I've said) to govern differently. That is his "context."

7 Cosmopolitical Criticism in Deep Time

In 1970, critics tended to assume that their interpretations were universally valid. They knew, of course, that their interpretations were open to dispute from rival critics, but there was no additional anxiety that those interpretations might also be open to dispute from *rival social positions*. Fifty years later, that anxiety has become unavoidable. When the critic faces the text, she has to assume that there are other people in the room with her, that those people have not checked the baggage of their histories at the door, and that they may take something out of their bag that will make a difference to everyone. It also may not. No one knows in advance what will be decisive. But when interpretive conclusions are being drawn, no one's historical baggage can be ignored. As we saw in the last chapter, this relativizing of interpretation, while anxiogenic, does not mean that incomprehension or disaccord is taken for granted. The premise of translatability and of shared ground between different standpoints has by no means been discarded. Recognition of different standpoints means only that universal shareability cannot be assumed in advance any more than can mutual incomprehension. The relativizing is real, but it is not absolute, and on the whole it has arguably been productive of more and better interpretation.

It seems likely that one cause of this relativizing was a new geography, itself a product of the 60s: the irresistibly global scale on which thinking was now assumed to happen. In any case, that relativizing has expressed itself in geographical terms. Since roughly 1970, the premise has come to be that attention must be paid to perspectives from social locations outside Europe and Europe's settler colonies, or what has come to be called the Global North. On one thing, at least, criticism has reached a consensus: it wants to avoid Eurocentrism. What exactly it entails to avoid Eurocentrism, however, is by no means a settled matter. This chapter will make some suggestions but will not try to settle the question of what a non-Eurocentric criticism should look like.

Another way to describe what has been more or less generally agreed is that criticism is or ought to be cosmopolitan. Unsurprisingly, there are different versions of cosmopolitanism.[1] Intellectual historian David Hollinger distinguishes between "old" and "new" versions.[2] According to the "old" or normative version, Hollinger argues, all of the earth's inhabitants must be understood to matter, and perhaps even to matter equally, whether they are located near you (which for anti-cosmopolitans makes them more important) or far enough from you to be invisible. According to the "new" versions of cosmopolitanism, which are descriptive or empirical rather than singular and normative, cosmopolitanisms are as plural as cultures. The "new" cosmopolitanism starts out from the empirical existence of social groups who enjoy, or are burdened with, multiple and overlapping experiences and loyalties. A key example is the diaspora. Diasporic subjects have often left their homelands because of harsh economic necessity rather than by choice. Here the focus is on the creative friction between loyalty to the society of origin and loyalty to the society of destination. This friction may do some of the same work as the normative version of cosmopolitanism—the work of shaking people loose from any one loyalty (for example, from their nation's nationalism) and allowing them to factor in the welfare of strangers. Yet it also may not. As descriptive rather than normative, the "new" cosmopolitanism comes closer to the defensive particularism of some of the 60s movements. In both cases, however, it is considered inadvisable to take the values of those near you as universal.

Agreement that criticism must now be more cosmopolitan cannot be dissociated from capitalist globalization, an inevitable background to any and all projects involving movement across national borders. But it was a more direct outgrowth of the antimilitarist and anticolonial movements of the 60s, another major fact of these same fifty years. It was certainly so comprehended in the culture wars of the 1980s and 1990s when the right, claiming to be both patriotic and universalistic, presented its enemies (those demanding that peoples of color who were being kept from political independence, bombed, and otherwise abused should be consulted as to their own fate) as traitors at once to their nation, to Western civilization, and to civilization as such. At that time, champions of the right like Dinesh D'Souza also claimed to be speaking in the name of cosmopolitanism. This suggests a further ambiguity in the term that might be either dangerous or productive.

The New Left of the 60s defined itself, at the scale of global politics, by rejecting what it saw as a false Cold War choice between East and West: Soviet-style totalitarianism and capitalist-style freedom. As the veterans and inheritors of the 60s worked their way into the academy's decision-making strata, they gradually replaced that bipolar division with another: the binary of colonizer and colonized. The new subdiscipline of postcolonial studies, which arose in the 1980s, used that map of the world to channel into a scholarly and pedagogical program the political energies of the movements of national liberation, resistance to US militarism, solidarity with the Latin American victims of US-sponsored military dictatorships, and similar transnational causes. That program is ongoing. One unmistakable event of the period since 2000, however, is the questioning of the colonizer/colonized binary. As the struggles that created so many newly independent states have faded into a lesser urgency and have been largely overshadowed by the sordid realities of independence, not all of which can be blamed on the former colonizers (and for other reasons as well), it has become obvious that criticism's newfound sense of responsibility to the world as a whole—an enormous and hopefully a lasting achievement of that generation—is too large and too varied to be comfortably housed within the colonizer/colonized paradigm.[3]

Edward Said's premise in his 1978 classic *Orientalism* was the existence of "an ontological and epistemological distinction" between "Orient and Occident, or the West and the rest."[4] More precisely it was "the idea of European identity as a superior one in comparison with all the non-European peoples and cultures."[5] This proposition named a primal and ongoing injury inflicted by Europe on the rest of the world, an injury that was part of Europe's historical self-constitution while it has also continued to impose various constraints on the development and expression of non-European peoples and cultures.

It hardly needs to be said that Said's proposition has been richly productive for scholarship. Material for research has not been lacking. As the direct pressure of the colonial moment has abated (with exceptions like Palestine), the moral landscape colonialism laid out has been sustained by fresh

outbursts of racism and xenophobia in Europe, the United States, and elsewhere as well as by new military interventions outside Europe. Still, as a field-
defining logic it has come to seem a bit timid, as if afraid to face the process
by which, with the passage of time, colonialism and the sufferings it imposed
are inevitably becoming less central to or representative of the total spectrum
of cultural activity and human injustices. As the moment of decolonization
recedes further from the headlines, as public opinion in the West tends more
and more to dismiss colonialism as ancient history and as irrelevant to the
understanding of today's most urgent dilemmas, it has been tempting for the
field to hunker down in a self-definition that merely reverses the mainstream
view: because society at large refuses to remember colonialism's outrages and
devious long-term effects, we tell ourselves, we will stay at our post, ready
to remind it and remind it again. It is no secret, however, that in the Global
South anti-imperialism has become the refuge of a great many scoundrels, as
Fanon predicted it would. And in the Anglo-American academy, anti-imperialism has become a frequent refuge for the politically lazy. Said, who was
never lazy, reconsidered both the effects of the argument of *Orientalism* for
the practice of criticism (in *Culture and Imperialism*) and his own political
commitments, in Palestine and in general. He insisted on self-critique, with-
drew somewhat from the core-periphery paradigm, and gave momentum to
others also trying to think beyond it.

An alternative logic was already latent in the critique of Eurocentrism. In
Orientalism's wake, there was a natural rush to pay more scholarly attention
to cultures that had been misrepresented, excluded, or marginalized. This
entailed recognizing that many, like the cultures of China and India, had canons and traditions going back thousands of years. It is self-evident that scholars cannot do justice to such cultures without attending to their full history.
But this is a problem for the premise of constitutive European injury. Much of
that longer history belongs to the period before European power had had any
significant impact on such cultures. Although the modern politicized model
of European core and non-European periphery is obviously relevant for the
past five hundred years, as Alexander Beecroft points out, it simply doesn't
apply for most of the world's culture during most of the world's history.[6] Thus
the great historical outrage of European colonialism cannot be central to the
study of culture as such, and indeed finds itself scrambling to renegotiate a
new and perhaps diminished role for itself. It would be temporally provincial to assume the particular inequalities and injustices of the modern period

were universal. Beecroft's argument is one of the pillars of the emergent for-mation of world literature, which works in an expanded temporal field, no longer focused solely on the period of European colonialism after 1500 and often skeptical about the usefulness of the concept of modernity itself.

The postcolonial paradigm generates a demand for respectful attention to non-European cultures that have heretofore been erased or neglected. But to supply the missing attention is to find oneself moving away from the key (though not the sole) postcolonial premise of a unique and defining European injury to those cultures. All cultures must be listened to. But when you listen, what do you hear? For most of them, most of the time, Europe was not what they were speaking about. And when they were, were they less prone to cari-cature those not like themselves than Europeans were to caricature them? Did the Persians think in less stereotypical terms of the Greeks than the Greeks thought of the Persians?

Note that speaking up for hitherto silenced cultures was not Edward Said's own method in *Orientalism*, as a number of his critics complained at the time; he did not counter Western stereotypes about the East by letting Eastern cultures speak for themselves. And in retrospect, this looks like it was a smart move. When these cultures do speak for themselves, there is no guarantee that they will sound any more secular, humanist, humane, or otherwise palat-able in what they say about the West, or about each other, than the West has sounded when it talked about them. Would it be surprising to find in them appreciable amounts of essentialism, more or less poisonous misrepresenta-tion, what might be called racism? The charge of Orientalism in reverse, or "Occidentalism"—a symmetrical stereotyping of the West by the rest—has not been slow to arise. You could always answer that Orientalism was dif-ferent because of the greater power it wielded. But turning from a culture's content to its power would not end the debate, especially if (in the expanded temporal frame of world literature) earlier periods and other non-European empires were suddenly not only permissible but compulsory topics, as they have increasingly become, within the same conversation. It seems unlikely that there exists such a thing as an empire without the coercive exercise of power—less euphemistically, without slaughter, enslavement, rapine, pillage, and plunder. Those activities have never been restricted to Europeans. Taking non-European pre-modernity seriously changes the moral landscape.

The magnification of timescale beyond the modern period, coupled with a diluting of European colonial blame, can also be traced back to another, entirely distinct logic: the emergence of Indigenous peoples as an international political movement. In an earlier essay on timescale in the humanities and human rights, I cited the Algerian French writer Assia Djebar, writing a history of the French conquest of Algeria in the nineteenth century in her book *Fantasia: An Algerian Cavalcade*.[7] Djebar chose to forget the earlier conquest of the Berbers, many centuries earlier, by the Arabs. That earlier conquest would have been a distraction, as would the conquest of the Arabs by the Ottomans in 1510. On the other hand, Djebar did not *entirely* forget them. The Ottoman conquest is mentioned in the "Chronology" that stands just outside the text—in fact it's the first date mentioned. And the Berbers are alluded to when Djebar talks about writing her book "in a foreign language, not in either of the native tongues of my native country—the Berber of the Dahra mountains or the Arabic of the town where I was born."[8] There were good reasons for Djebar's almost complete forgetting of these earlier acts of conquest: they would unavoidably relativize the European conquest, and it was the European conquest that made the most urgent political demands on her memory, especially since the actions and sufferings of the women who fought against the French occupation very largely remained unmemorialized. And yet there were also good reasons for remembering the conquest of the Berbers by the Arabs. The reasons are present and political: Indigenous peoples of North Africa have now mobilized in political movements demanding self-determination or linguistic and cultural equality. The Berbers or Amazigh have brought their second-class status in a predominantly Arab culture before the UN Permanent Forum on Indigenous Issues. One former member of the Permanent Forum, Hassan Id Balkassm, is himself a Berber.

The international mobilization of Indigenous peoples has reinvigorated the term "colonialism," extending into the present a concept that was arguably in danger of shutting down. In so doing, however, the new Indigenous politics has also stretched the concept in one way that, though obvious, needs to be underlined. If a (European) conquest that happened in the nineteenth century now appears in the same temporal frame with a (non-European) conquest that happened in the seventh and eighth centuries, then those accused of being colonizers can no longer be exclusively Europeans. That could not conceivably be the case for a movement that includes not just the Ojibwa of the United States and the Maori of New Zealand but also the Berbers of Algeria and Morocco, the Maasai of Kenya and Tanzania, and the Chakma people in the Chittagong Hill Tracts of Bangladesh, among many others. It seems unlikely that colonialism will ever count again as an exclusively European phenomenon.

At the United Nations, some states have argued that colonialism is only colonialism if it involved the crossing of water in a boat. Conquest by land would not then be colonialism at all. Unsurprisingly, this "salt water" or "blue water" hypothesis has been strongly urged by the People's Republic of China, which posits that it possesses no Indigenous peoples.[9] But the hypothesis has not gotten a lot of traction, even in Asia. It would of course deny the convergence between America's westward expansion in the nineteenth century and Russia's symmetrical eastward expansion, each of them resulting in the subjugation of many local populations, a subjugation that is ongoing. The effort to maintain the unique guilt of Europe would force us to declare, absurdly, that European Russia was not a colonial power. This position would sacrifice the Indigenous status of the peoples of the Caucasus and Siberia along with all the Indigenous peoples of Asia who are currently striving to protect themselves against the majorities around them. That would be too large a sacrifice.

If this ethical blurring or dispersion and the expanded time frame associated with it are conclusions to which we are led by such different lines of thought, each compelling in its own right, it would seem to follow that the destination is mandatory, whatever the inconveniences. In short, there is a new moral landscape. It rules out the European monopoly of blame, which is of course also a claim to causal primacy, hence a mode of European self-aggrandizement. Criticism will have to learn to find its way around in this landscape, aware of its perils as well as its opportunities.

One influential attempt to map it is Arjun Appadurai's postmortem for the center-periphery model, "Disjuncture and Difference in the Global Cultural Economy," first published in 1990.[10] The global cultural economy "can no longer be understood in terms of existing center-periphery models," Appadurai argues, and the reason is the disjuncture "between economy, culture, and politics."[11] In order to grasp the consequences of this disjuncture, Appadurai takes the metaphor of landscape and fractures it into what he calls "scapes." Each scape is distinct and relatively autonomous: ethnoscapes, technoscapes, mediascapes, financescapes, and ideoscapes. "These landscapes," Appadurai goes on, "are the building blocks of what (extending Benedict Anderson) I would like to call *imagined worlds*"[12]: imagined *worlds*, and not just imagined communities, in that they describe how different local or national communities imagine their connections to other such communities. And yet these are worlds, plural, without the oneness or unity at the level of the planet that Anderson assumed to exist at the level of the nation. Separating these various scapes from each other highlights real and important disjunctions— stories within one scape, for example, might have no analogue in other scapes and might not therefore even be visible. But the multiplicity of the terms suggests that Appadurai rejects in advance the hypothesis of a single landscape or meta-structure whose power-saturated relations would determine how the various contexts might be linked to each other. In some cases they *are* linked to each other, whether the linkages add up to a single landscape or not. And where there is linkage, there is also politics—not as the inhabitant of only one scape but as a potential arbiter between the scapes.

Appadurai's rejection of the core-periphery model allowed him to display cultural flows that ran from one so-called periphery to another, bypassing the supposed center or Global North entirely. Playing up these South–South connections was a large contribution to fresh knowledge of the world. Another was to show how what looks like homogenization (a power-laden flow from the core outward to the periphery) might often be better described as Indigenization, a process by which the periphery, receiving cultural flows from the core and yet also actively exercising its own power, resignifies and in effect remakes what it receives. Here the periphery is effectively core-like in its powers, at least in the sphere of culture. And yet Appadurai's key concept of disjuncture—which sought and won for the imagination, wherever it operated, a certain autonomy from other social determinants—left no room for the arguably all-important question of how autonomous culture actually is or isn't: how autonomous it might be from, say, finance or military and political power. It's not as if we always know that in advance. A world divided into scapes cannot simultaneously be seen as a single landscape, which is to say a landscape where the materialities and inequalities of ethnicity, technology, finance, and so on would be recombined into a single reductive and therefore morally operative picture, a picture that, precisely because it does simplify, would bring into relief the injustices that arguably continue to structure the world and the terrain on which moral and political choices (for example, about the planetary dilemma of climate change) have to be made.

It is a hard lesson of the 60s movements that this simplified moral landscape is at best a hypothesis. It is not an established fact. Whether or not the scapes are distinct, the subject positions produced by racism, patriarchy, and homophobia are irreducible to one another or to any other category. All have distinct pre-capitalist roots; they were around too long before the advent of capitalism for capitalism to take the full blame for them. Even if capitalism has since managed to incorporate and derive advantage from them, and from many other differences as well, and even if capitalism on a global scale has done so in a way that criticism cannot ignore, it cannot be taken for granted that power has a single center, a single goal, a single operating principle. In positing on the contrary that power is irreducibly decentered, Appadurai's model of disjunct, fragmented scapes, like Foucault's influential discussion of the subject, might be seen as faithful to the side of the 60s that never trusted that the social movements, plural, could or would come together in a singular capitalized Movement.

So what then? One option would be for criticism to adopt the fragmented, case-by-case perspective of human rights, which takes up one violation at a time and in the same cool nonpartisan spirit, even if it was committed by a collectivity that has itself been victimized and thus makes a legitimate claim on the critic's solidarity. This would risk giving up on the synthesis, the persistence, the (at least provisional) taking of sides, and the (irreplaceable) vision of a better collective life that are distinguishing marks of politics. Giving up on these aspects of politics has always seemed attractive to criticism's self-righteous, morally purist, happily negative side. Under pressure from the irreducible diversity of forces arrayed at the global scale, perhaps politics will give way to ethics.

Another option, also aiming at the global scale, would be to try to politicize humanitarianism, for example by focusing on the vectors of economic causality, like commodity chains, that make the rich rich and make them something more than sympathetic spectators of the misery of the poor.[13] This option too risks settling for something less than politics as traditionally conceived. The same holds for a politics centered on the peremptory plight of refugees. Can it be, in the strong sense, a politics?

In the absence of a genuine internationalism, cosmopolitanism cannot be assured of functioning as a cosmopolitics. Eyes open, critics who want to do work of political significance will thus have to keep looking about them, prepared to question models that may no longer serve and alert to the possible emergence of better ones. The core-periphery model has not been definitively superseded, as the three-worlds theory has. A cosmopolitical criticism that wants to be adequate to its era will have its work cut out for it. It will have to ask whether criticism is better off *without* any such simplifying and comprehensive world-picture. And if not, then what will the replacement or replacements be for our existing moral landscape, such as it is?

Recontextualizing World Literature

Joseph North credits the subdiscipline of world literature with an effort to escape the prison house of context in which postcolonial studies had confined itself. The tribute is substantially accurate in the sense that, as argued above, world literature takes into account an expanded temporal field and the challenge of producing a new set of moral imperatives that correspond to that expanded field. Criticism doesn't have the choice of ignoring that challenge. But is this really an escape from context? Or is it a choice *between* contexts?

In shifting away from the field's former center in Europe and therefore also away from its origin in classical Greece, the new world literature has been sensitive in its fashion to the postcolonial context of its own birth. The 2004 *Longman Anthology of World Literature*, for example, of which I am one of the authors, declares in the general introduction to its first volume: "One important way to understand literary works in context is to read them in conjunction with the broader social and artistic culture in which they were created."[14] One notices, however, that while the anthology is enthusiastic in its pursuit of transnational comparisons and the displaying of global connections and cross-currents, here the "broader social and artistic culture" offered as context is strictly local. What counts as context is the society in which a given work was created—actually, more the culture than the society. This is a context that any traditional history could have provided. What is *not* meant by historical context here is the new scale or kind of transnational context that might help explain, say, where the global crosscurrents and connections come from, what significance they have, for whom, and so on—the issues raised in particular by historians working over the past two decades to create what is sometimes called global or world history.

It is theoretically possible, of course, that the new world literature has no real need for the new world history. That would follow from the assumption that literature by its nature enjoys considerable or even absolute autonomy from history. If the field's practitioners believe, say, that literature is sufficiently autonomous so as to make mandatory or reflex contextualization seem like a mistake, then perhaps, so the argument would go, the new world literature should continue to resist historical contextualization in much the same way that the old world literature did.[15] This line of reasoning accords well with the sense of cheery liberation from the weight of an over-moralized and over-politicized context that pervades much of the enthusiasm for world literature. It also accords with some of the Longman's preliminary contextual materials. If "ancient writing is urban in origin," it says on page 1 of volume 1, even if "the great majority of all people in antiquity were engaged in growing crops and raising livestock,"[16] then in a sense the point has already been made. How the majority of people make a living is something to which writing, and the history of writing that will follow, cannot be profitably tied. From the first page, literature disengages from how the majority of livings are made.

This means that literature is also likely to disengage from the relations of power that structure the world in which literature is produced and received. Consider the Alexander Beecroft argument cited above. Beecroft sweeps away the moral landscape of postcolonial studies, which had taken planetary power relations as its organizing principle. As Beecroft correctly observes, it would be provincial in the extreme to consider cultures that go back thousands of years, like those of India and China, before either had any substantive contact with Europe, from the viewpoint of a politicized planetary division between European core and non-European periphery or a primal injury inflicted by the former upon the latter. That largely happened, to the extent that it did, after 1500. It is a hypothesis about Western modernity. If Western modernity is no longer at the center, the global balance of power drops out, at least as a default position. Beecroft goes on to list some languages that have been powerful without the backing of a powerful country of origin: Chinese in Japan, Persian in the Mughal and Ottoman courts, and Greek in the eastern Mediterranean, which "likewise has little to do with imperial power."[17] The implication is that yes, there were empires, but the fact that literature was written in empires *did not matter* to the literature. It's as if only the nation worked, as a context, to invest its values in the literature produced within it—as if the fact of literature coming into existence within an empire somehow had a weaker political effect and did not make literature into, say, a vehicle for imperial values. This hypothesis seems both questionable in itself and symptomatic of a fake decontextualization—fake in the sense that (although Beecroft is clear that not all literature before 1500 was produced in empires) its effect is to insinuate that pre- or non-modern literature is autonomous and that the sole exception to that autonomy is literature produced in the modern nation-state, reflecting as it does its national context and demanding to be evaluated accordingly. The long-term truth of literature is its autonomy from context.

As literature departments have seen a turn to world literature, so history departments have seen a turn to world history. And there too, the most likely effect of the temporal expansion back before (European) modernity seems to be a move away from politics. Kenneth Pomeranz observes that studies of rebellious social movements are much more difficult to assimilate to world history than studies of, say, daily life or large-scale social organizations. To say that social movements, as "intentional efforts at social change,"[18] resist the perspective of world history is to admit that scaling up to world or global or big history is likely to give a lesser role to the sort of politics that matters to many of us. In "writing of the social history of empires," Pomeranz says, he means "to de-emphasize some of the concerns that are necessarily front and center in a political history of empires—for example, how a particular place in West Africa wound up being ruled from Paris rather than London (or neither)."[19] This looks like a slippery way of saying that the concerns of postcolonial studies—what it meant for West Africa and places like it to be ruled from Paris or London—are going to be pushed out of the picture. Again the effect is to depoliticize.

The same might be said of the approach to world history by Jerry Bentley, founding editor of the *Journal of World History*. In an essay entitled "Hemispheric Integration, 500–1500 CE.," Bentley argues that modern nation-centered history has neglected the considerable cross-cultural interaction and "integration" that happened in the pre-modern period. He's therefore interested, he says, in "processes, such as long-distance trade, biological diffusions, and cultural exchanges, that profoundly influenced the lives of individuals and the development of their societies throughout the eastern hemisphere during the millennium 500–1500 CE."[20] This includes attention to "nomadic Saljuqs, Khitans, Jurchens, Tanguts, Mon and others," who from the tenth through the sixteenth century "embarked on a remarkable round of empire building that shaped Eurasian affairs from the China seas to the Danube River."[21]

What unites the agricultural settlers of the first half-millennium to the nomads of the second half-millennium, in this account, is the activity of empire-building. But words like "empire" and "imperial" appear here without any ethical or political inflection of the sort that would be expected if we were discussing the modern European empires. If their ethical neutrality seems entirely natural and normal, it's because modern readers assume that in this case ethical or political judgments would be anachronistic. After all, this happened a long time ago. In that far-off time, wasn't it literally unimaginable for such ethical or political judgments to be formulated? Was there any language in which such formulation could occur? Did any notion exist of refraining from the full exercise of powers of conquest, with all that exercise entails, including the attendant massacres of what of course had not yet come to be called civilians?

Bentley claims that he is virtuously rejecting presentism by refusing to use the ethical vocabulary of the as yet unborn nation-state—the vocabulary of democracy, rights, freedom, and so on. He argues, correctly, that too much world history is in fact patriotic world history, its endpoint something like a complacent reaffirmation of American democracy. We don't want that. But does Bentley really avoid presentism? It's true that presumably anachronistic political objections to empire have no place in his account. On the other hand, trade, circulation, cross-cultural contact, and integration, which are all ethically positive terms for mainstream opinion today, are also positive terms for Bentley. Indeed, they are his key terms. What he wants (along with many other historians) is to show that a kind of cross-border or large-scale intercultural contact that we value positively now but think is quite recent actually began much longer ago. He likes the idea of a world that is united, but is trying to show that it was united earlier. In this sense he is not being any less presentist than anyone else; he's just dropping one set of value terms while retaining another: unity, cross-cultural contact, integration. But how is it possible that "cross-cultural interaction" can be a positive but massacre, say, can't be a negative? Why do massacres have to become invisible? From the perspective of core-periphery, West/rest models, Bentley is trying to equalize things, but he equalizes them by eliminating the element of coercion on both sides. Empire for him is not about coercion; it's about the free circulation of commodities. In offering us one thousand years of empire with not a drop of blood spilled, he paints a picture of globalization today as it is wishfully imagined by its champions: thriving commerce, creative interaction, and free choice, all of it accomplished without state intervention or coercion.

The danger here is that a newly deepened temporality will sponsor moral evasiveness. Early manifestos of world literature by Franco Moretti, Pascale Casanova, and David Damrosch were more or less indifferent to the old-fashioned practice of moral judgment, and understandably so. The field's main inspiration lay elsewhere: in the expansion of the literary map to include non-European materials that might or might not be influenced by or responding to Europe. And on that expanded map, the excitement was generated by the new intertextual relations that demanded to be named and explored and the research methods that needed to be developed for them. It was perhaps inevitable that literature, viewed from a greater distance, would come to seem liberated from any and all contexts—liberated from context as such. For some would-be practitioners, it seems natural that one of the field's attractions would be renewed enjoyment of a literary autonomy that some had come to feel was too constrained by criticism's historicist/contextualist paradigm, local as well as global, a paradigm that (for example, according to the center-periphery model) made some degree of moral and political judgment seem inevitable.

As argued in the previous chapter, context cannot be allowed absolute sovereignty over interpretation. The fact that literature manages to communicate across vast tracts of time and equally vast differences of moral code is itself a historical fact, and it loosens the interpretive hold of any one code or context. Critics will recognize the complications, which are a felt burden on interpretation; they live with those complications every day. And yet they cannot be liberated from those complications by simply rejecting context. Rejecting context is debilitating even when the critic's will to speak politically is unmistakable. The first page of Wai Chee Dimock's influential *Through Other Continents: American Literature Across Deep Time* juxtaposes the destruction of the Iraqi National Library as well as the Islamic library in the Religious Ministry in April of 2003, both of which had been left unprotected by the conquering American forces, with the destruction of the Baghdad archives by the conquering Mongols in 1258, led by Genghis Khan's grandson Hulugu.[22] "Modern Iraqis," Dimock commented, "see the actions of the United States as yet another installment of that long-running saga." This continuity "made no sense to the Marines," Dimock goes on: "The year 1258 was long ago and far away. It was separated by 745 years from 2003. The United States has nothing to do with it."[23]

Dimock's outrage against the American invasion of Iraq is timely and inspiring. And yet it is arguably not as well aimed as it might be. It makes history disappear as an explanatory tool. Dimock makes no effort to understand either the American invasion of Iraq or the Mongol invasion of Iraq.

It's as if the obvious, unquestionable barbarism of the first invasion somehow removed all pressure to explain the barbarism of its American reincarnation. Dimock is content to point the finger at barbarians, wherever and whenever she thinks she can find them. Politics cannot be more than gestural. She appears to assume that barbarism is inexplicable, perhaps a manifestation of an eternal propensity to cruelty, perhaps an aspect of an eternal human nature. For her, barbarians simply *are* barbarians.

In the presence of atrocity, it is tempting to lay down the tools of analysis and simply feel what one has to feel. And yet critics who want to be professional in what they do have a professional responsibility to resist this temptation. In putting the events of the present into significant relation with the events of the past, we are obliged to do some hard thinking—about the events, and also about the paradigms within which we evaluate those events. Dimock's denunciation of the forgetfulness of American presentism assumes that, once remembered, historical events exist simultaneously in the present, like great works of literature for T. S. Eliot. But this makes history as process vanish. And without it, Dimock cannot in fact condemn the American invasion as severely as it deserves to be condemned.

When she says that Americans overestimate the 745 years that have passed between 1258 and 2003 and should learn from the Iraqis that 745 years of linear time don't really count, she is neglecting one sense in which the 745 years of linear time clearly *do* count. At the time of the Mongol invasion, it seems likely—I await the verdict of intellectual historians on this point—that no moral norm existed that would have defined invasion and conquest of someone else's territory as a moral violation. On the contrary, conquest was widely held to bestow the right to territorial possession.[24] Conquerors were admired. Conquest conferred legitimate possession not just when the Europeans arrived in the New World but also within Europe, where the sacking and pillaging and raping that accompanied conquest were of course already a long-established routine. One thing that happened during those 745 years that Dimock assumes to be effectively empty is the rise of moral norms that did define invasion and conquest as violations, however difficult to punish or prevent. Those norms may not have been much respected in practice, but their emergence is nevertheless a cultural fact that cultural critics, of all people, should be hesitant to ignore. The Americans could and should have known better. History had made the relevant knowledge available to them. One might conclude, therefore, that the Americans are much guiltier than the Mongols. This is one sense in which Fredric Jameson is a better guide to "progress" than Walter Benjamin.

Despite the activist edge of *Through Other Continents* (a series of links leading from the *Bhagavad Gita* to Thoreau to Gandhi to Martin Luther King), its idea of history is that history does not matter. What you see is eternal repetitions of the same. There will always be authorities trying to get populations to go to war. There will always be a few good men and women trying to resist them. Such people are like literary masterpieces who speak across the centuries, centuries that are otherwise empty. They are allegorical figures of world literature itself as Dimock would like us to conceive it. In her entirely ahistorical account of pacifism in the *Bhagavad Gita* and Thoreau, Dimock ignores the fact that competence in inflicting violence no longer enjoys the same prestige today that it once did. In so doing, she misses out on the opportunity to say that there were secular and historical contexts and motives for the development of modern pacifism. The fact that these contexts and motives didn't exist in the time of the *Bhagavad Gita*—perhaps didn't exist, one might surmise, before modernity—helps explain why the debate between Arjuna and Krishna disappoints Thoreau by going the way it goes, overturning the noble decision to renounce warfare.

If there truly existed no vocabulary for resistance to empire during the thousand years from 500 to 1500, as Jerry Bentley seems to assume, if there was no vocabulary that could serve to condemn not just those attempting to conquer us but also our own attempts to conquer others, then cosmopolitical critics would have at a minimum two options. First, we could self-consciously impose that vocabulary from outside, knowing that in so doing we are being no more presentist than those who celebrate circulating commodities and cross-cultural contact. Or, we could treat the emergence of such a vocabulary and thus criticism's possibility of using it as a historical event, an event around which history could perhaps then be reorganized, and this even if the language of resistance to empire was honored only selectively and intermittently. This second option seems not only preferable but unavoidable.

Cosmopolitical criticism would thus inherit the task of reinvestigating what is called Western civilization and might even find it can do so with unexpected if only intermittent pride. Hence the fact that champions of the right in the culture wars like Dinesh D'Souza could also claim to be speaking in the name of cosmopolitanism, as can more recent liberal pluralists like

David Hollinger and Anthony Appiah. Complacency is an obvious danger, but it is outweighed by the need to see things as they are.

Taking a fresh look at Western civilization is the task laid out in Robert Young's *Postcolonialism: An Historical Introduction*, originally published in 2001 and reissued in an anniversary edition in 2016.[25] Young summarizes what the colonizer/colonized model omits. "Partly because of the dominance of attention given to colonial discourse," he writes, "and the degree to which the notion of a discourse, certainly in Said's formulation in *Orientalism*, does not really allow for antithetical ideologies, there is a tendency to produce a level of ideological uniformity that is a travesty of the historical record."[26] Trying to set the record straight, Young gives his Part II the title "European Anti-Colonialism" and begins it with a section on "Las Casas to Bentham."

Today Bartolomé de Las Casas is frequently taught, though perhaps not frequently enough. It is less generally known that as early as 1793 Jeremy Bentham delivered a speech in Paris called "Emancipate Your Colonies!" A renewed canon needs both, and all those like them. Even if figures like Las Casas and Bentham (and Burke on India, Multatuli on Java, and Tolstoy on the Caucasus) turn out to be a small metropolitan minority, dwarfed by a mainstream opinion that had little if any objection to Europe's killing and conquering of supposed barbarians, scholars adding to and deepening our knowledge of the exceptions would, first of all, be doing something very like what literary scholars have traditionally done with writers classified as great, who were always a minority. This would not require much if any departure from existing critical habits.

It would keep us, however, from making the kind of mistake exemplified by Dimock's reflections on the two widely separated invasions of Iraq: the airbrushing out of a historical context that would make a moral difference to our interpretation. Laura Doyle notes that there were slave revolts in the Abbasid empire of the ninth century,[27] just as there were "anticolonial movements" in the twentieth century. She takes for granted that the two movements rhyme with each other. But do they? Doesn't one have to ask whether the slave revolts of the ninth century might have been different in kind—more precisely, whether they *were* in fact anticolonial or anti-imperialist? They may have been, and they may not have been. These may have been slaves who not unreasonably preferred (in terms of the code of the time) to *have* slaves rather than to *be* slaves. The difference makes a difference. In order to know, you would have to be interested not just in the history of slavery, but in the history of *anti*-slavery—not just in the history of imperialism, but in the history of anti-imperialism. You would have to decide that anti-slavery and anti-imperialism *have* a history. It's the difference between asking when people were merely complaining that *we* suffer under imperial rule (there have probably been such complaints for as long as there have been conquests) and when they began saying that *others* may have suffered under *our* rule—a universalizing moment that is probably more recent. To repeat: one context of which world literature is in urgent need is the history of those cultural norms that have made it possible to condemn violence even when it is we who commit it against someone else. Wherever, whenever, and however such norms developed, we and our students need to know more about them, if only because the texts of world literature are almost certainly entangled with their development in rich and interesting ways.

Which means that cosmopolitical criticism also has to be more curious about the Global South. We know that as attention shifts from "us and them" to "them without us," a certain degree of bad conduct arises in the foreground as characteristic of "them" when "we" were not around. But what about the good conduct? After all, why should anyone assume that, if colonialism was not a uniquely European phenomenon, that the history of colonial self-criticism, as in Multatuli's *Max Havelaar* (1860), was a uniquely European phenomenon? It is true that even Tolstoy could not publish in his lifetime his astonishing novella *Hadji Murat*, which described the destruction of Indigenous villages of the Caucasus by the Russian army. But there is at least one Japanese novel about the slaughter of civilians during the Japanese invasion of China that came out within months of the 1937 Rape of Nanjing. If we were to look, it seems likely that we would find more of this sort of thing in other colonialisms, other empires—in Turkey, in Persia, in China, in North Africa. Perhaps even among the Mongols. In order to know, of course, we would have to forgo the infinite forgiveness or condescension that takes ethical and political considerations out of play and seek resistance to empire in places where we wouldn't have expected to find it.[28]

Self-scrutiny demands that another part of this history should not be neglected. This is the history leading up to a piece of common sense I would posit as an achievement of "ours," in the metropolis and outside it: the knowledge that the "barbarian" is really just a construct and that those who are so labeled deserve historical understanding as much as anyone else. If this is indeed today's common sense, though it can be selectively ignored, and if we think it is more desirable than the durable old distinction between the barbarian and the civilized, it would seem to follow that we would want to know how it *became* common sense—that is, where "we" come from.[29] To treat that question as an irrelevance would also be a serious failing of self-consciousness even if the apparent motive was to avoid the appearance of self-congratulation. Humility can be carried too far. Without that chapter, the moral history of humanity is missing something essential.

Stuart Hall: Theoretical Gains

Criticism's resistance to narratives of progress, discussed at length in the previous chapter, has always had its unacknowledged exceptions. One lies at the very heart of the project of world literature: a story in which the blossoming of cultural plurality, with its many new and unique flowers of local expressiveness, condenses into a single happy narrative of increasing cultural democratization. If Whiggish metanarrative is a problem, then so is this.

But scholars do not seem unanimous that triumphal narratives *are* always a problem. Laura Doyle calls on literary critics to "incorporate the new historical scholarship on early world systems and states."[30] It's as if what gave this scholarship an unquestionable authority, leaving literary critics with nothing to do but "incorporate" it, is its newness. The new is understood to be authoritative. That's a progress narrative, though not a very convincing one. Just as different literary critics have their different takes on world literature, so different historians have their different takes on world history.[31] For what it's worth, Sebastian Conrad in *What Is Global History?* dismisses the "new" scholarship Doyle is recommending as bad history. The field has been too caught up, he says, in making "token gestures towards connectivity" and needs to pay more attention to what he calls integration, meaning exchanges that were "regular and sustained, and thus able to shape society in profound ways."[32] Conrad is emphatic: most exchanges and networks, including those that both historians and literary critics are spending much time on, did *not* shape society in profound ways. "A global history that aspires to more than an ecumenical and welcoming repository of happy stories of cross-border encounters, then, needs to engage systematically with the issue of structured global transformations and their impact on social change."[33]

Narratives of progress *within scholarship* seem to evade the unconscious strictures that forbid narratives of progress in the real world. One reason is perhaps that scholars assume scholarship is not a real-world activity. That assumption is consonant with world literature's uncritical enthusiasm for that which comes before (and after) the modern nation-state. That propensity more or less guarantees neglect of the historical rise of those moral norms mentioned above, which cannot be understood without some appreciation of what distinguished the modern nation-state, with all its imperfections, from pre-modern empires; but it also suggests that politics, an activity that is still mainly defined by the nation-state, is a waste of time and that the reader's time would be better invested in reading literature (because literature is not nationally defined) than in otherwise trying to change the world within which literature is (or more likely isn't) read. Here scholarship is not an activity on a continuum with other activities in the world. It is not "worldly," to use Edward Said's term.

The volume entitled *Cultural Studies*, which gathered contributions to the cultural studies conference that took place in 1990 on the campus of the University of Illinois at Urbana-Champaign, records a question Stuart Hall was asked after his presentation.[34] Andrew Ross asks,

> "I have a query about a term which you invoked throughout your history of cultural studies—'theoretical gains.' Exactly how does one recognize what theoretical gains are? The term seems to appeal to a narrative of progress which was almost completely problematized by those moments which you described in vivid detail when gender and race came crashing in through the window."[35]

In response, Hall concedes that yes, there was a narrative of progress "smuggled into" his talk, perhaps unconsciously, and he can see why this might seem problematic. He spends some time on the need to recognize limits and to remain open-ended. But as he warms up to the question, he also accepts as a self-conscious position what he had perhaps first said only instinctively:

> "To be quite honest about your criticism, I guess I do think that some terrain is gained, otherwise I won't make those moves. I don't think those gains are guaranteed, but I do think the work is better when someone understands those complexities that one wrestles to gain insight into."[36]

Three decades ago, in the immediate aftermath of the 1960s, it did indeed seem problematic to affirm that intellectual work could result in "theoretical gains," or any gains at all. It was rare to speak of gains in insight or in terrain that mattered to the culture at large or in the Gramscian domain of main-stream common sense. No one used the word "progress." On the other hand, reconstructing or rediscovering or revaluing the popular could obviously have been thought of as progress, progress in the direction of cultural democracy. The paradox was that at other times, or to other people, this very move toward cultural democracy seemed to have de-legitimized the concept of progress. That's what happens, Andrew Ross suggests, when gender and race come crashing through the window. The moral seems to be—though again, no one drew that moral until the rise of post-secularists like Talal Asad—that so-called progressives really ought to find something else to call themselves.

In the discipline of literary criticism, suspicion of narratives of progress did not wait for gender and race and the other 60s constituencies to come crashing through the window. As I've suggested above, suspicion of progress was there at the discipline's birth. That's one reason why it could switch so smoothly from Matthew Arnold to Michel Foucault, for whom apparent reform is only the ruse of another regime of power; and it's one reason why literary studies resisted ethnic studies and cultural studies, which (again, this point is made above) do not share its full predisposition to melancholy. One should therefore be suspicious of the suspicion of progress, and on the alert for further moments, like the exchange between Stuart Hall and Andrew Ross, where a commitment to measurable achievement, as the indispensable foundation of politics, makes itself felt within the hostile environment of criticism. Examples do present themselves. In her book *The Deaths of the Author,* Jane Gallop notices that when Gayatri Chakravorty Spivak talks about her work as the author of *A Critique of Postcolonial Reason,* she uses the word "progress," as in the sentence, "'My book charts a practitioner's progress.'"[37] "'Progress,'" Gallop goes on, "does not seem like a word one would expect Spivak to use. The word 'progress' generally denotes the most triumphant relation to temporality. 'Progress' here represents the least troubled or troubling, the most positive version of a writer's change over time"; in fact, she concludes, this somewhat conventional phrasing is "quite atypical of the book."[38]

A similar inconsistency pops up in Max Weber's famous lecture "Scholarship as a Vocation" (Wissenschaft als Beruf).[39] It is the strong and prophetic argument of that lecture that we have fallen into what Weber calls "polytheism," a somewhat melancholic condition in which progress is impossible because each collectivity follows its own gods and there is no commonly shared membership, no overarching religious or political principle that would adjudicate among them or mark out any course of action as an advance over any other. And yet Weber also says that scholars-to-be must resign themselves to seeing their work rendered obsolescent by those researchers who come afterwards. Unlike art, where "there is no progress," Weber says, scholarship or *Wissenschaft* "is yoked to the course of *progress.*"[40] "In science," as a result,

> we all know that everything we've done and are doing will be obsolete in ten or twenty or fifty years. That is the destiny of such work—what's more, that is the *point* of such work. . . . Every scholarly work that "accomplishes" its goal produces new questions; it *wants* to be "surpassed" and left behind. Anyone who hopes to serve the cause of scholarship has to come to terms with that fact.[41]

If our work will be surpassed and outdated, that is not just something to which we have to resign ourselves; it's not just a grim fate to which we are "yoked." It's also a fact that ought to give us a certain satisfaction. It means we belong to a collectivity that recognizes the value of our work, takes advantage of it, and builds on it. The suggestion here is that you would need to feel you belong to a relatively tight collectivity in order to be able to experience progress. So there is such a thing as progress after all—progress at the level of research, progress within the community of scholars, provided that the community of scholars really is in a strong sense a community.

This is also the sort of quiet, almost unacknowledged progress that sneaks into the revisionist account of human rights offered by Peter de Bolla in his book *The Architecture of Concepts.*[42] Histories of human rights have been kicking the foundations out from under the older, Whiggish, self-congratulatory histories by insisting on an extreme discontinuity, as Samuel Moyn does in *The Last Utopia.* Instead of locating the significant point of origin for human rights in the revolutions of the eighteenth century, with the most significant later development happening in the wake of World War II, as in Lynn Hunt's *Inventing Human Rights* (2007), Moyn argues that human rights really only emerge in the 1970s, and they emerge "seemingly from nowhere." De Bolla's version also puts the emphasis on discontinuity, though in a different way. His argument, like Moyn's, assumes a radical discontinuity between the eighteenth century and the present. For de Bolla, there was an extraordinary eighteenth-century moment, associated with Tom Paine, when the rights of man were imagined outside the model of property rights. But that moment was lost, and the dominant tradition of human rights has seen rights as specifiable, actionable possessions—in many ways, not a good thing. So there has been no progress in the domain of human rights.

And yet as soon as de Bolla begins to speak about *scholarship* about human rights, progress suddenly reappears. If one finds the dominant narrative of human rights compelling, de Bolla argues, one will see "the movement from 'natural rights' to the 'rights of man'" as "simply a further refinement or extension of [the] long tradition of rights discourse. But, as recent studies have begun to show . . ."[43]

I pause at "recent studies have begun to show" to note the incongruity between, on the one hand, the rejection of any single, progressive tradition in the history of human rights and, on the other hand, what looks very much like an uncritical embrace of such a progressive tradition in the history of human rights scholarship. It's as if the recentness of the scholarship could be taken as a guarantee that it is reliable, authoritative, even uncontroversial. In other words, there is a strange meta-critical return here to history as progress—on condition (as with Weber) that the progress be restricted to the world of scholarship.

One might say that Weber is after all comfortable enough with linear history, but only to the extent that the linear history in question represents regress rather than progress—as long as it represents a disenchantment of the world, our entrapment in an "iron cage," or some other sort of melancholic decline. Again, there is something similar in de Bolla. De Bolla, unlike Moyn, sees the eighteenth-century antecedents of human rights discourse as very real. That is, human rights discourse in the present is determined by them. But the past is determining in an undesirable way. The bad sense of "right(s)" as specifiable entitlements on the model of property rights has continued from the eighteenth century, de Bolla argues, and has helped render the present concept of human rights incoherent and unhelpful. But there did exist a good or at least a better sense of human rights in the eighteenth century—that's de Bolla's point about Tom Paine and his "rights of man." De Bolla shows by digital word searches that Paine's sense of rights did not catch on nearly as much as the popularity of the phrase "rights of man" would suggest it did. On the contrary, it was lost sight of and thus was not historically determining. Thus today it remains as "aspirational"—an ideal resource offered up by the past to the present, one that might guide human rights discourse today out of the mess it's in. Its untimeliness of course fits within a very traditional structure of argument for the humanities, going back through T. S. Eliot to

Matthew Arnold. It offers a heroic rationale to people like ourselves who, rich in our knowledge of the untimely, reach back for those neglected antecedents and bring them forward to rescue an otherwise misguided present.

Consider the temporal structure of this argument. On the one hand, history is indeed a determining agent, continuous with the present, its effects still visible in the present—but it is continuous with the present only in a constraining and objectionable way. On the other hand, history offers to the present nobler alternatives it can draw on—but only on the condition that the present has to reach across the abyss of time in order to seize those alternatives, alternatives that are not allowed to be already available within it. What seems to be absolutely taboo here is the other combination of the same terms: history as *continuous* with the present, but continuous in a *good or desirable* way. Of course, such a narrative should never be assumed in advance. But if the evidence in a given case seems to support it, why should it be taboo? Notice that it's not historical continuity as such that's being ruled out—it's only history that comes bearing good news. Why can't we listen to news if and when it happens to be good? Why should historical continuity pass without comment if it leads to catastrophe, while it's a no-no when it seems Whiggish or triumphalist? This is incoherent. It's also very familiar.

If critics acknowledge progress in their scholarship, they ought to be more willing to acknowledge progress in the real world as well. This argument brings me back to Stuart Hall and his refusal to give in on the idea of making "theoretical gains."

I've already suggested that the inconsistency between being anti-progress on one scale and pro-progress on another might after all be resolvable if scholarship were considered a worldly activity on a continuum with other activities. Perhaps that, in a nutshell, is the argument this book is trying to make about criticism. Another possible resolution follows from this. Perhaps scholars in general and critics in particular can acknowledge progress within scholarship but not outside it because they feel themselves to belong, as critics and scholars, to a collectivity, but collectivity is not something that they ordinarily experience as citizens, or experience with the same intensity and solidarity. If this is right, then something might change for the better if scholars who want real-world progress could find or foment real-world, larger-scale equivalents for the scholarly experience of collectivity.

As we know, Stuart Hall always seemed to be writing in collaboration with others; he carried that intellectual practice further than any intellectual in modern memory. But what most distinguishes him from the rest of us, even those of us who admire him most, is that he did not think of himself first as a writer or scholar but as a member of a movement. As a member of a movement, he thought in terms of making gains, theoretical and practical. Recently it has seemed that every day's news, like news of police violence, has given us reasons to question the gains we thought we had made. What scholars and critics get from Stuart Hall, arguably the most complete and accomplished example of the organic intellectual that the 60s movements produced, is a reminder that you can know all those reasons and still think about progress, that being scholars and critics is not the only thing we are, that whether or not we feel we are members of a movement, we can be committed to having an impact beyond the world of scholarship, and we don't have the luxury of not thinking about what we collectively have to gain.

Given that solidarity is already so hard and so precious at the national level, where politics took its modern form, solidarity beyond the borders of the nation may seem like aiming too high. But once upon a time, the same was felt about solidarity that departed from the level of the family or the village or the guild and rose to the level of the nation. If there is a silver lining in the dark cloud of global capital, it is the potential that the multiplying of global connectedness has to transform itself into the basis for presently nonexistent world-scale solidarities. Yes, cosmopolitanism's forbidding distances discourage criticism from committing itself to politics. But even thinking in strictly disciplinary terms, there is a big disadvantage to dropping this commitment. It's the loss of the sense that Hall never fails to convey: that his work as a scholar, however specialized, is also oriented.

Conclusion

Once upon a time, before the canon was invented, critics believed in progress. As Jonathan Kramnick writes, making his personal contribution to the booming "invention of X" genre,

> [T]he idea that older English writers composed a trinity of classics [Spenser, Shakespeare, Milton] was new to the mid-eighteenth century. Before then, the literary past was typically considered a progressively unfolding lineage. One writer followed another in a steadily flourishing line of achievement. Like the exuberant economy and military, England's literature improved with time.[1]

The idea that the great works of the past set an unreachably high standard that the works of the present could never match, let alone improve on—that anti-progressive paradigm had to be dreamt up. Why and by whom? In answering that question, Kramnick disputes John Guillory's picture of eighteenth-century critic/journalists as organic intellectuals of the rising middle class. For Kramnick, the critic/journalists were really looking out for their own professional self-interest. In a "battle over professional expertise," they discovered that they could make a case for their specialized knowledge by offering a positive "revaluation of English antiquity," an antiquity to which they had access but the *hoi polloi* did not.[2] For them, it was not inconvenient to think of the present as a proto-wasteland. "Modern culture seemed beleaguered by the book trade, literacy, and rationality. In contrast, the past shone with value and achievement"; patterned on "the prior notion of the classical age of Greece and Rome," their self-serving picture of "the antiquity of English writers" as "a golden age of cultural achievement" was set up to shine against the putative cluelessness of an aspiring but barely literate "nation of consumers," and they shared in its radiance.[3] According to the anti-progressive story the critics began to tell, a society imperiled by anarchic and unprincipled democratization required the guidance of past greatness, which they themselves could luckily provide. Thus was the canon invented.[4]

As Kramnick suggests, all this should sound familiar. It "set the terms for literary study as we know it."[5]

And now? Is it plausible to think that the earlier, pre-canonical paradigm might be retrieved, and with it the idea that cultural flourishing and improvement over time are at least possible, even if there is no guarantee that cultural progress may actually be happening and no special incentive from national pride to believe that it must be happening? National pride is not the only kind of solidarity that makes collective progress worth celebrating. Other solidarities might have the same effect. From this admittedly iffy angle, the fight over the canon during the culture wars could perhaps be reframed as an effort, on one side, to restore the early eighteenth-century's belief in the possibility of general cultural progress, spurred now by the entry into the academy of previously excluded social collectivities, previously unknown or neglected cultural work, and the unusual excitement of seeing scholarship itself enlisted in the cause of democracy. In that case, the struggle could be seen as ongoing.

Commitment to that struggle would not require taking up arms against the concept of a canon. If the canon is simply a set of cultural materials that at any given moment are felt worthy to be preserved, transmitted, and interpreted—a definition that even Matthew Arnold might find acceptable, at least in some moods—then canonicity as such need not stand in criticism's way. (Consider, as one small but indicative example, the significance of the Roman classics to the young Frederick Douglass.[6]) What does stand in the way is Kramnick's assumption—it can fairly be called cynical—that critics are motivated only by personal or corporate self-interest, which can be disguised but will always dominate. Recall that this is also Guillory's assumption—but an assumption that he restricts to criticism today. What Kramnick seems to be disputing is Guillory's failure to apply the assumption of self-interest to criticism in the past. In writing about the eighteenth century, Guillory turns instead to the Gramscian model of the organic intellectual. For that model, the critic/journalists were not merely cynically self-interested. However invested they may or may not have been in their careers, they could not be accurately described as entrepreneurs; they were also contributing to the purposes of a social collectivity. To repeat Guillory's words: they "assumed large political significance" by allowing the new middle class to "identify itself as a class with common interests."[7]

Common interests. It would be silly to claim that criticism is somehow disinterested or altruistic by nature. Like everyone else, critics want jobs, if possible jobs with security, benefits, and a decent salary. They also want personal recognition. But it does not go without saying, as is so often assumed, that the claim to represent common interests is merely camouflage for personal or professional self-aggrandizement. Note, for example, the characteristic sarcasm that Kramnick directs at the notion that the new eighteenth-century public sphere was "a bourgeois encroachment on aristocratic institutions":

> The appeal of this narrative for late twentieth-century readers is clear. For a criticism that now sees itself as bereft of a public vocation, Eagleton's story provides a contrasting relief. If we are now functionless for a technocratic age, at least we were once an agent of bourgeois hegemony,[8]

Like everyone else, critics want only to reign, even it means reigning in hell—reigning, that is, as agents of bourgeois hegemony. The fact that this cynical translation has become the default position for so many can perhaps be understood as still another legacy of the 60s, the coincidence of the 60s critique of representation, as in Foucault, and the 70s advent of neoliberalism (unfortunately not irrelevant to Foucault), whose model was the individual representing nothing but her or his own interests. It's the same model that underlies the right-wing critique of the American Democratic Party as a party of so-called liberal elites. Liberal elites, for the right, are those who claim to represent women and minorities but in fact profit from them. The quiet assumption (often shared with the left) is that women and minorities do *not* profit from any of the changes proposed in their name. But the louder argument is that this alliance of minorities and educated elites comes at the expense of the uneducated majority, most often presumed to be white and male. There is a clear response to this: benefits *do* accrue to women and minorities as well as to educated elites. These benefits are not the cause of increasing economic inequality (which is very real), but rather one bright spot in that massive dark injustice that continues to inspire critics to be critical.

The fact remains, however, that the right's analysis is not entirely wrong. On the one hand, critics, most of them not tenured or on a tenure track, do not live the life of hedge fund managers or doctors specializing in cosmetic surgery or owners of a used car franchise—all of whom most likely vote on the right. On the other hand, the highly educated do have a material and ideological relationship with women and minorities, legatees of the 60s movements, that is neither an illusion nor a scandal. There are real common interests that link them. Both sides benefit, if unequally. Representation is not a figment of the imagination or a self-aggrandizing lie. It is the work that critics do—whether they are preserving, transmitting, and reinterpreting the diverse cultural heritages to which the future needs to be introduced, or pointing out the limits of anyone's knowledge of anyone else, or, for that matter, asking its interlocutors to pause over everything in life that is "wild as the wind, hot as fire, swift as lighting," and therefore "errant, incalculable," at least for the moment.[9]

In his introduction to *Stuart Hall: Selected Writings on Marxism*, Gregor McLennan writes that Hall

> can best be appreciated as a peerless dialectical mediator . . . . He mediated within Marxism—structuralism/culturalism; economism/ideologism; class/nonclass social forces—and he mediated between Marxism and various non- and post-Marxist discourses and movements.[10]

McLennan's account of mediation also suggests the possibility of slotting Hall into Gramsci's concept of the organic intellectual, which was introduced into the argument of this book via John Guillory and criticism's lost centrality, was discussed vis-à-vis Edward Said as a figure of 60s antimilitarism, returned in the previous chapter, and now returns again thanks to Jonathan Kramnick. The obvious objection to describing Stuart Hall as an organic intellectual, aside from Hall's own repudiation of the idea, is that what Gramsci had in mind was intellectuals thrown up by the working class and helping to organize that class's consciousness and sense of common interests. It's in this sense, I assume, that Hall says, speaking with his signature modesty about his work at the Birmingham Center: "we were organic intellectuals without any organic point of reference"[11] —meaning, without a special relationship to the working class. As argued above, the premise that we would have to accept in order to make the concept of the organic intellectual work in the 1960s and after, when Hall was active, is that what defines the concept—relationship with and accountability to a political constituency—can be stretched beyond the working class so as to cover the diverse social collectivities that composed the New Left, which included the working class but did not give it priority. In other words, it included the "non- and post-Marxist discourses and movements" that McLennan sees Hall as mediating between.

For many of the collectivities that animated these discourses and movements, the idea of the organic intellectual is obviously a challenge. It would entail trying to discover or impose a political unity on groups that didn't just happen to be diverse; for many of them, diversity or difference was a major principle of self-definition. This is a bigger job than trying to bring together the "class fractions" that, for Gramsci, might be expected to resist identification with a unified working class. In the context of race, gender, and sexuality, the very idea of political unity can no longer be taken for granted. As Hall says,

> Isn't the ubiquitous, the soul-searing lesson of our times the fact that the political binaries do not (do not any longer? Did they ever?) either stabilize the field of political antagonism in any permanent way or render it transparently intelligible?[12]

It's the challenge posed by the multiplicity of the post-60s movements: if political antagonism can't be defined in binary terms, do you still *have* political antagonism? Can you have a common vision of a better life?

Hall did not seem to think these things were out of reach. He knew that multiplicity or difference was not the exclusive defining principle of the 60s movements. It was certainly not the defining principle, for example, of the antiwar, anti-imperialist, and environmental movements, all of which made their case in universalistic terms. And even the movements associated with race, gender, and sexuality were not committed in an absolutist way to tearing down Western morality and rationality and replacing them with identity, subjectivity, or culture. Which means that when Hall expressed his impatience with those who would like to replace an economic reductionism with an exclusive or overriding concern with identity, subjectivity, or culture, he knew he had an audience. It's also a reason why, along with his pathbreaking work on racism and mugging, youth music cultures, diasporic identity, and kindred topics, he continues to enjoy the kind of humanities-wide authority he does.

To call Hall a mediator suggests that he might just have been asking the 60s constituencies to compromise a little in the interest of peace and tranquility, asking them to listen to everyone else, to play nice. That's clearly inadequate. As McLennan says, what he means by a "mediator" corresponds to what Bruno Latour means by it. It's not merely an "intermediary," who takes the social and its problem fields as given—let's say, who takes identities as given. True mediators "*reconstitute* the very concerns being addressed; in effect, they propose and co-produce a *new* 'social' in and through their acts of problematization and the network effects they trigger."[13] Mediators are "game-changers."[14] In this sense, one might also say—though Latour would probably not—that the work of mediation Stuart Hall did was the work of the Gramscian organic intellectual. It was doing something *to* the players and the identities, helping to create a collective self-consciousness, trying to reconstitute them with a common and a larger purpose in mind.

For Gramsci, the organic intellectual was defined by a "capacity to be an organizer of society in general, including all its complex organism of services, right up to the state organism, because of the need to create the conditions most favorable to the expansion of their own class."[15] The function to which the organic intellectual aspired, in other words, was "organizing social hegemony and state domination."[16] The phrase "state domination" is not sloppy or accidental. Gramsci's abstract description of the working class is "any group that is developing toward dominance." The phrase "any group" may have been there only to avoid censorship, but it also leaves the door open for us to shift the notion of the organic intellectual from class to the 60s constituencies, including class but not restricting ourselves to it. The problem is that most if not all of the 60s constituencies did not see themselves as "developing toward dominance." Dominance was what they suffered from, not what they were seeking.

The project of "developing toward dominance" also makes sense, retrospectively, of Hall's trademark concern with the state. The prospect of successfully taking over the state was of course never close enough to make the articulating of that goal seem like anything other than a bad joke. But as a long-term aspiration the putting together of a coalition that would be capable of governing, and capable of governing differently, seems a better guide to Hall's career than, say, his supposed concern for culture at the expense of economics, which has frequently sucked all the oxygen out of the discussions of his work. About the state, there was no established Marxist orthodoxy in the name of which Hall could be dismissed as a shameless revisionist. There was controversy, as McLennan points out, and Hall contributed meaningfully to it. There was also controversy, maybe even more of it, on the other side of his mediating efforts. The philosopher who was most consistently affirmed by the "new social movements" was Foucault, who as McLennan reminds us refused to trace "power . . . back to any single organizing instance, such as 'the State.'"[17] Whether you think of Foucault's anti-statism as sinister and neoliberal or as "anarcho-libertarianism" (which might also be a bit sinister), there is no doubt that it was utterly alien to the project of "developing toward domination." This means that, in effect, Hall was fighting Foucault for the soul of the movement.

Cultural studies, the most visible fruit of Hall's efforts, began by trying to understand the British working class and in particular why so many Labor voters shifted their allegiance to Margaret Thatcher, thereby voting, it seemed, against their economic interests. Efforts to answer this question led to investigations of popular attitudes toward race, gender, and sexuality. Investigations of race, gender, and sexuality led from politics in the narrow sense to identity formation generally. Critical tools developed to deal with Henry James (the subject of Hall's unfinished thesis) were suddenly turned toward television, pop music fandom, hairstyles, tattoos, shopping. Hall analyzed the prepositions of the Hippies (tune *in*, drop *out*) as less a symptom than as part of a symbolic political project. It was easy enough to caricature, and the stubborn fact remained that the forward march of Labor seemed to have halted.

Cultural studies is not the ideal form of a politically significant criticism. At any rate, it did not succeed in becoming a solid, fully realized ideal. Even as it has thrived as a zone of publication, often also generating the kind of writing most prized in traditional literature departments, it did not satisfy the hunger for literary value that many of those departments felt, and feel, and in part for that reason it by and large failed to remake existing departments in its own image. There are multiple ironies in this situation. One is that critiques of the market sell on the market. This is evidence that the market, like everything else, is better thought of dialectically than with a simple yes or no. Another is that the characteristic willingness of cultural studies to lend an ear to the opinions of "fans" of popular culture has paradoxically helped nurture the "limits of critique" backlash, which accuses criticism of being too negative and too political, makes a populist case against critical expertise, and in its extreme form threatens to turn criticism into nothing but a consumer advice branch of corporate publishing.

On the question of criticism as negativity, however, Stuart Hall's example is again clarifying. He spent little time denouncing that which, from a progressive point of view, might seem to deserve denunciation. His analysis of what he named "authoritarian populism," the political strategy of what had not yet come to be called neoliberalism, did not sputter with pious indignation over the massive cruelty the neoliberals had already begun to enact. For his critics on the left, that meant Hall was not too negative, but too positive. If there was perhaps some excess in his fascination with Thatcherism's success, the most likely reason would be that, like Gramsci, he thought the left could learn from the right's ideological creativity, its capacity to bring devious but powerful popular feelings into a new synthesis and a new ruling coalition. If the right could ride popular feelings into power, so the logic went, why couldn't the left? The idea of governing might have seemed to him grandiose, ruled out for the moment both because it was too far from the immediate concerns of the "new social movements" and because of the weakness of the organized working class. But whatever the subject on the table, his interpretation was informed and oriented by that ultimate concern, that very positive project. The world needs to be governed differently. And, he insisted, it can be.

For better or worse, here Marxism does not enter in as an insistence that other constituencies should follow the lead of the working class. It does not insist on "economic determination in the last instance," though there are certainly places where that's what Hall seems to assert, and perhaps rightly. It comes in as the simple if mainly unarticulated proposition that all of our differences should not stop us from forming ourselves into a coalition, that the eventual goal of that coalition is to create a better form of life for ourselves, and that in order for this to happen no one can rest content with affirming their own identity, their own subjectivity, their own experience. To put this more generally: academic work had and has a larger and more important goal than merely reproducing culture, and reproducing *academic* culture, which is to say making careers for academics. That larger goal applies to critics who do not share all of Gramsci's politics, or all of Hall's, which were not identical with Gramsci's. It should catch the eye even of those who feel closer to what Gramsci called "traditional" intellectuals: those who see themselves as first and foremost autonomous (as we would say now, critically detached) and who identify with eternal values, which is to say the eternity of the materials they preserve and transmit and their own guild continuity over time. Historically speaking, critics have never been autonomous. Who has? Nothing about criticism is eternal. But if you think of the actual targets at which criticism has so often chosen to aim its critical detachment, a valuable continuity does appear, a continuity worth trying to sustain. It is not a glaringly radical proposal to envisage reframing that critical detachment as a form of solidarity and to aim it at the goal, however delayed, of learning to govern differently.

Notes

Introduction

1. Emma Goldberg, "The 37-Year-Olds Are Afraid of the 23-Year-Olds Who Work for Them," *New York Times* (October 28, 2021): https://www.nytimes.com/2021/10/28/business/gen-z-workplace-culture.html Thanks to Lee Konstantinou for the reference.

2. Christopher Beha, "Thomas Mann on the Artist Versus the State," *New York Times Sunday Book Review* (September 19, 2021): https://www.nytimes.com/2021/09/17/books/review/reflections-of-a-nonpolitical-man-thomas-mann.html Beha is reviewing the re-publication: Thomas Mann, *Reflections of a Nonpolitical Man*, trans. Walter D. Morris and others, introduction by Mark Lilla (New York: New York Review Books, 2021).

3. Lilla, "Introduction," ix.

4. Ibid.

5. Ibid.

6. Ibid., xvi.

7. Ibid., xx.

8. Ibid., xxi.

9. Joseph Conrad, *Nostromo: A Tale of the Seaboard,* foreword by F. R. Leavis (New York: New American Library, 1960 [1904]), Part 1, chap. 6, 53.

10. Tobias Boes, *Thomas Mann's War: Literature, Politics, and the World Republic of Letters* (Ithaca: Cornell University Press, 2019), 20.

11. Ibid. For Boes, Mann's defining commitment in *Reflections* was "to consider all sides of any given issue" (106). This sounds innocent enough, but Boes does not ask here whether Mann's commitment to the German side in World War I was consistent with it or, more abstractly, whether considering all sides of any given issue would

preclude making a decision about that issue (for example, about Nazism) once the consideration had been completed.

12. William E. Connolly, *The Terms of Political Discourse*, 3rd ed. (Princeton: Princeton University Press, 1993 [1974]).

13. A. O. Scott, *Better Living Through Criticism: How to Think About Art, Pleasure, Beauty, and Truth* (New York: Penguin, 2016).

14. Rita Felski, *Hooked: Art and Attachment* (Chicago and London: University of Chicago Press, 2020), ix. See also *The Limits of Critique* (Chicago and London: University of Chicago Press, 2015).

15. A straw in the wind: "I have never argued that the aesthetic and the political should not be allied with each other or that such an alliance has been unproductive. I have simply advocated for distinguishing the two as carefully as possible in the moments when they get entangled": Timothy Aubry, *Guilty Aesthetic Pleasures* (Cambridge, MA: Harvard University Press, 2018), 201.

16. "Not So Well Attached," roundtable on Rita Felski's *The Limits of Critique*, *PMLA* 132:2 (March 2017): 371–376. Readers may also want to consult Bruce Robbins, "Fashion Conscious Phenomenon," a review of Rita Felski and Elizabeth Anker's *Critique and Postcritique*, *American Book Review* (special issue on "Postcritique") 38:5 (July/August 2017): 5–6 or "But What About Love"? *Symploke* 28:1–2 (2020): 542–545.

17. Michel Foucault, "What Is Critique?" in *What Is Enlightenment? Eighteenth-Century Answers and Twentieth-Century Questions*, ed. James Schmidt (Berkeley: University of California Press, 1996), 382–398, at 384.

18. "The Function of Criticism at the Present Time" is probably the most widely reprinted of Arnold's essays. It is my pleasure to cite it from the place where I first encountered it: Walter Jackson Bate, ed., *Criticism: The Major Texts*, enlarged edition (New York: Harcourt Brace Jovanovich, 1970 [1952]), 455–456.

Chapter 1

1. Christopher Caldwell, *The Age of Entitlement: America Since the Sixties* (New York: Simon & Schuster, 2020), 3, 6, 7.

2. Walter Benn Michaels, *The Trouble with Diversity: How We Learned to Love Identity and Ignore Inequality* (New York: Metropolitan Books, 2006), 7. As I argued in a review, anyone who takes inequality as seriously as Michaels does ought to realize that there are rather more important politico-economic forces imposing it, and resisting any change to it, than concern with diversity in the humanities. See "On the Trouble with Diversity" *n+1* (online) (December 2006), with response from Michaels and my response to the response: https://nplusonemag.com/online-only/online-only/magical-capitalism/

3. Richard Rorty, "Intellectuals in Politics," *Dissent* (Fall 1991): 487; Russell Jacoby, *The Last Intellectuals: American Culture in the Age of Academe*, 2nd ed. (New York: Basic Books, 2000), 139. The flavor of the times can be sampled by taking a quick look

at *New York Times* correspondent Richard Bernstein's over-the-top extension of the military metaphor:

> what might be called the MLA liberation army was sending its cadres out to the hinterlands to spread the message of poststructuralism, of feminist scholarship in its several varieties, of the new historicism, social constructionism, gay and lesbian studies, Marxism, ethnic and Third World studies—in sort, all of the various regiments in the army of ideological multiculturalism.

Richard Bernstein, *Dictatorship of Virtue: Multiculturalism and the Battle for America's Future* (New York: Knopf, 1994), 321.

4. "The cultural Left has had extraordinary success. . . . they have decreased the amount of sadism in our society" (80–81). Richard Rorty, *Achieving Our Country: Leftist Thought in Twentieth-Century America* (Cambridge, MA: Harvard University Press, 1998).

5. Walter Jackson Bate, ed., *Criticism: The Major Texts*, enlarged edition (New York: Harcourt Brace Jovanovich, 1970 [1952]), 692. The reconciliation between Blackmur's New Criticism and Arnoldian humanism is logical in the sense that both believed that history poses no obstacle to literature. The New Criticism attached much the same conservative social values to a new, modern, more democratic pedagogy.

6. Bate made his views on the influence of the 60s on literary criticism more explicit ten years later in "The Crisis in English Studies," *Harvard Magazine* (September/October 1982): 46–53. Topics like deconstruction as politics, lesbian feminist poetry in Texas, and the trickster figure in Black and Chicano literature, he argued, had made the MLA "a laughingstock in the national press" (52).

7. Stefan Collini, *Matthew Arnold: A Critical Portrait* (Oxford: Clarendon Press, 1988/1994), 5, 52, 53.

8. Fredric Jameson, "Periodizing the 60s," in *The 60s Without Apology*, eds. Sohnya Sayres, Anders Stephanson, Stanley Aronowitz, and Fredric Jameson (Minneapolis: University of Minnesota Press, in cooperation with Social Text, 1984), 178–209, at 180.

9. Ibid.

10. Kristin Ross, *May '68 and Its Afterlives* (Chicago: University of Chicago Press, 2004), 10–11.

11. Mark Greif, *The Age of the Crisis of Man: Thought and Fiction in America, 1933–1973* (Princeton: Princeton University Press, 2015), 263.

12. Ibid., 265, 265, 266.

13. On universalism today, one useful reference is Souleymane Bachir Diagne and Jean-Loup Amselle, *In Search of Africa(s): Universalism and Decolonial Thought*, trans. Andrew Brown (Cambridge, UK: Polity, 2020).

14. The judgment of literature in terms of "life," which has to be distinguished from the "literature for its own sake" aestheticism of the New Critics, runs in a line from Wordsworth through Arnold to Henry James, Virginia Woolf, D. H. Lawrence,

F. R. Leavis, and Raymond Williams. Thanks on this point (and others) to Jonathan Arac.

15. Bate, *Criticism*, 438.

16. See the forthcoming work of Anthony Alessandrini against "critical thinking."

17. Bate, *Criticism*, 441.

18. See Rebecca Meade, "*Sexual Politics* and the Feminist Work That Remains Undone," *New Yorker* (February 4, 2016): https://www.newyorker.com/books/page-turner/sexual-politics-and-the-feminist-work-that-remains-undone

19. The question is posed by Agnes Callard, "Should We Cancel Aristotle?" *New York Times* (July 21, 2020): https://www.nytimes.com/2020/07/21/opinion/should-we-cancel-aristotle.html?action=click&module=Opinion&pgtype=Homepage

20. Matthew Arnold, *Culture and Anarchy*, ed. J. Dover Wilson (Cambridge, UK: Cambridge University Press, 1971), 76.

21. Sontag is cited in Greif, *Age of Crisis of Man*, 279.

22. Bate, *Criticism*, 692, 600, 600.

23. Ibid., 600.

24. This may not hold for Arnold's chiding of the "machinery" of reform by his fellow liberals, but what about T. S. Eliot's shamelessly reactionary royalism, Anglo-Catholicism, and anti-Semitism? The easy assumption that the society of the present is problematic, as the saying goes, is a comfortable assumption for critics, but it could make room for quite uncomfortable particulars.

25. To be fair, note that what Arnold valued in ancient Greek drama did not include all Greek values. The famous exception is the moral obligation to bury a fallen brother in *Antigone*, which Arnold said could no longer be expected to work on a nineteenth-century audience.

26. Bate, *Criticism*, 440.

27. In *Bleak Liberalism* (Chicago: University of Chicago Press, 2016), Amanda Anderson quotes the sociologist Daniel Bell on his generation, and that of Lionel Trilling. According to Bell, that generation "finds its wisdom in pessimism, evil, tragedy, and despair" (24).

28. Francis Mulhern, *Culture/Metaculture* (London and New York: Routledge, 2000), 170–171.

29. Arnold, *Culture and Anarchy*, 40.

30. Ibid.

31. Stefan Collini, *Matthew Arnold: A Critical Portrait* (Oxford: Clarendon Press, 1988/1994), 55.

32. Ibid.

33. Edmund Burke, *Thoughts on French Affairs* (1791), quoted in Bate, *Criticism*, 457.

34. Matthew Arnold quoted in Bate, *Criticism*, 456.

35. Fredric Jameson, "Periodizing the 60s," in *The 60s Without Apology*, eds. Sohnya Sayres, Anders Stephanson, Stanley Aronowitz, and Fredric Jameson (Minneapolis: University of Minnesota Press, in cooperation with Social Text, 1984), 178–209.

36. Ibid., 204.

37. Ibid., 205.

38. Lionel Trilling, *Sincerity and Authenticity* (Cambridge, MA: Harvard University Press, 1971/1972), 171.

39. R. P. Blackmur, "The Politics of Human Power," *Kenyon Review* 12:4 (Autumn 1950): 663–673, at 663.

40. Trilling, *Sincerity and Authenticity*, 41.

41. Ibid., 98.

42. Ibid., 159.

43. Ibid.

44. For a nuanced and interesting update on Trilling, see Daniel Rosenberg Nutters, "Modernism in the Classroom: Lionel Trilling and the Experience of Literature," *College Literature: A Journal of Critical Literary Studies* 48.4 (Fall 2021): 677–707. Another essential resource on Trilling's politics is Daniel O'Hara, *Lionel Trilling: The Work of Liberation* (Madison: University of Wisconsin Press, 1988).

45. Anderson, *Bleak Liberalism*, 164.

46. Gerald Graff, *Professing Literature: An Institutional History* (Chicago: University of Chicago Press, 1987), 173–174.

47. Ibid., 165. Graff describes Douglas Bush's 1948 presidential address to the Modern Language Association as "the last defiant roar" (185) of the historical scholars feeling themselves submerged by the tide of New Criticism. As Graff notes, this tone is parodied in the final chapter of *The Pooh Perplex*. That chapter makes much of Bush's attachment to gentlemanliness and his attendant anxiety about the "swarms of industrious and ingenious little graduate students—many of them, I must say, looking as if they were scarcely off the boat from Eastern Europe, or worse" (139).

48. Ross, *May '68 and Its Afterlives*, 6.

49. Lauren Berlant, "'68, or Something," *Critical Inquiry* 21:1 (Autumn 1994): 124–155, at 126.

50. Jacoby, *The Last Intellectuals*, 141.

51. Richard Rorty, "The People's Flag Is Deepest Red," in *Audacious Democracy: Labor, Intellectuals, and the Social Reconstruction of America,* eds. Steven Fraser and Joshua B. Freeman (Boston and New York: Houghton Mifflin, 1997), 57–63, at 62. Rorty quotes from Todd Gitlin's *Twilight of Common Dreams.*

52. Barbara and John Ehrenreich, "The Professional-Managerial Class," in *Between Labor and Capital,* ed. Pat Walker (Montreal: Black Rose Books, 1979), 33.

53. Ibid., 39.

54. Anderson, *Bleak Liberalism*, 112–113.

55. Ibid., 105. Whatever its other political merits or demerits, Anderson's bleak liberalism is, as she here admits, a secular rewriting of the Christian conviction that human beings are ineradicably sinful.

56. Pierre Bourdieu, *Homo Academicus*, trans. Peter Collier (Stanford: Stanford University Press, 1988), xiii. I'm grateful to Michael Trask's *Camp Sites* for reminding me of this point.

57. Another side of that fundamental commitment to autonomy is a perpetual friction with society-at-large. That friction is one reason for the oppositional streak that runs through the discipline from Arnold to the present.

58. On attachment, see Rita Felski, *Hooked: Art and Attachment* (Chicago and London: University of Chicago Press, 2020).

59. Amanda Anderson, *The Way We Argue Now: A Study in the Cultures of Theory* (Princeton: Princeton University Press, 2006), 172.

60. Ibid., 116.

61. Ibid.

62. This would presumably be the position of the so-called dirtbag left, though for better or worse that position seems better represented on social media than in the academy.

63. Susan Sontag, "Notes on 'Camp,'" in *Against Interpretation and Other Essays* (New York: Octagon, 1978 [1966]), 276.

64. Ibid., 290.

65. Ibid., 291–292.

66. Ibid., 279.

67. Michael Trask, *Camp Sites: Sex, Politics, and Academic Style in Postwar America* (Stanford: Stanford University Press, 2013), 12.

68. Ibid.

69. Berlant, "'68, or Something," 129–130.

70. Ibid., 127.

71. Ian Hunter, "Literary Theory and Civic Life," *South Atlantic Quarterly* 95:4 (Fall 1996): 1099–1134.

72. Viet Thanh Nguyen, "The Emergence of Asian American Literature as an Academic Field," in *The Cambridge History of Asian American Literature*, eds. Rajini Srikanth and Min Song (Cambridge, UK: Cambridge University Press, 2015).

73. The claim that the humanities and democracy have something important to offer each other, though it was not invented in the 1960s, has become an increasingly important one. Helen Small points out its weaknesses, including the fact that much of what literary criticism purports to offer is also offered by other disciplines or by education in general. Helen Small, *The Value of the Humanities* (Oxford: Oxford University Press, 2013), chap. 4. As Small points out, the claim that democracy needs the humanities has much less support among the educational reformers of the nineteenth century than one might have expected.

Chapter 2

1. An analogue to the criticizer, imprecise but resonant, is the early modern "corrector" or, even more resonantly, "castigator." See Anthony Grafton, *Inky Fingers* (Cambridge, MA: Harvard University Press, 2020).

2. See, for example, Ellen Schrecker. "The Roots of the Right-Wing Attack on Higher Education," *Thought and Action: The NEA Higher Education Journal* 26 (Fall

2010): 71–82. Schrecker's point is that the crises facing higher education in the twenty-first century are about "the ghosts of the 1960s" (71):

The enormous changes that took place on the nation's campuses during that tumultuous decade not only opened those campuses to new constituencies and new ideas, but also created a powerful conservative movement that sought to reverse those changes. . . . From the start, the general public disliked what was happening on the nation's campuses during the 1960s. The media fed that aversion. (71)

3. Raymond Williams, *Keywords: A Vocabulary of Culture and Politics* (Fontana/Croom Helm, 1976), 75.

4. Ibid.

5. Ibid.

6. See, for example, John K. Wilson, *The Myth of Political Correctness: The Conservative Attack on Higher Education* (Durham: Duke University Press, 1995).

7. Lionel Trilling's takedown of V. L. Parrington's *Main Currents in American Thought*, three full decades before Williams, is another interesting moment of objection to the politicization of criticism.

8. But see Stefan Collini's critique of *Culture and Society* in *The Nostalgic Imagination* (Oxford: Oxford University Press, 2019), 156–182. Collini argues that most of the references to the word "culture" had "no connection to the Industrial Revolution" (159). The nineteenth-century critique of industrialism was largely expressed in and through themes like "the whole against the fragmented, the general against the specialized, the common against the individual, and so on" (176), including an "idealized Hellenism," themes that are as much mainstream as oppositional:

The danger in trying to impose this division on nineteenth-century thought is that in the end the only people left to represent the alternative to his "tradition of English social thinking"—that is, the "culture-and-society tradition"—would seem to be a few strictly orthodox political economists, a travesty of Victorian social thinking . . . that has now outlived its day. (179)

9. Pertinent here is Frederic Harrison's critique of Arnold on culture, quoted by Arnold in his introduction to the book: culture "means simply a turn for small fault-finding" (39). Matthew Arnold, *Culture and Anarchy*, ed. J. Dover Wilson (Cambridge, UK: Cambridge University Press, 1971).

10. The published version of Butler's "What Is Critique?" is in David Ingram, ed., *The Political: Readings in Continental Philosophy* (London: Basil Blackwell, 2002).

11. Talal Asad, Wendy Brown, Judith Butler, and Saba Mahmood, *Is Critique Secular? Blasphemy, Injury, and Free Speech* (Berkeley: Townsend Center for the Humanities, UC Berkeley, 2009), 139.

12. Ibid., 140.

13. Butler's response is in "The Sensibility of Critique: Response to Asad and Mahmood," in *Is Critique Secular?* 103.

14. Ibid., 105.

15. Ibid., 106.

16. Ibid., 109.

17. Butler, "What Is Critique?"

18. Here she returns to the distinction between criticism and critique: "Criticism usually takes an object, and critique is concerned to identify the conditions of possibility under which a domain of objects appears" (*Is Critique Secular?* 108–109). Note the difference: here what distinguishes criticism is taking an object, not applying to that object a pre-established category. Also, Butler is selling ordinary criticism down the river.

19. Asad, *Is Critique Secular?* 24.

20. Todd Gitlin, *The Sixties: Years of Hope, Days of Rage* (New York: Bantam, 1993), xxii.

21. Richard Rorty, *Achieving Our Country: Leftist Thought in Twentieth-Century America* (Cambridge, MA: Harvard University Press, 1998), 76–77.

22. Mark Lilla, *The Once and Future Liberal: After Identity Politics* (New York: Harper, 2017), 70, 88.

23. For background on Lilla's politics and his critics, see David Remnick, "A Conversation with Mark Lilla on His Critique of Identity Politics," *New Yorker* (August 25, 2017): https://www.newyorker.com/news/news-desk/a-conversation-with-mark-lilla-on-his-critique-of-identity-politics

24. Simon During, "When Literary Criticism Mattered," in *The Values of Literary Studies: Critical Institutions, Scholarly Agendas,* ed. Ronan McDonald (Cambridge, UK: Cambridge University Press, 2016), 120–136, 122.

25. Ibid., 134.

26. There is a parallel here with John Guillory's analysis of the self-legitimating vision of the New Critics. Guillory is extremely critical of what he sees as Cleanth Brooks's power play yet is no happier to conclude at the end that if Brooks's "program to restore literary culture to a position of power" no longer works, it's because "'difference' has become our central critical category" (359). John Guillory, "The Ideology of Canon-Formation: T. S. Eliot and Cleanth Brooks," in *Canons*, ed. Robert von Hallberg (Chicago: University of Chicago Press, 1983), 337–362.

27. During, "When Literary Criticism Mattered," 136.

28. A rhetorically cruder and even ugly example comes from Ronan McDonald's *The Death of the Critic* (London: Continuum, 2007). When he tells the 1968-and-after story, McDonald makes pious noises about how "the political turn in the humanities" has "performed a scholarly service that has greatly enriched world culture. Who would not welcome the rediscovery of unjustly forgotten women writers, or the efforts to hear the voices of the marginalized and disempowered?" (21). Then he continues: "It is an entirely different proposition, however, to do away with the idea of quality and canonicity altogether" (23). Did anyone ever propose doing away with canonicity or (the mind boggles) with *quality*? McDonald quotes no one. The impression is therefore left hanging that marginalized and disempowered writers *have* no literary quality but are being read now simply because they had not been read before. It would have been better for McDonald's argument if he had not pretended to a respect for them that he was about to demonstrate he does not possess.

29. Joseph North, *Literary Criticism: A Concise Political History* (Cambridge, MA: Harvard University Press, 2017), 3.

30. For a corrective, see Bruce Robbins, "Neoliberalism Is Not Everything," *American Literary History* 31:4 (October 4, 2019): https://doi.org/10.1093/alh/ajz034

31. North, *Literary Criticism,* 86.

32. Terry Eagleton, *Literary Theory: An Introduction* (Minneapolis: University of Minnesota Press, 1983), 12. Eagleton's book is not perfect, but it is itself an admirable monument to a generation's sensibility.

33. For those with a taste for this sort of dead-on satire, there is also Eagleton's reading of the (ambiguous) imperative, borrowed from nonliterary discourse, "Dogs must be carried on the escalator":

> One could let oneself be arrested by the abrupt, minatory staccato of the first ponderous monosyllables; find one's mind drifting, by the time it had reached the rich allusiveness of "carried," to suggestive resonances of helping lame dogs through life; and perhaps even detect in the very lilt and inflection of the word "escalator" a miming of the rolling, up-and-down motion of the thing itself. (Eagleton, *Literary Theory,* 7)

In his commentary on I. A. Richards, Eagleton notes that all the participants in the experiment recorded in his *Practical Criticism* (1929) "were, presumably, young, white, upper- or upper-middle-class, privately-educated English people of the 1920s, and how they responded to a poem depended on a good deal more than purely 'literary' factors" (ibid.,15).

34. North, *Literary Criticism,* 45; John Paul Russo, "Ivor Armstrong Richards," in *Encyclopedia of Aesthetics,* Vol. 3, ed. Michael Kelly (New York: Oxford University Press, 1998), 160.

35. Gitlin, *The Sixties,* xxi.

36. Russell Jacoby, *The Last Intellectuals: American Culture in the Age of Academe,* 2nd ed. (New York: Basic Books, 2000), 141.

37. Rita Felski, *The Limits of Critique* (Chicago and London: University of Chicago Press, 2015), 149.

38. Ibid.

39. See, for example, Gitlin, *The Sixties.* Gitlin takes a dark and perhaps even tragic view of the effect of identity politics on "the movement." For identity politics, he argues, "the principal purpose of organizing is to express a distinct social identity rather than to achieve the collective good. In this radical extension of the politics of the late Sixties, difference and victimization are prized, ranked against the victimization of other groups." Gitlin's tone sours into sarcasm: "We crown our good with victimhood" (xxii).

40. Edward W. Said, *The World, the Text, and the Critic* (Cambridge, MA: Harvard University Press, 1983), 83.

41. Ibid.

42. Ibid., 84.

43. On the divisions within the 60s New Left over Israel and Palestine, see Michael R. Fischbach, *The Movement and the Middle East: How the Arab-Israeli Conflict Divided the American Left* (Stanford. Stanford University Press, 2020).

44. "The troubling side of the movement's most counter-cultural, participatory spirit is a certain tendency toward know-nothing leveling. One hears the assumption that all knowledge is bankrupt, all claims to authority or objectivity fraudulent, all expertise is a mask for raw power." Gitlin, *The Sixties*, xxi.

45. Bruce Robbins, *Perpetual War: Cosmopolitanism from the Viewpoint of Violence* (Durham: Duke University Press, 2012).

46. Williams, *Keywords,* 79.

47. Colin MacCabe, Holly Yanacek, and others, eds., *Keywords for Today: A 21st Century Vocabulary* (New York: Oxford University Press, 2018), 270, 271.

48. Ibid., 269.

49. Ibid., 270.

50. Ibid.

51. Ibid., 270–271.

52. Rorty, *Achieving Our Country,* 76–77, 78.

53. Francis Mulhern, *Culture/Metaculture* (London and New York: Routledge, 2000), 165.

54. Ibid., 170–171.

55. Ibid., 171.

56. Rorty, *Achieving Our Country,* 80–81.

Chapter 3

1. The preferred translation of "The Order of Discourse" (by Ian McLeod) is in Robert Young, ed., *Untying the Text: A Post-Structuralist Reader* (Boston, London, and Henley: Routledge & Kegan Paul, 1981), 48–78, at 56.

2. Ibid., 57.

3. Ibid.

4. Isobel Armstrong, *The Radical Aesthetic* (Oxford: Blackwell, 2000), 11.

5. The reference is to Hans Vaihinger's *The Philosophy of As If* (1911/1924), a philosophical synthesis of Kant and Nietzsche, ethics and aesthetics. For a brilliant (and equally synthetic) updating, see Kwame Anthony Appiah, *As If: Idealization and Ideals* (Cambridge, MA: Harvard University Press, 2017).

6. Simon During notes that Foucault "often complained" about commentary. "When he criticized commentary he was dissociating himself from a procedure close to the heart of the modern humanities" (2). Simon During, *Foucault and Literature: Towards a Genealogy of Writing* (London and New York: Routledge, 1992).

7. Foucault in Young, *Untying the Text,* 58.

8. Ibid., 54.

9. See, for example, *The Norton Anthology of Theory and Criticism* (2001), further discussed below, which gives *Ion* pride of place in a modernized metanarrative of

theory. The first reference I know of, and the one to which I am personally indebted, comes from Harold Bloom.

10. As translated by Paul Woodruff in the *Norton Anthology of Theory and Criticism* (New York and London: Norton, 2001), 37–48, the dialogue goes like this. Ion: "Really, Socrates, it's worth hearing how well I've got Homer dressed up ..." Socrates: "Really, I shall make time to hear that later. Now I'd just like an answer to this" (38).

11. Ibid., 41.

12. Ibid., 43.

13. Ibid., 42.

14. Conor Friedersdorf, "Is 'Victimhood Culture' a Fair Description," *The Atlantic* (September 19, 2015): https://www.theatlantic.com/politics/archive/2015/09/the-problems-with-the-term-victimhood-culture/406057/

15. Fredric Jameson's model of criticism as the fitting of one narrative into another narrative could also be described as a performative evasion of Foucault's dilemma of commentary, but without recourse to first-person testimony.

16. See Grace Lavery, "On Being Criticized," *Modernism/Modernity* 25:3 (September 2018): 499–516.

17. Jeffrey J. Williams, "The New Modesty in Literary Criticism," *Chronicle of Higher Education* (January 5, 2015): https://www.chronicle.com/article/the-new-modesty-in-literary-criticism/

18. Stephen Best and Sharon Marcus, "Surface Reading: An Introduction," *Representations* (special issue: "The Way We Read Now") 108 (Fall 2009): 1–21, 15–16.

19. Ibid., 16.

20. Ibid.

21. Foucault in Young, *Untying the Text,* 59.

22. Ibid.

23. Ibid., 60.

24. Ibid., 61, 61, 60.

25. In *The Limits of Critique* Rita Felski proposes that it is critique alone that submits to the secondariness of commentary. In her eagerness to gather everything and anything that can be said against her straw-man adversary, she ignores the fact that for Foucault this paradoxical secondariness would clearly apply to criticism as such, not to any particular version of it.

26. These lines are quoted from Bruce Robbins, "Less Disciplinary Than Thou: Criticism and the Conflict of the Faculties," *Minnesota Review* 45/46 (1996): 95–115, at 106; reprinted in E. Ann Kaplan and George Levine, eds., *The Politics of Research* (New Brunswick: Rutgers University Press, 1997), 93–115. The quotation from John Gross is from *The Rise and Fall of the Man of Letters* (New York: Macmillan, 1969), 297–298. Relevant here also is Stanley Fish's argument on anti-professionalism.

27. Gross, *Rise and Fall,* 302.

28. Andrew Abbott, *The Chaos of Disciplines* (Chicago and London: University of Chicago Press, 2001), ix.

29. Consider the field of rhetoric, as discussed by Dilip Gaonkar. Some histories of rhetoric look forward to a moment when "rhetoric would reclaim its lost glory as 'the queen of the human sciences,'" when it "would preside over other disciplines as the metascience of culture in the Isocreatean sense" (361). See Dilip Parameshwar Gaonkar, "Rhetoric and Its Double: Reflections on the Rhetorical Turn in the Human Sciences," in *The Rhetorical Turn: Invention and Persuasion in the Conduct of Inquiry*, ed. Herbert Simons (Chicago: University of Chicago Press, 1990), 341–366. Rhetoric's true disciplinary history is much more contingent, Gaonkar insists modestly. But the modesty has its own claims to press—very like Gross's for literature.

> The fortunes of rhetoric, more than any other discipline, turn on the roll of the cultural dice. Rhetoric has good days and bad days, mostly bad days. This is one of the good days. If there is a myth about rhetoric, it is that of an outside whose day of reckoning is deferred, time and again. (360—my emphasis)

If rhetoric seems weaker than other disciplines, this weakness is again really a strength. Once again, a claim to disciplinary power masquerades as an admission of disciplinary frailty and lack of substance. It emptiness, its lack of substance or grounding, is finally the discipline's animating principle—that is to say that rhetoric *has* such a principle, which not every discipline can boast. Emptier than other disciplines, it has also survived a lot longer. I borrow this point from my "Less Disciplinary Than Thou," 106–107.

30. Derek Attridge, *Peculiar Language: Literature as Difference from the Renaissance to James Joyce* (London: Methuen, 1988), 1.

31. This passage borrows from Bruce Robbins, "Epilogue: The Scholar in Society," in *Introduction to Scholarship in Modern Languages and Literatures*, 3rd ed., ed. David G. Nicholls (New York: Modern Language Association, 2007), 312–330.

32. John Guillory, "Literary Critics as Intellectuals: Class Analysis and the Crisis of the Humanities," in *Rethinking Class: Literary Studies and Social Formations*, eds. Wai Chee Dimock and Michael T. Gilmore (New York: Columbia University Press, 1994), 107–149, at 115. I owe a great deal to this essay, one of the most intellectually serious and ambitious pieces of work spawned by the fury of the culture wars.

33. Ibid., 114.

34. Ibid., 115.

35. Ibid.

36. Ibid.

37. Ibid., 116.

38. Ibid.

39. Ibid., 115.

40. Terry Eagleton, *The Function of Criticism: From The Spectator to Post-Structuralism* (London, Verso, 1984), 10.

41. Guillory, "Literary Critics as Intellectuals," 116.

42. The "and other forms of collectivity" complicates the story, as I have already suggested, but too seriously to be dealt with here. For example, it includes the working class, though to a lesser extent, and it includes the victims of American militarism abroad, a larger constituency than the American working class. The argument that follows—that criticism also involves learning how to govern—obviously does not apply in anything like the same way to the victims of American militarism abroad as it does to racial and sexual minorities in the United States.

43. John Guillory, *Cultural Capital: The Problem of Literary Canon Formation* (Chicago and London: University of Chicago, 1995), 38–39.

44. I develop this argument at greater length in Bruce Robbins, "'Real Politics' and the Canon Debate," *Contemporary Literature* 35:2 (Summer 1994): 365–375.

45. But see Niall Ferguson, *Empire: How Britain Made the Modern World* (London. Allen Lane, 2003), 184–186, on the specific content of the Indian civil service exam.

46. John Bender and David E. Wellbery, eds., *The Ends of Rhetoric: History, Theory, Practice* (Stanford: Stanford University Press, 1990), 17.

47. Eagleton, *Function of Criticism*, 106–107.

48. Ibid., 123.

49. Guillory, "Literary Critics as Intellectuals," 126.

50. In another vocabulary, one might say that unlike intellectuals, academics are asked to write without solidarity—without solidarity, that is, for anyone but fellow academics.

51. On the pertinence of Gramsci's model of the organic intellectual to class formation in eighteenth-century Britain, see for example the discussion of Adam Smith in Kate Crehan, *Gramsci's Common Sense: Inequality and Its Narratives* (Durham and London: Duke University Press, 2016). Thanks to James Livingston for the reference.

52. Francis Mulhern, *Culture/Metaculture* (London and New York: Routledge, 2000), 17.

53. Chris Baldick, *The Social Mission of English Criticism, 1848–1932* (Oxford: Clarendon Press, 1987), 95.

54. Bill Readings, *The University in Ruins* (Cambridge, MA: Harvard University Press, 1996), 3.

55. Ibid, 5.

56. Ibid, 193.

57. Gauri Viswanathan, *Masks of Conquest: Literary Study and British Rule in India* (New York: Columbia University Press, 1989).

58. Ibid, 23.

59. Ibid., 142.

60. How different this story is from the British state's intervention in England remains an interesting question. At home, the nineteenth-century state intervened in education (reluctantly) because of violent disputes between the various religious denominations over who would control popular education. See During, *Foucault and Literature*, 189–190.

61. Viswanathan, *Masks of Conquest*, 10.

62. David Lloyd and Paul Thomas, *Culture and the State* (New York and London: Routledge, 1998), 19.

63. Ibid., 6.

64. Ibid., 10.

65. Guillory, "Literary Critics as Intellectuals," 115.

66. According to the *New York Times* (July 9, 2020), Black Lives Matter may be the largest popular movement in United States history.

Chapter 4

1. Richard Ohmann, *English in America: A Radical View of the Profession,* with a new introduction and a foreword by Gerald Graff (Hanover, NH, and London: Wesleyan University Press, 1995 [1976]).

2. Ibid., xiv.

3. Antonio Gramsci, *Selections from the Prison Notebooks*, trans. and eds. Quintin Hoare and Geoffrey Nowell Smith (New York: International Publishers, 1971), 7.

4. Michel Foucault, "Intellectuals and Power," in *Language, Counter-Memory, Practice: Selected Essays and Interviews by Michel Foucault,* ed. Donald F. Bouchard (Ithaca: Cornell University Press, 1977), 205–217, at 207–208.

5. Ibid., 206.

6. Dinesh D'Souza, *Illiberal Education: The Politics of Race and Sex on Campus* (New York: Free Press, 1991), 72.

7. At the same time, one might say that Foucault's recoil from representation of or accountability to a constituency also reflects a commitment to intellectual autonomy that *is* a symbolic consolidation of the diverse constituencies' diverse aims and impulses. The worry about being subordinated to or absorbed by someone else's agenda or simply told to wait one's turn was not baseless. For all their diversity, the movements thus shared a commitment to autonomy, and sharing it would make it easier for their representatives to make themselves at home in the university, where autonomy has had its lonely, ever-precarious refuge.

8. Michel Foucault, "What Is Critique?" in *What Is Enlightenment? Eighteenth-Century Answers and Twentieth-Century Questions,* ed. James Schmidt (Berkeley: University of California Press, 1996), 382–398, at 384.

9. In "The Order of Discourse," Foucault had taken aim at the most seemingly innocent of norms, arguing that the real work of governing has come to be done by these norms and not by the cruder and more visible means of violence or prohibition. The hierarchy of primary text and secondary text, hidden away in the "normal" functioning of criticism, is one example. As Arnold I. Davidson puts it in his introduction to *Abnormal,* the norm "founds and legitimizes a certain exercise of power, and is 'always linked to a positive technique of intervention and transformation'" (xxi). Michel Foucault, *Abnormal: Lectures at the Collège de France 1974–1975,* eds. Valerio Marchetti and Antonella Salomoni, trans. Graham Burchell (New York: Picador, 2003).

10. I am not speaking here about writers like James Baldwin or Adrienne Rich personally, but about the academic stands that purported to represent them, and not without reason.

11. The assumption that aesthetic taste serves a conservative social function is also associated with the French sociologist Pierre Bourdieu. For Bourdieu's very different uptake in the United States, see John Guillory, "Bourdieu's Refusal," *Modern Language Quarterly* 58:4 (December 1997): 367–398.

12. George Levine, "Introduction: Reclaiming the Aesthetic," in *Aesthetics and Ideology*, ed. George Levine (New Brunswick: Rutgers University Press, 1994), 1–28, at 19.

13. Regina Gagnier, "A Critique of Practical Aesthetics" in Levine, *Aesthetics and Ideology*, 264–282, at 264.

14. John Rajchman, *Michel Foucault: The Freedom of Philosophy* (New York: Columbia University Press, 1985), 25. This gives the arts the function that Kant attributed to critique. See also Kandice Chuh, whose endorsement of Jacques Rancière's aesthetics goes back through Foucault to Kant: art serves the function of critique, getting at the structures that frame what can be seen, including what is seen as political (22). Kandice Chuh, *The Difference Aesthetics Makes: On the Humanities After "Man"* (Durham: Duke University Press, 2019).

15. Rajchman, *Michel Foucault*, 23.

16. Michel Foucault, "An Aesthetics of Existence," in *Politics, Philosophy, Culture: Interviews and Other Writings, 1977–1984*, ed. Lawrence D. Kritzman, trans. Alan Sheridan and others (New York: Routledge, 1988), 47–53, at 49. The original interview with Alessandro Fontana appeared in the Italian journal *Panorama* and then in *Le Monde* on July 15–16, 1984. See also, in the Kriztman volume, "The Functions of Literature" (1975), 307–313.

17. Ibid., 49.

18. Simon During, *Foucault and Literature: Towards a Genealogy of Writing* (London and New York: Routledge, 1992), 179.

19. Michel Foucault, "What Is an Author?" in *The Foucault Reader*, ed. Paul Rabinow (New York: Pantheon, 1984), 101–120, at 114.

20. Ibid. David Macey, one of Foucault's biographers, notes that the "commentary" section of "The Order of Discourse" is one of the projected topics of research on which he never followed through: he "had little more to say about literary criticism" (245). David Macey, *The Lives of Michel Foucault* (London: Hutchinson, 1993). Literary criticism seems to have returned the favor by withholding commentary on that essay.

21. In another interview, conducted three months earlier, Foucault was asked whether his new interest in "the care of the self" entails a shift away from a practice that is "coercive" and toward "a practice of self-formation of the subject" (282). The question suggested diplomatically that aesthetic self-fashioning is in fact the *same* practice that Foucault had earlier seen as coercive. Michel Foucault, "The Ethics of the Concern of the Self as a Practice of Freedom," in *Ethics: Subjectivity and Truth*, Vol. 1 of *Essential Works of Michel Foucault, 1954–1984*, ed. Paul Rabinow (New York: New

Press, 1997). The interview was conducted on January 20, 1984, at the very end of his life, by H. Becker, R. Fornet-Betancourt, and A. Gomez-Müller and first published in *Concordia: Revista internacional de filosofia* 6 (July–December 1984): 96–116. In "What Is Critique?" Foucault had argued, in a familiar vein, that "there is meaning only through effects of coercion" (Schmidt, *What Is Enlightenment?* 390). Hence knowledge and power cannot be separated from each other.

22. Michel Foucault, *Power,* Vol. 3 of *Essential Works of Michel Foucault, 1954–1984,* ed. James D. Faubion (New York: New Press, 2000), 341.

23. Presented with the proposition that "the care of the self is in a certain sense care for others," Foucault agrees—"*Ethos* always implies a relationship with others"— but he also insists that "Care for others should not be put before the care of oneself. The care of the self is ethically prior" (ibid., 287). If you take proper care of yourself, you should not have to worry about dominating others: "the risk of dominating others and exercising a tyrannical power over them arises precisely when one has not taken care of the self and has become a slave of one's desires" (ibid., 288).

24. Foucault, "Intellectuals and Power," 207.

25. Ibid., 216.

26. Judith Butler, *Gender Trouble: Feminism and the Subversion of Identity* (New York and London: Routledge, 1990).

27. Ibid., 143.

28. Foucault, "Ethics of the Concern of the Self as a Practice of Freedom," in *Ethics,* vol. 1 of *Essential Works of Foucault,* ed. Rabinow, 294.

29. Butler noticed the compulsive signaling of this incompleteness in the conclusion to *Gender Trouble.* Diversity is not an ideal; it can also be described as incoherence and as a political liability. But (as Butler points out) it is also a source of collective self-knowledge, and it does generate a distinct sort of politics.

30. David Lloyd, *Under Representation: The Racial Regime of Aesthetics* (New York: Fordham University Press, 2019), 12.

31. Ibid., 7.

32. Audre Lorde, "Poetry Is Not a Luxury," first published in *Chrysalis: A Magazine of Female Culture* 3 (1977). Reprinted in *Sister Outsider: Essays and Speeches by Audre Lorde,* ed. Cheryl Clarke (Berkeley: Crossing Press, 2007), 37.

33. Ibid.

34. Chuh, *The Difference Aesthetics Makes,* xi–xii.

35. Ibid., xii.

36. Ibid., 3. The choice of the adjective "illiberal" for the (largely minority) sensibilities Chuh values (5) is unfortunate, as it reminds her reader of the common ground between similarly illiberal positions that Trump's America shares with "minorities" in Modi's India, Erdogan's Turkey, and Bolsonaro's Brazil, all of them highly undesirable. Trying to eat her cake and have it too, Chuh has little to say about whether what is distinctively aesthetic about minority writing is distinct from what is distinctively aesthetic about majority writing. Nor does she confront the risk that by giving due credit to minority works, critics might diminish their difference

from majority ("liberal humanist") works, thereby putting them back on the same ground.

37. Ibid., 3.

38. Ibid., 16–17.

39. Quoted in Lauren Berlant, "Claudia Rankine," *Bomb* (October 1, 2014): https://bombmagazine.org/articles/claudia-rankine/ I borrow this from Kenneth Warren, "The Poetics and Politics of Black Lives Matter," *Nonsite* 32 (September 10, 2020): https://nonsite.org/the-poetics-and-politics-of-black-lives-matter/

40. On intersectionality, see Keeanga-Yamahtta Taylor, "Until Black Women Are Free, None of Us Will Be Free: Barbara Smith and the Black Feminist Visionaries of the Combahee River Collective," *New Yorker* (July 20, 2020) and Keeanga-Yamahtta Taylor, ed., *How We Got Free: Black Feminism and the Combahee River Collective* (Chicago: Haymarket Books, 2017).

41. Terry Eagleton, *The Ideology of the Aesthetic* (Oxford: Basil Blackwell, 1990), 97.

42. Ibid.

43. Ibid., 98–99.

44. Ibid., 76.

45. Lloyd, *Under Representation,* 35.

46. I borrow this theme from *Hegemony and Socialist Strategy: Towards a Radical Democratic Politics* (1985) by Ernesto Laclau and Chantal Mouffe, a book that was widely praised for offering a political theory that was organically attuned to the new social movements.

47. Charles M. Blow, "Allies, Don't Fail Us Again," *New York Times* (June 8, 2020).

48. Hannah Arendt, *Lectures on Kant's Political Philosophy*, ed. Ronald Beiner (Chicago: University of Chicago Press, 1992).

49. In Arendt's words: "What Kant said is—to vary the Aristotelian formula—that a bad man can be a good citizen in a good state" (ibid., 17).

50. Chris Baldick, *The Social Mission of English Criticism, 1848–1932* (Oxford: Clarendon Press, 1987), 24.

51. Ibid.

52. Ibid., 35–36.

53. See John Storey, "Matthew Arnold: The Politics of an Organic Intellectual," *Literature and History* 11:2 (Fall 1985): 217–228 and Sebastian Lecourt, "Matthew Arnold and the Institutional Imagination of Liberalism," *Victorian Literature and Culture* 49:2 (2021): 361–375.

54. Fredric Jameson, "Periodizing the 60s," in *The 60s Without Apology*, eds. Sohnya Sayres, Anders Stephanson, Stanley Aronowitz, and Fredric Jameson (Minneapolis: University of Minnesota Press, in cooperation with Social Text, 1984), 178–209, at 195.

55. Jonathan Arac, "Why Does No One Care About the Aesthetic Value of *Huckleberry Finn*?" *New Literary History* 30:4 (Autumn 1999): 769–784.

56. David Lloyd and Paul Thomas, *Culture and the State* (New York and London: Routledge, 1998), 147.

57. Ibid.

58. Ian Hunter, *Culture and Government: The Emergence of Literary Education* (New York: Macmillan, 1988).

59. Ibid., 5.

60. Foucault, "Ethics of the Concern of the Self as a Practice of Freedom," 298.

61. Ian Hunter, "Literary Theory in Civil Life," *South Atlantic Quarterly* 95:4 (Fall 1996): 1099–1134, at 1099.

62. Lloyd, *Under Representation,* 11.

63. Francis Mulhern, *Culture/Metaculture* (London and New York: Routledge, 2000), 170.

64. Bill Readings, *The University in Ruins* (Cambridge, MA: Harvard University Press, 1996), 21–43.

65. Ibid., 22.

66. Ibid., 180–193.

67. By harping on power in this way, I expose my position to caricature—for example, as a wonkish identification with bullies, which is to say a hunger for power on the part of a weak social position that makes such a claim to strength outlandish and absurd. My wish is for it to be taken, rather, as a plea for progressives to take their own progressive goals seriously.

Chapter 5

1. Craig S. Womack, Daniel Heath Justice, and Christopher B. Teuton, eds., *Reasoning Together: The Native Critics Collective* (Norman: University of Oklahoma Press, 2008), 3.

2. Ibid., 5.

3. Ibid.

4. See Elizabeth Cook-Lynn, "Who Stole Native American Studies?" in *Wicazo Sa Review* 12:1 (Spring 1997): 9–28. For a global overview, see "Study on How the Knowledge, History and Contemporary Social Circumstances of Indigenous Peoples Are Embedded in the Curricula of Education Systems. Note by the Secretariat," United Nations Economic and Social Council, Permanent Forum on Indigenous Issues, Twelfth Session, New York (May 20–31, 2013).

5. University of Minnesota, College of Liberal Studies, American Indian Studies: https://cla.umn.edu/ais/about/history (accessed April 26, 2021)

6. Exemplary defenders of the canon are Allan Bloom, *The Closing of the American Mind* (New York: Simon & Schuster, 1987) and E. D. Hirsch Jr., *Cultural Literacy: What Every American Needs to Know* (Boston: Houghton Mifflin, 1987). On the other side, Paul Lauter in *Canons and Contexts* (New York: Oxford University Press, 1991) points out: "of things Latino Hirsch includes little more than señor, señora, señorita, wetback, 'La Cucaracha (song),' and Zapata; but . . . he excludes Cesar Chavez, migrant worker, barrio, and La Raza" (264). Hirsch did not object to expanding his list but

added that "if items had been left out, that reflected their relative *unimportance* to what [he] describes as the 'national culture'" (ibid.).

7. Of course, not everything has changed. This is hardly surprising, given how rare it was for anyone to call for the burning down of the Western tradition in its entirety, as Amiri Baraka did when the Department of English tried to hire him at Rutgers–New Brunswick in the mid-1980s. As one Baraka supporter observed, his lecture had to be understood, in the context of his writing career, as an example of the theater of cruelty.

8. According to Google Ngram, "coopted" began a precipitous climb in 1960 and reached a peak in 2000. It then fell almost as precipitously and has only recently begun to rise again. For a sharp examination of the issues it raises, written amid the term's ascent, see Gerald Graff, "Co-optation," in *The New Historicism,* ed. H. Aram Veeser (New York and London: Routledge, 1989), 168–181.

9. Elizabeth Cook-Lynn, *Wicazo Sa Review* 12:1 (Spring 1997): 5.

10. Aimee Carrillo Rowe, "Romancing the Organic Intellectual: On the Queerness of Academic Activism," *American Quarterly* (2012): 799–803, at 799.

11. Ibid., 800–801.

12. Ibid., 800.

13. Hortense J. Spillers, "The Crisis of the Negro Intellectual: A Post-Date," *boundary 2* 21:3 (Fall 1994): 65–119. Spillers accuses Cornel West of appealing to "the two most powerful (and predictable motifs of African American cultural life: '*the black Christian tradition of preaching* and *the black musical tradition of performance*'" (83 n12). And this because West's idea of the Black intellectual is so "firmly rooted in the romantic ground of organicity" (83 n12).

14. Ibid., 68–69.

15. Ibid., 73.

16. Ibid., 92.

17. Ibid., 101 n31.

18. *The Norton Anthology of Theory and Criticism,* eds. Vincent B. Leitch and others (New York and London: Norton, 2001). Placing the Norton next to Walter Jackson Bate's *Criticism: The Major Texts* (1970), thirty years earlier, the first thing that leaps into view is that, while preserving Plato and Aristotle and most of the other landmarks of the classical tradition, the Norton also makes room for a great number of critics and theorists, not all of them recent, who are women and people of color. There is even one Indigenous woman: the poet Paula Gunn Allen (1939–2008). I am grateful to one of Stanford University Press's anonymous readers for suggesting the juxtaposition with Bate's anthology.

19. *Norton Anthology,* 1136.

20. For the record, class is also relativized, at least in appearance, in Gramsci's prison notebooks themselves, where it is replaced by "social group" and "fundamental social group" (5). Gramsci's editors maintain that this was to avoid censorship. Antonio Gramsci, *Selections from the Prison Notebooks,* trans. and eds. Quintin Hoare and Geoffrey Nowell Smith (New York: International Publishers, 1971).

21. *Norton Anthology*, 1987.

22. Ibid.

23. Keeanga-Yamahtta Taylor, ed., *How We Got Free: Black Feminism and the Combahee River Collective* (Chicago: Haymarket Books, 2017), 4.

24. Ibid., 61.

25. Ibid.

26. Timothy Brennan, *Places of Mind: A Life of Edward Said* (New York: Farrar, Straus and Giroux, 2021), 124.

27. Ibid., 125.

28. At Columbia, according to Ellen Schrecker, "only 5 percent [of the faculty] supported [the student] takeover of the campus" (75). Ellen Schrecker, "The Roots of the Right-Wing Attack on Higher Education," *Thought and Action: The NEA Higher Education Journal* 26 (Fall 2010): 71–82.

29. Brennan, *Places of Mind*, 140. Noam Chomsky, *The Essential Chomsky*, ed. Anthony Arnove (New York and London: New Press, 2008). For more on Chomsky, see Nicholas Allott, Chris Knight, and Neil Smith, eds., *The Responsibility of Intellectuals: Reflections by Noam Chomsky and Others After 50 Years* (London: UCL Press, 2019).

30. Chomsky, *Essential Chomsky*, 49.

31. Ibid., 39–40.

32. Ibid., 40.

33. Edward W. Said, *Representations of the Intellectual: The 1993 Reith Lectures* (New York: Pantheon Books, 1994), 67.

34. Brennan, *Places of Mind*, 299.

35. Ibid., 300. Said himself refused to play the identity game, stoutly opposing the idea that what you are capable of knowing depends on where you are from. This fact does not imply, of course, that he embodies the deeper truth of the 60s legacy. It suggests only that that legacy is divided, has been contested at every step, and is still up for grabs.

36. Such claims would look a good deal weaker if there was recognition of the small but heroic tradition of anticolonial voices that came from within the metropolis, like Bartolomé de las Casas. See my work-in-progress on the literary history of atrocity.

37. Frantz Fanon, *The Wretched of the Earth*, trans. Constance Farrington, preface by Jean-Paul Sartre (New York: Grove Press, 1963). See also James Ferguson, *Global Shadows: Africa in the Neoliberal World Order* (Durham: Duke University Press, 2006).

38. For a particularly eloquent statement, see Olúfémi O. Táíwò, "Being-in-the-Room Privilege: Elite Capture and Epistemic Deference," *The Philosopher* 108:4 (2020): https://www.thephilosopher1923.org/essay-taiwo

39. The pressure of democratic inclusiveness can get out of hand. It is arguably that pressure, and not genuine concern for the state of the planet or its live inhabitants, that has led to some advocacy of the "post-human," including expressions

of admiration for the agential force and concern for the moral value of inanimate objects, including stones.

40. Benjamin Schreier, *The Rise and Fall of Jewish American Literature: Ethnic Studies and the Challenge of Identity* (Philadelphia: University of Pennsylvania Press, 2020).

41. Ibid., 63.

42. Kenneth Warren, *What Was African American Literature?* (Cambridge, MA: Harvard University Press, 2011), 9.

43. Ibid., 8.

44. Ibid., 9. Warren does not seem displeased that the "conditions" that produced African American literature as a field "no longer obtain" (9). This saves African American critics from "the temptation to shore up a specialized intellectual undertaking by insisting on its efficacy as a contribution to the race as a whole" (139–140). In other words, he embraces intellectual specialization and autonomy at the expense of shouldering the "burden of political responsibility" (141). This burden would perhaps seem lighter, and thus more worth shouldering, if it were not placed disproportionately on the shoulders of African American scholars.

45. Schreier, *Rise and Fall of Jewish American Literature*, 64.

46. See Bill Readings, *The University in Ruins* (Cambridge, MA: Harvard University Press, 1996). The theoretical difficulty is a different thing, as Guillory points out. John Guillory, *Cultural Capital: The Problem of Literary Canon Formation* (Chicago and London: University of Chicago, 1995):

[T]he temptation to regress to a theoretical position which construes valuing within local communities as "in effect" universalizing and exclusive by virtue of the homogeneity of experiences, beliefs, or "values" attributed to such communities, a problem she [Barbara Herrnstein Smith] identifies with good reason in Richard Rorty's appeal to community as the only basis of a consistent pragmatism. (277)

47. Schreier, *Rise and Fall of Jewish American Literature*, 55.

48. See Nada Elia and others, eds., *Critical Ethnic Studies: A Reader* (Durham and London: Duke University Press, 2016).

Chapter 6

1. Walter Benjamin, *Illuminations,* trans. Harry Zohn, ed. Hannah Arendt (New York: Schocken, 1969), 257–258.

2. Roderick A. Ferguson, *The Reorder of Things: The University and Its Pedagogies of Minority Difference* (Minneapolis: University of Minnesota Press, 2012), 140.

3. Lee Edelman, *No Future: Queer Theory and the Death Drive* (Durham: Duke University Press, 2004), 3.

4. Ibid., 4. For a commentary on Edelman and an important and distinctive contribution to the same theme, see Judith Halberstam, *The Queer Art of Failure* (Durham: Duke University Press, 2011).

5. See Frank B. Wilderson III, *Afropessimism* (New York: Liveright, 2021).

6. Lisa Lowe, "Metaphors of Globalization," in *Interdisciplinarity and Social Justice: Revisioning Academic Accountability*, eds. Joe Parker, Ranu Samantrai, and Mary Romero (Albany: SUNY Press, 2010), 37–62, at 45. Another problem to note in Benjamin's famous passage, to which Lowe also refers, is that it does not actually disavow progress. In this passage progress is indisputably happening. It has a misleading name; it should not be *called* progress. It should not be welcomed as something desirable. But the storm blowing out of Paradise is very real. It is blowing the angel with outspread wings backwards into the future, and it is piling wreckage at the angel's feet. Benjamin disapproves of the direction in which history is moving, to put it mildly, but there is no doubt that history *has* a direction. It is linear. If so, then those who are satisfied with Benjamin's critique of progress will have to make do without one element of that critique: the idea that what's wrong with the belief in progress is its dependence on the idea of history as linear and unidirectional.

7. Benjamin is a central figure for Enzo Traverso's *Left-Wing Melancholia: Marxism, History, and Memory* (New York: Columbia University Press, 2016). Traverso ingeniously translates Benjamin's melancholy as "the obstinate refusal of any compromise with domination" (45).

8. Benjamin, *Illuminations*, 261.

9. Ibid., 261, 263.

10. Stephen Greenblatt, *Shakespearean Negotiations: The Circulation of Social Energy in Renaissance England* (Berkeley: University of California Press, 1988).

11. Ibid., 1.

12. Ibid.

13. I try to justify the neologism "pastism" in "Presentism, Pastism, Professionalism," *Victorian Literature and Culture* 27:2 (Summer 1999): 457–463.

14. Catherine Gallagher, "Marxism and the New Historicism," in *The New Historicism*, ed. H. Aram Veeser (New York: Routledge, 1989), 37–48, at 38. It is worth noting that Joseph North is similarly cynical about "the claim that there really *is* a relationship between, on the one hand, New Historicism as a movement within the academy and, on the other, actual political struggles outside the academy, feminism in particular." Joseph North, *Literary Criticism: A Concise Political History* (Cambridge, MA: Harvard University Press, 2017), 89.

15. Gallagher, "Marxism and the New Historicism," 40. Gallagher goes on to suggest, after denying the charge of quietism, that the kind of historicist criticism she endorses "can develop independently of political concerns; there may be no political impulse whatsoever behind her desire to historicize literature" (46). For the relation to the new social movements of the 1960s, see also the Jean Franco essay, "The Nation as Imagined Community," in the same volume, *The New Historicism*, 204–212.

16. Gallagher, "Marxism and the New Historicism," 41.

17. Jean-Paul Sartre, *What Is Literature?* trans. Bernard Frechtman, introduction by Wallace Fowlie (New York: Harper, 1965), 22. This was originally published in *Situations 2* in 1948. Though Sartre would go on to spend much time and effort writing critically about Flaubert and Genet, here he has no qualms about his playful metaphor of the critic as invested in death.

18. Terry Eagleton, *The Meaning of Life* (Oxford: Oxford University Press, 2007), 64.

19. Ibid., 53.

20. Ibid., 55.

21. Ibid., 74, 76.

22. Bonnie Honig, *Political Theory and the Displacement of Politics* (Ithaca and London: Cornell University Press, 1993), 60.

23. It is perhaps worth noting here that this wisdom had been challenged by the increasingly persuasive contention, in and around the trans community, that an individual's sexual identity is not in fact constructed but given at birth, though it is of course often distinct from biological sex.

24. Ian Hacking, *The Social Construction of What?* (Cambridge, MA: Harvard University Press, 1999), 7.

25. Terry Eagleton, *Literary Theory: An Introduction* (Minneapolis: University of Minnesota Press, 1983), 11. Eagleton is building on the arguments of Raymond Williams in *Culture and Society* and in *Keywords*. The original sense of the word "literature" is polite learning. Its modern sense as creative or imaginative writing—in particular poems, plays, and novels—was the result of a drastic specialization, it is "a matter of social and cultural history" (153).

26. Ernesto Laclau and Chantal Mouffe, *Hegemony and Socialist Strategy: Towards a Radical Democratic Politics*, trans. Winston Moore and Paul Cammack (London, Verso, 1985).

27. Hayden White, "The Value of Narrativity in the Representation of Reality," in *The Content of the Form: Narrative Discourse and Historical Representation* (Baltimore and London: Johns Hopkins University Press, 1987).

28. Ibid., 6–7.

29. Page duBois, *Trojan Horses: Saving the Classics from Conservatives* (New York: New York University Press, 2001).

30. Ibid., 25.

31. Ibid., 19, 18–19.

32. Ibid., 30, 31.

33. Ibid., 39, 41.

34. Ibid., 54.

35. Ibid., 54–55.

36. See Rachel Poser, "He Wants to Save Classics from Whiteness. Can the Field Survive?" *New York Times Magazine* (February 2, 2021): https://www.nytimes.com/2021/02/02/magazine/classics-greece-rome-whiteness.html

37. Eric Hobsbawm and Terence Ranger, eds., *The Invention of Tradition* (Cambridge, UK: Cambridge University Press, 1983), 14.

38. Rita Felski, *The Limits of Critique* (Chicago and London: University of Chicago Press, 2015), 154. In their introduction to the edited volume *Critique and Postcritique*, Felski and Elizabeth Anker state that critique is "poorly equipped to engage seriously with spiritual beliefs, sacramental practices, and attachments to the sacred" (14). Given the inspiration that the project of postcritique takes from Bruno Latour,

an explicit defender of Christianity, given its own lack of serious critical engagement with love of country (and patriotism's victims at home and especially abroad), and given its programmatic attachment to existing loves and attachments, it does not seem unfair to associate postcritique with the Nixon-era platform of "family values." Elizabeth A. Anker and Rita Felski, eds., *Critique and Postcritique* (Durham and London: Duke University Press, 2017).

39. Family values" are worth pausing over. After his bestselling assault on the 60s generation, *Tenured Radicals* (1990), conservative art critic Roger Kimball published a book called *The Rape of the Masters* (2004) on what academic criticism does to great art, and then *The Fortunes of Permanence* (2012), in which he does not hesitate to describe permanence as a religious value. Taken together, the titles speak volumes. If art is a stand-in for femininity in peril, then the moral is clear: anything less than permanence (that is, the sacrament of marriage) should be seen as rape.

40. Felski, *Limits of Critique*. esp. chap. 4.

41. Carolyn Dinshaw, *How Soon Is Now? Medieval Texts, Amateur Readers, and the Queerness of Time* (Durham: Duke University Press, 2012), xiv. "Asynchrony," for Dinshaw, means "different time frames or temporal systems colliding in a single moment of *now*" (5). Dinshaw is speaking on behalf of "our lived sense of time," which differs from "the measured time of successive linear intervals" (9). She argues that it is experience itself, and not just the experience of literature, that is asynchronous. But she could make the case about literature without having to add the case about the putative timelessness of experience as such. The obvious disadvantage of the full argument is that it denies the linearity that progressive politics requires. One searches in vain in Dinshaw's index for the word "democracy."

42. Barbara Herrnstein Smith, *Contingencies of Value: Alternative Perspectives for Critical Theory* (Cambridge, MA: Harvard University Press, 1988). "What is commonly referred to as 'the test of time,'" Smith writes,

> is not, as the figure implies, an impersonal and impartial mechanism for the cultural institutions through which it operates (schools, libraries, theaters, museums, publishing and printing houses, editorial boards, prize-awarding commissions, state censors, and so forth) are, of course, all managed by *persons* (who, by definition, are those with cultural power and commonly other forms of power as well); and, since the texts that are selected and preserved by "time" will always tend to be those that "fit" (and, indeed, have often been *designed* to fit) their characteristic needs, interests, resources, and purposes, that testing mechanism has its own built-in partialities accumulated in and thus *intensified* by time. (51)

Characteristically, Felski drops needs, interests, and power from her account of this process and instead opts for the neutral "structures of gatekeeping and evaluation" and "institutional inertia" (*Limits of Critique*, 160).

43. Smith, *Contingencies of Value*, 52–53.

44. duBois, *Trojan Horses*, 22.

45. Ibid., 2.

46. Ibid., 22–23.

47. Ibid., 23.

48. Felski, *Limits of Critique*, 154, 155, 156.

49. Fredric Jameson *The Political Unconscious: Narrative as a Socially Symbolic Act* (Ithaca: Cornell University Press, 1981), 19.

50. Ibid.

51. Ibid.

52. One simple thing Jameson no doubt means by "great" is big. But even there, note the complexities. Before it applied to monarchs of extraordinary ability, "great" meant (in Old English) coarse, thick, stout, big. Of particles like grain, it meant coarse. Of the air, it meant thick or dense. Of women, it meant pregnant. Of the human body, it meant corpulent. Of the sea, it indicated high tide. By figurative extension, it then came to mean elevated social position as well as famous or important.

53. Fredric Jameson, *Allegory and Ideology* (New York: Verso, 2020), 50.

54. The struggle between freedom and necessity is perhaps visible within Jameson's criticism itself. One the one hand, there is necessity: it says that taking sides in history makes no sense, because there has not been enough freedom to choose. Choice is morally meaningless. On the other hand, there is freedom: the freedom to choose a side within the limits of necessity is still freedom, in fact the only real freedom that exists. In every epoch there have been choices that are meaningful, meaningful in the sense that they add to the realm of freedom for those who come afterwards.

55. Jameson, *Allegory and Ideology*, 49.

56. Ibid.

57. Ibid.

58. Ibid., 49–50.

59. Ibid., 40.

60. Ibid., 37.

61. Ibid., 16, 22.

62. Ibid., 11–12.

63. According to the *Dictionary of Global Culture*, edited by Kwame Anthony Appiah, Henry Lewis Gates Jr., and Michael Colin Vazquez (New York: Vintage, 1996), Timur (Tamarlane) was "the last of the great nomadic conquerors" (645).

64. I say more on this subject in my work-in-progress on the literary history of atrocity.

65. Jameson, *Allegory and Ideology*, 71.

Chapter 7

1. See Bruce Robbins and Paulo Horta, eds., *Cosmopolitanisms*, afterword by Kwame Anthony Appiah (New York: NYU Press, 2017).

2. David A. Hollinger, "Not Universalists, Not Pluralists: The New Cosmopolitans Find Their Own Way," *Constellations* 8:2 (June 2001): 236–248.

3. This recognition has come in various shapes and sizes. One striking example is Jini Kim Watson's argument that in Singapore, Malaysia, Korea, and other Asian countries, no account of decolonization will work that does not factor in the enormous impact of the Cold War and the radical alternatives that were foreclosed by anti-communism. Jini Kim Watson, *Cold War Reckonings: Authoritarianism and the Genres of Decolonization* (New York: Fordham University Press, 2021).

4. Edward W. Said, *Orientalism: Western Conceptions of the Orient* (New York and London: Penguin, 1995 [1978]), 2.

5. Ibid., 7.

6. See Alexander Beecroft, "World Literature Without a Hyphen: Towards a Typology of Literary Systems," *New Left Review* 54 (2008): 87–100, and the ambitious expansion of that argument in *An Ecology of World Literature: From Antiquity to the Present Day* (London: Verso, 2015).

7. Assia Djebar, *Fantasia: An Algerian Cavalcade*, trans. Dorothy S. Blair (London: Quartet, 1993 [1985]).

8. Ibid., 204.

9. See Bruce Robbins, "Blue Water: A Thesis," *Review of International American Studies* 8:1 (2015): 47–66.

10. Arjun Appadurai, "Disjuncture and Difference in the Global Cultural Economy," reprinted in Appadurai's *Modernity at Large: Cultural Dimensions of Globalization* (Minneapolis: University of Minnesota Press, 1996).

11. Ibid., 32, 33.

12. Ibid., 33.

13. That is the argument in brief in Bruce Robbins, *The Beneficiary* (Durham: Duke University Press, 2017). The subtitle that I failed to affix to it was "Cosmopolitanism from the Viewpoint of Inequality."

14. *The Longman Anthology of World Literature* (New York: Longman, 2004), 1: xxi.

15. A more traditional way of assuring literature's autonomy is to declare or simply assume that the only proper context for literature is other literature. This argument for an absolutist intertextuality is spelled out by Simon During in "When Literary Criticism Mattered":

> [F]rom its beginning, a core strand of literary studies—which I will call "modern literary criticism" —sought to find standards without appealing either to value in the singular, to expressive values in the plural, or indeed to "worth," or substantive qualities like right, good, or beauty. It turned rather to the literary heritage. It was committed to immanence: to finding what had worth in the heritage just as a result of comparative acts of attention to works in that heritage, as if to make judgments inductively on grounds supplied by the heritage. (121)

In Ronan McDonald, ed., *The Values of Literary Studies: Critical Institutions, Scholarly Agendas* (Cambridge, UK: Cambridge University Press, 2016).

16. *Longman Anthology*, 1: 1.

17. Beecroft, "World Literature Without a Hyphen," 95.

18. Kenneth Pomeranz, "Social History and World History: From Daily Life to Patterns of Change," *Journal of World History* 18:1 (2007): 69–98, at 84.

19. Ibid., 87.

20. Jerry H. Bentley, "Hemispheric Integration, 500–1500 C.E.," *Journal of World History* 9:2 (1998): 237–254, at 239.

21. Ibid., 240–241.

22. Wai Chee Dimock, *Through Other Continents: American Literature Across Deep Time* (Princeton and Oxford: Princeton University Press, 2006).

23. Ibid., 2.

24. Yves Winter, "Conquest," *Political Concepts* (Winter 20212): https://www.politicalconcepts.org/conquest-winter/

25. Robert J. C. Young, *Postcolonialism: An Historical Introduction* (Chichester and Malden: Wiley-Blackwell, 2016 [2001]).

26. Ibid., 74.

27. Laura Doyle, "Inter-Imperiality and Literary Studies in the Longer *Durée*," *PMLA* 130.2 (2015): 336–347, at 345.

28. There is a parallel here with the history of secularism, at least for those for whom secularism would count as a measure of progress. In South Asia, among other places, secularism was long treated as an alien import that came with the colonizers. More recently, however, a native pre-history has been exposed; secularism has been established as a tendency of Indian thought that developed through the cohabitation of Hindus and Muslims. Current debates over European immigration and identity would look and sound different if secularism were no longer seen as the exclusive possession of Europe. And it could not be a bad thing to try out the same hypothesis with regard to anti-imperial self-critique. It may not be there. But we won't know unless we look.

29. On *Cloud Atlas* and the barbarian, see Bruce Robbins, "Barbarians: Cosmopolitanism Beyond the Center-Periphery Model," in *Handbook of Anglophone World Literatures*, eds. Stefan Helgesson, Birgit Neumann, and Gabriele Rippl (Berlin: DeGruyter, 2020), 102–117.

30. Doyle, "Inter-Imperiality and Literary Studies in the Longer *Durée*," 336.

31. For a further development of this argument see Bruce Robbins, "What World History Does World Literature Need?" in *The Routledge Companion to World Literature and World History*, ed. May Hawas (London and New York: Routledge, 2018), 194–206.

32. Sebastian Conrad, *What Is Global History?* (Princeton and Oxford: Princeton University Press, 2016), 6, 9.

33. Ibid., 70–71.

34. Lawrence Grossberg, Cary Nelson, and Paula Treichler, eds., *Cultural Studies* (New York: Routledge, 1992). Stuart Hall's contribution is "Cultural Studies and Its Theoretical Legacies," 277–294.

35. Ibid., 289.

36. Ibid.

37. Jane Gallop, *The Deaths of the Author: Reading and Writing in Time* (Durham: Duke University Press, 2011), 130.

38. Ibid., 130, 131.

39. For a better translation and useful commentary, see *Max Weber, Charisma and Disenchantment: The Vocation Lectures*, trans. Damion Searles, eds. Paul Reitter and Chad Wellmon (New York: New York Review Books, 2020).

40. Ibid., 15.

41. Ibid., 16.

42. Peter de Bolla, *The Architecture of Concepts: The Historical Formation of Human Rights* (New York: Fordham University Press, 2013).

43. Ibid., ch. 2, 61.

Conclusion

1. Jonathan Kramnick, *Making the English Canon: Print-Capitalism and the Cultural Past, 1700–1770* (Cambridge, UK: Cambridge University Press, 1998), 2.

2. Ibid., 5, 3.

3. Ibid., 2, 3.

4. Kramnick's argument might be assimilated to the genre laid out in the previous chapter: once again, *progress for critics and scholars* can be affirmed without the possibility of progress being affirmed for society in general.

5. Kramnick, *Making the English Canon*, 6.

6. Cornel West and Jeremy Tate mention the example in their indignant op-ed about Howard University's decision to eliminate its classics department in the spring of 2021. Cornel West and Jeremy Tate, "Howard University's Removal of Classics Is a Spiritual Catastrophe," *Washington Post* (April 19, 2021): https://www.washingtonpost.com/opinions/2021/04/19/cornel-west-howard-classics/

7. John Guillory, "Literary Critics as Intellectuals: Class Analysis and the Crisis of the Humanities," in *Rethinking Class: Literary Studies and Social Formations*, eds. Wai Chee Dimock and Michael T. Gilmore (New York: Columbia University Press, 1994), 107–149, at 115.

8. Kramnick, *Making the English Canon*, 5.

9. Virginia Woolf, *Orlando: A Biography* (London: Granada, 1977 [1928]), 175.

10. *Stuart Hall: Selected Writings on Marxism*, edited, introduced, and with commentary by Gregor McLennan (Durham and London: Duke University Press, 2021), 14.

11. Ibid., 13. The sentence comes from "Cultural Studies and Its Theoretical Legacies," in Stuart Hall, *Critical Dialogues in Cultural Studies*, eds. David Morley and Kuan-Hsing Chen (London and New York: Routledge, 1996), 267.

12. *Hall: Selected Writings on Marxism*, 295.

13. Ibid., 342.

14. Ibid.

15. Antonio Gramsci, *Selections from the Prison Notebooks*, trans. and eds. Quintin Hoare and Geoffrey Nowell Smith (New York: International Publishers, 1971), 5.

16. Ibid., 10.

17. *Hall: Selected Writings on Marxism*, 269.

Index